## What People Are Saying about *Parenting for the GENIUS*

*Amy Alamar dispenses parenting advice with humor, compassion, and wisdom. This is a confidence-boosting book for parents and one that will be useful from cradle to college.*
**Daniel H. Pink**
**Author of *Drive* and *To Sell Is Human***

*The brilliance of this book is how it blends real-to-life vignettes with practical advice, allowing parents to reflect on what is best for their children. Parents will develop strategies to develop the character, values, and resilience in their children that will prepare them to thrive now and far into the future.*
**Kenneth R. Ginsburg, MD, MS Ed**
**Author of *Building Resilience in Children and Teens: Giving Kids Roots and Wings***

*Like a good parent, Amy doesn't adopt a judgmental or scolding tone. She approaches her reader like the good, experienced friend every parent needs. Her practical, realistic advice acknowledges the realities of balancing work, personal health, and relationships. I thought I'd heard every bit of parenting advice, yet this book kept surprising me.*
**Peter Hartlaub**
**Father, Parenting Blogger (*The Poop*), and Journalist (*San Francisco Chronicle*)**

***Parenting for the GENIUS*** *is a practical resource for parents of children from infancy through adolescence. Through insightful and heartfelt examples, Amy points out how to think through the challenges parents face on a daily basis.*
**Mike Riera, PhD**
**Head of Brentwood School and Best-Selling Author**

*What a treasure! A parenting book that shines with heartfelt appreciation for the privilege of parenting without sugarcoating the challenges of helping kids develop a moral compass. Thank you, Amy Alamar, for this timely and timeless resource.*
**Annie Fox, MEd**
**Author of *Teaching Kids to Be Good People***

*Most parenting books focus on children; this one is different. In her fresh, accessible style, Amy helps readers reflect upon themselves and upon their practice as parents and thoughtful human beings. Combining compelling vignettes and research, Amy presents a must-read approach to values-based parenting—and to life.*
**Susan Eva Porter, PhD**
**Author of *Bully Nation: Why America's Approach to Childhood Aggression Is Bad for Everyone***

## What People Are Saying about *Parenting for the GENIUS*...

*You will come back to consult this book again and again as you and your family grow and change. Dr. Alamar offers a pragmatic, values-based approach to parenting. Her candid tone and rich examples make this approachable and enjoyable reading for every parent.*

**Rabbi Carla Fenves**
**Congregation Emanu-El of San Francisco**

*Well informed and encouraging,* **Parenting for the GENIUS** *is a comprehensive guide for navigating parenting. Alamar's judgment-free, family-focused approach will help you engage your kids in becoming responsible, resilient, and happy members of your household and community. A compelling read with suggestions you can incorporate immediately and refer to time and again.*

**Hannah Denmark**
**Full-Time Mother and Board Member of SPEAK (Speakers for Parents Educators and Knowledge)**

*I am confident Dr. Alamar is able to help any parent become successful in parenting with the use of her principals and the knowledge she freely gives in her book. This is a book that is worth having in your library!*

**Rev. Emmett J. Neal Sr., MSW**
**Child Protective Services Worker, San Francisco Human Services Agency, and Pastor, Macedonia Missionary Baptist Church**

*Amy Alamar's values-driven parenting style offers guidance for parents seeking to nurture their children to become thoughtful, grounded, compassionate individuals and community members. She offers many tips and insights to assist parents confronting the unique parenting challenges of contemporary society. It's a gentle manual, and Alamar's steady commitment to educating rather than blaming is a relief.*

**Lonnie Stonitsch**
**Cochair and Programming Chair, Family Action Network**

*Alamar unites what we know about great teaching and learning with common-sense knowledge. She reminds us that effective parenting is not about having perfect children but about making reasoned, reflective decisions. She helps us understand we can all be genius parents by making sure the desire to do what is best for our children drives our decisions.*

**Peter Williamson**
**Associate Professor, Teacher Education, University of San Francisco**

# Parenting

Developing Confidence
in Your Parenting through
Reflective Practice

FOR THE GENIUS IN ALL OF US™

Amy Alamar, EdD

Parenting for the GENIUS™

One of the **For the GENIUS®** books

Published by
For the GENIUS Press, an imprint of CharityChannel LLC
30021 Tomas, Suite 300
Rancho Santa Margarita, CA 92688-2128 USA

ForTheGENIUS.com

Library of Congress Control Number: 2014947757
ISBN Print Book: 978-1-941050-10-1 | ISBN eBook: 978-1-941050-11-8

Printed in the United States of America
10 9 8 7 6 5 4 3 2

This and most For the GENIUS Press books are available at special quantity discounts for bulk purchases for sales promotions, premiums, fundraising, or educational use. For information, contact CharityChannel, 30021 Tomas, Suite 300, Rancho Santa Margarita, CA 92688-2128 USA. +1 949-589-5938

## Publisher's Acknowledgments

This book was produced by a team dedicated to excellence; please send your feedback to Editors@ForTheGENIUS.com.

Members of the team who produced this book include:

*Editors*

**Acquisitions Editor:** Amy Eisenstein

**Comprehensive Editor:** Susan Schaefer

**Copy Editor:** Jill McLain

*Production*

**Book Design:** Deborah Perdue

**Illustrations:** Kimberly O'Reilly

**Layout Editor:** Jill McLain

*Administrative*

**For The GENIUS Press:** Stephen Nill, CEO, CharityChannel LLC

**Marketing and Public Relations:** John Millen and Linda Lysakowski

# About the Author

Amy Alamar, EdD, is the director of school partnerships at Girard Education Foundation, where she works with K–12 schools on integrating Activate Instruction, an interactive, online curriculum tool. In this role, she gathers and disseminates best practices and works with teachers, administrators, parents, and students to implement this tool. Previously, she served as the schools program director for Challenge Success at Stanford University. In her role there, she oversaw all the programming for member schools and conducted professional development for middle and high school faculty and parent education presentations.

Amy has been working and researching in the field of education as a teacher, teacher educator, researcher, and reformer for over fifteen years, with a focus on underresourced students, literacy, curriculum design, and constructivist education. She has also done additional research in the areas of utilization of multimedia in education and student stress. In her role as an educator, Amy has been in classrooms ranging from elementary all the way through higher education.

In her role as a frequent speaker for parent and faculty groups, Amy has facilitated parent education sessions focused on student stress and well-being as well as faculty development workshops focused on engagement with learning, professional communication, and curriculum design.

Amy is the mother of three of her very own research subjects whom she learns from and enjoys each and every day.

To Teddy, May, Alex, and Ben, who have taught me the most important part of being a parent is being a part of this family.

Enjoy this fabulous New Adventure.

Much love,

# Author's Acknowledgments

I have had the great honor and privilege of being a teacher, friend, mother, daughter, sister, and wife and would like to express thanks to those who have supported, inspired, and encouraged me in all the roles I play.

I am grateful for the opportunity to have learned from many educators and students—all of whom have taught me something dear and true about myself. Much of this book is based on my experiences with them.

Thank you to Susan Anderson, Alexandra Ballard, and Gina Morris for your valuable insight through the writing process.

Thank you, Madeline Levine, for cheering me on, modeling strong parenting and writing, and taking a chance on me.

Thank you, Jim Lobdell and Denise Pope, for seeing potential in me and helping me grow as a professional and as a parent.

Thank you to Stephanie Raphanelli, who started out on this journey with me and whose contributions to the manuscript were extremely valuable. I am so grateful for our conversations and our collaboration.

A very special thank-you to Amy Eisenstein, my dear, longtime friend, fellow mother, and editor. I knew you were special when we met in fourth grade, and I've enjoyed your friendship and support ever since.

Thank you to my lovely and loving sisters, Lisa and Lora. The two of you have had a hand in my parenting from day one, and you get me through the fun and the sorrow. You remind me of how loved I am in this world and that I am not alone. Your admiration of my children gives me great pride, and you also show me that parenting is more than just what I make of it. You are amazing mothers and role models for me.

Thank you to my fantastic parents. You are two of my biggest supporters. You have helped me develop into the mom and wife I am today. Your parenting and love are a constant compass in my day-to-day decisions and in my big-picture thinking.

Alex, May, and Teddy, you are the reason I wrote this book. You are my teachers, my colleagues, and my coconspirators. Thank you for your endless supply of love and support. Thank you for encouraging me to do this project and for cheering me along.

Ben, you're an incredible editor, shoulder to cry on, die-hard fan, and friend. You are the one I want to share each joy of parenting with and the one I need when I am at my lowest points. Thank you for the emotional support required to raise our children in a strong community. I consider our three the luckiest in the world to have you as a dad, and I consider it an honor to play the role of their adoring mother and your adoring wife!

# Contents

# Summary of Chapters

## Chapter 11
### Moderation: When Enough's Enough . . . . . . . . . . . . . . . . . . . . . . . . . . . 115
It's okay for your kids to want material goods, so long as they understand and are grateful for the things they already have. Be a discerning consumer of material and digital goods.

## Chapter 12
### Perseverance: Pushing Through and Sticking With It . . . . . . . . . . . . . . 127
Know that you're in this parenting thing for the long haul. Don't try to do it all just to check things off your list. Follow your child's interests and not necessarily success.

## Chapter 13
### Resilience: Bouncing Back . . . . . . . . . . . . . . . . . . . . . . . . . . . . . . . . . 137
Learn to parent out of love instead of fear. Be sure to praise the process and not the product.

## Chapter 14
### Responsibility: Raising a Self-Respecting Adult . . . . . . . . . . . . . . . . 149
Responsibility is about caring for oneself and accepting burdens along with enjoyment and success. We are forced as adults to act responsibly, and your child will learn from your example, but there are also things you can do to help nurture responsibility.

# Part 3—Nurturing Well-Being . . . . . . . . . . . . . . . . . . . . . . . . . . . 163
The chapters in this section will address the overall well-being of you and your child. We'll look at ways to increase your family's health and wellness both in mind and body.

## Chapter 15
### Balance: The Teeter-Totter of Life . . . . . . . . . . . . . . . . . . . . . . . . . . 165
It's okay to take a moment for yourself. It's okay to love your job and stay up late working on something important. It's

okay to have a date night or go to book club. If you don't
honor your own individuality and preserve what is most dear
to your heart, no one else will.

## Part 4—Fostering Community.........................251
The chapters in this section will deal with how we as parents relate to the community around us and how to support our children's entry into that community. We'll look at ways to build, enjoy, and benefit from the people and institutions around them.

### Chapter 21
#### Collaboration: Parenting with a Partner and/or Community ........253
Parenting is a team sport. Get in good with your teammates; trust and enjoy each other. Learn from each other and support each other.

### Chapter 22
#### Competition: It's How You Play the Game.....................267
Go for the gold and enjoy the journey along the way. An urge to win is healthy, and an understanding of loss is practical.

### Chapter 23
#### Relating: Your Relationship with Your Child ...................279
Connecting with your child is all about talking and listening. Maintain the connection through awkward transitions and difficult challenges by talking and listening more.

### Chapter 24
#### Socializing: The Good, the Bad, and the Ugly...................291
Enjoy your relationship with your child, and enjoy that your child will have many more relationships outside of yours. Help nurture intimacy and fun in your child's relationships.

### Chapter 25
#### Raising a Family.........................................305
Parenting is more than just raising a child. It's about the relationships you nurture with your child and your family and the relationships and experiences you support for your child.

Parenting books tend to come in two flavors. We start reading and, before long, either feel worse about how we're handling our kids or understand what we're doing right and what we could improve but are given no practical solutions on how to improve. Dr. Amy Alamar, researcher, teacher, school reform expert, and—most importantly of all—mother of three, neither flogs us nor abandons us. Quite the contrary, she's right there in the trenches with us, and like the invaluable friend who meets you for coffee when times are tough, she is present and ready to help out with a good dose of empathy and the kinds of practical solutions that are easily implemented.

Most importantly, she provides us with a structure for thinking about parenting challenges so that long after you read this book, you will feel guided by what you have learned here. Cultivating patience, perseverance, and gratitude in our children may look different at different ages, but *Parenting for the GENIUS* helps us look at the bedrock of each of these kinds of character traits and how to further them in our kids, regardless of their ages. Using principles that can easily be incorporated into our everyday parenting (principles such as resilience, balance, and responsibility), Amy illuminates each of these with thoughtfulness, expertise, and concrete examples that provide the reader with practical tools they can use in their own parenting.

All parents today are challenged. Some of our challenges are as old as Adam and Eve, and others are as fresh as the latest social network newly launched on the Internet. As we confront each new stage of development, each new challenge with our children, we also must navigate the world of our peers and a culture that often misses the boat on what constitutes good parenting. There is often conflict between what we know in our hearts to be the better course for our kids and what everyone around us seems to be doing. Peer pressure doesn't belong to adolescents alone, and we may often feel pressured by our own adult peers into making poor decisions. Alternately, we may find ourselves short on time to really think about the best course of action—both for our children individually and for our family as a whole. I have worked with parents and their kids for thirty years and generally find, given the space to be reflective and a bit of wise advice, that most parents are quite capable of being thoughtful and figuring out what is truly in the best interests of their children.

*Parenting for the GENIUS* gives us that space and time to sit back with a good friend who just happens to be an expert in parenting and education and who guides us thoughtfully through the thicket of parenting challenges that, while expectable and inevitable, often feel less than manageable. You'll come away a better parent for it.

**Madeline Levine, PhD**
Author of *Teach Your Children Well* and *The Price of Privilege*

I had a speaking engagement one night that was an hour and a half away from my home. My husband was traveling on a last-minute trip. My three children had to be in three different places that afternoon. There was homework. Dinnertime. Bedtime. I can handle this, right? I picked up my daughter and had friends come together to help coordinate getting my other two kids home from their activities. I was preparing dinner for the kids and running through the evening out loud with my daughter as I was simultaneously applying lipstick and shoving some form of dinner into my mouth.

"And don't forget you need to finish your homework, do your dance practice, and help your younger brother get ready for bed." In the midst of my talk, my daughter opened the back door and made for the yard. I said, "Oh good, so you're going to start with dance practice?" She looked up at me and said, "No, I need to go play now." I was stunned. My first thought was, "Play? What do you mean you are going to go play?" but luckily I had a second thought before I opened my mouth. My second thought was to be stunned by her brilliant understanding of what she needed in that moment.

It wasn't about my handling it after all. It was about my children. All my stress revolved around what I needed to accomplish, and my daughter, who had just come home from a very full day of her own, complete with her own stress and perspective, knew what she needed. I couldn't have been prouder of my daughter in that moment of clarity.

*Parenting for the GENIUS* presents values you can proudly parent and live by. I will present reflective practice as applied to parenting. This book is a resource for parents of children of all ages. It's a how-to book geared toward the parents who would rather spend time with their children than read a parenting book but who also realize the importance of creating strategies based on informed decisions. Each of the four parts presented discusses a variety of values that I have found to be important and recurrent themes in my own parenting. It is also designed for busy parents; thus, each chapter stands on its own as a quick fix. This book will go through the basics of child rearing with a sympathetic and understanding tone. Educators know that positive reinforcement and constructive criticism go much further than finger pointing and instilling fear. There are enough books and popular news articles out there accusing parents of what they are doing wrong. Here's a book about what you can do (and might already be doing) right and how you can enjoy your parenting and be proud of your decisions.

From the moment a parent even thinks about conceiving, adopting, or fostering a child, questions begin to form. On top of that, parents (expectant, current, new, and old hat) find themselves in the thick of popular criticism. There is constant press out there about what parents are doing wrong and how parents are shortchanging their children (from overindulging to deprivation). There was the story that highlighted a woman sending her child on the New York subway system, and she was met with accusations of neglect. The self-proclaimed Tiger Mom was criticized for overparenting. These conflicting messages, along with others, are out there as reminders of what we should be doing or what we're doing wrong as parents, and it can often feel like there's no common ground. What parents need is support and understanding. It truly does take a village; yet, in this fast-paced world in which families live apart from each other, it can seem impossible to find a village.

Parenting today can often feel like a rat race of its own. Parents are pressured to push their kids and yet not stress them out. They are expected to raise responsible and hard-working kids yet shower them with unconditional love and praise rather than acknowledgment. Given the incessant stream of mixed messages, it is not surprising that it is often hard to find our way. This book is written to inspire values-based parenting. It is broken into four parts: Character, Independence, Well-Being, and Community. The values in the book are connected to one another, and you will see some constant themes that weave the four parts together, including taking a deep breath, making time and space for reflection, and learning from your mistakes.

At any playdate, birthday party, or carpool line, you will find parents apologizing for or defending their decisions. "We were watching *Dancing with the Stars*. Of course, we don't let the kids watch too much television. It's the one thing we watch, and..." Why is it that parents have to defend their decision to enjoy a moment of television with their kids? Why can't they enjoy dessert (even if it does have high fructose corn syrup in it)? It's good to be concerned about your choices, understand them, and second-guess them from time to time, but on average, we should be able to trust our decisions. It's okay that sometimes the choices we make are not ideal. We don't live in vacuums, and we have constant stimulation influencing our choices. We have to be able to embrace the fact that we will mess up and learn from our mistakes—just as we tell our children. Maybe you don't worry so much. And kudos to you if that's the case. If you're like me and you do worry, try to use your worrying as an opportunity to reflect on what's really important.

There are many parenting books out there with good advice (and I even list several of them in the **Appendix**). This book is from a fellow parent— in the trenches with you. I offer you sound and productive advice based on research in child development and education, years spent in multiple education levels, and my own experiences as a parent—advice you can start using in the moment. This book is designed to help you make informed decisions with confidence and to deal with the fact that sometimes your decisions won't actually be the best choice. In that event, I will talk about how to use the experience to make the next one even richer.

Parenting is the perfect topic for the **For the GENIUS** series because, like Thomas Edison's definition of genius, the best parenting is 99 percent perspiration (i.e., a lot of hard work). You cannot master the art of parenting until you've done it, and it's really never over. Every day that you parent your child (no matter how many you've had or will have) will be different. You've never parented this particular child through this particular age before. It's literally all new, every day. That said, you can learn from your own experiences, and this book will help you do that.

I will talk about positive and productive self-reflection and the ability to learn from your mistakes. Additionally, every values-based chapter includes a "Character in Action" section that exemplifies the points of the chapter in real-life situations. The vignettes are structured to make you wonder, "What would I do in this situation?" I hope you will spend some time thinking about each of these as an opportunity to practice what I preach. There are three vignettes per chapter to help illustrate how the concepts of the chapter can be applied throughout different stages of development (the preschool/ elementary years, the elementary/middle years, and the adolescent years).

The book is written to help you to parent in a way that you can be proud and confident of. I am writing as a parent, as an educator, as a daughter, as a sister, and as a wife. I have three kids, ranging (from the time this project began to its publication) from toddler to teen. I have worked for fifteen years in education and have been married for seventeen years. I am hoping that my experience, both professional and personal, will encourage you to do all of these things:

- Make up your mind, not excuses.

- Be proud of your choices and learn from your mistakes.

- Resist parent peer pressure.

- Honor honesty (it *is* the best policy, after all).

- Choose your battles.

While I will share my points of view and experiences in a variety of situations, they are presented with the central theme of the book in mind: Reflective practice helps families keep the big picture in mind for everyday parenting and big decision making. Some of the decisions I will share I am very proud of, and others not so much. First and foremost, they are decisions I have learned from. You can learn from these, contrast them with your own experience, and—most importantly—use them as lessons to consider as you forge ahead. The discussions will hopefully broaden your perspective and help you think more constructively about your parenting. As you reflect on your parenting choices, try to learn from your mistakes, and keep a broad perspective in mind, odds are that you are parenting like you mean it.

# Developing Character

Your child's character will be determined, molded, and developed by how you embrace the values mentioned in this book. Beginning with the microlevel, we will look at your child's character development through your own moral compass and decision making. We will take a close look at acceptance, empathy, perspective, forgiveness, gratitude, integrity, and patience.

Acceptance creates a space for tolerance and enjoyment. Empathy and perspective allow us to understand how others experience the world. Forgiveness helps us let go and move forward. Gratitude gives us an appreciation for the tangibles and intangibles in our lives. Integrity grounds us and helps us build our internal moral compass. And patience—the sister of the other values—provides us the space and time to process.

# Chapter 1

## Parenting You Can Be Proud Of

### In This Chapter...

- How to view your role as parent as the job of a lifetime
- How to make smart mistakes
- Sudoku for parenting: Keep your mind fine-tuned for your child
- How to find pride in parenting

In my work with parents, I have seen too many treat parenting as a recreational activity. Often the time spent with children is superficial and filled with stuff and activities rather than authentic engagement and enjoyment of one another. Most of this comes from a place of honest concern for their kids. Parents worry that their kids have to excel in three different areas before high school or they'll never get into a decent college and their life will be ruined, all because they didn't make sure they found their passion by the sixth grade.

My advice to parents? Take a breath. Take your time and enjoy the moment. Parent with pride, and know that the time and energy you put in (and not the money and time you spend on activities and entertainment) will make the difference.

The beauty of parenting is the relationship you will build with your child and your family, not what your child can do. Spend time with your child and cultivate a true relationship—where you can connect authentically and communicate effectively. You can always buy your forty-year-old daughter that pair of designer jeans she always wanted as a kid, but you cannot ever go back and spend time with her and help her through her teenage angst.

## Parenting as an Art

Parenting is an art form that should be undertaken with care, caution, and conviction. How can anyone understand what it is to have children until they do? We jump into this new stage of life with eager anticipation, doing our best to purchase all the "best" and "right" items and eating "all organic" food, but we cannot understand the complexity that will ensue until we experience it.

And then, with our second, third, and fourth (and, oh, bless the ones with even more), we still get surprises because, thank goodness, each one is unique. Enthusiasm goes a long way, but reflection and refinement are necessary as well. The best parents reflect on their practice and improve it with these reflections. It doesn't help to mull over poor choices, but it does help to consider missteps in an effort to make better choices the next time. The good news is *you* can be a parenting genius because no one knows you, your child, or your family as well as you do!

Being a parenting genius is not about being a genius in the academic sense. Sure it's good to know the number of hours of sleep recommended for toddlers or adolescents (which this book will tell you). And it's important to understand why research suggests that a practice of gratitude helps develop character. But being a parenting genius is really about being the best you can be in the moment and being willing to be better tomorrow.

## Parenting as a Job

Think of parenting as a job—one you'll have for life. Yes, even when your child is off to college, married, working, and aging, you will still be concerned. You're in this for the long haul, so get comfortable. Keeping the big picture in mind is useful because the day-to-day can be overwhelming at times. It's nice to know that you're working toward a future.

The job description for parenting is similar to that of an administrator of a small organization. You have to do a little bit of everything, have a little knowledge about many things, be responsible for a lot, and get "credit" for the less successful of the lot. You have to be on time every day. You can't miss your infant's feeding, your toddler's nap time, your elementary student's concert, your middle schooler's science fair, or your high schooler's driving test. And when you do (which you will)—well, trust me, you won't forgive yourself easily.

You will experience a lot of on-the-job learning but very little training. You are responsible for feeding, sheltering, nurturing, and educating your child. All of a sudden, you're a chef, waiter, landlord, nanny, and teacher. And just when you've mastered one age or phase, you move on to the next. And when your second child reaches a new age, that child behaves nothing like the older one did at that same age, so the learning process starts all over.

The absolute most important aspect of the job is the knowledge that raising your child is all about raising your child with values. In this book, we will take a

### Professional Parenting

My friend was reworking her resume and joked that she should include her job as a mother, or "diplomat of familial relations. Skills: transportation management, education consultation, domestic negotiations, cultural communications, and logistical operations."

**Pure Genius!**

close look at a series of values that we have found to be important and what they mean. This book is written to provide you with a practical day-to-day application of values you can use in your parenting and that you will want to nurture in your child.

# Parenting as a Series of Mistakes

Make no mistake, you'll be making many mistakes. Sometimes there are no right answers, but often there are plenty of wrong ones. If you take nothing else from this book, know that mistakes (while they can present challenging situations) are extremely valuable and that you can view each one as a teachable moment.

I can't stand it when parents say things like, "I'm such a bad mom," or "I know, I'm the worst father in the world!" You will say the wrong thing. You will react too strongly, or not strongly enough. You will lack consistency. Tell yourself this is okay as long as you learn from it and make a better (but still maybe not the best) choice next time. It is very hard to move forward and enjoy the great moments of parenting when you feel stuck in the bad ones. Nobody's perfect, so why should you be any different? But you can be a terrific parent—as long as you make productive mistakes. Stop worrying about being the best or worst parent, and just focus on being the best parent you can be. Have good intentions, reflect on your practice, and forge ahead with knowledge.

I recall my mother's advice when I returned home from a show with my son. I had made a special day for him: dinner out, a live show. On the way home, he wanted to go for a treat. I said it was time for bed, and he pouted and whined—and that is a nice way of putting it. Well, I lost it. Really? How could he be so ungrateful? Why wasn't he thanking me for such a special day? As I went to bed, I was frustrated that I had spent so much time making it such a special day only to find it was all ruined. I was near tears with anger as my mother pointed out to me that just because we had a bad drive home didn't mean the whole day was ruined. It was a great day with one bad moment.

At some point, you have to let these things go. It's okay to be upset, of course, but you have to move forward and know that one imperfect experience doesn't make the whole day a failure. More importantly, it doesn't make you a bad parent—just a good parent who had a perfectly normal imperfect moment with your child.

# Parenting as an Intellectual Exercise

Ideally, as parents, we should always be mentally fit and ready for the next adventure with our kids. This does not mean that we know exactly what that next adventure will entail. What it means is that we are prepared to use our past experiences as teachers and are ready to face the unexpected.

This book focuses on reflective practice and implementing it into your parenting. As an educator, I was trained to use reflective practice. I would prepare, implement, reflect, revise, reimplement, repeat. Teacher training instilled in me the ability (and now the immediate expectation of myself) to reflect on my practice: to think about what worked, what didn't, and what could be better. True, sometimes reflection can highlight the negative, but the intention is to use your experience and prior knowledge to do what you do better. These chapters will help you apply this practice to your parenting.

## Reflective Practice

Through reflection, we can better understand what we do, how we do it, and why we do it. We can take moments in our parenting to step outside ourselves and see the situation for what it is and not for how we feel in it. It is with these reflections that we can make informed decisions moving forward. This self-awareness creates a space for growth.

**Definition**

Think of your small decisions as your training. Your infant has a rash; you learn not to use a certain brand of diapers or wipes. Your toddler throws a fit; you learn to count to ten before responding. Your elementary-aged child is having a hard time in a class; you work with the teacher and your child and supervise study sessions and organization. Your middle schooler lies to you; you enforce some serious consequences and allow for retribution. When your adolescent outright defies you and stays out overnight, you've done your training and you're ready! You've prepared for this moment. You've laughed, you've worried, you've contemplated, you've cried, you've collaborated, you've nurtured a special relationship. You are ready to parent at the next level.

# Parenting as a Privilege

You have the distinct privilege of being a parent to your child, and don't forget what an honor it is. Yes, you will encounter challenges, strife, annoyance, frustration, and more, but don't ever forget how lucky you are to have what you have. No matter how your family came to be, it is here and you are the parent. Be mindful of your duties and enjoy them as an honor. Stop and smell the roses (much nicer than the dirty diapers anyhow).

Speaking of dirty diapers, I recall one very stressful day. My family was in the midst of buying a house we could barely afford. My husband and I met the real estate agent at the title company to sign our final papers. We were in the middle of a large stack when our son announced he had to go to the bathroom. Unfortunately, he didn't make it all the way there. As I was getting him comfortably wrapped in the cardigan I had with me, my daughter apparently also needed to relieve herself, and it began to seep out of her diaper (and it wasn't yellow). I was midwipe on the floor of this lovely downtown office. I was a stay-at-home mom feeling extremely unglamorous. I was searching my diaper bag for something, anything that could help. Our real estate agent (a lovely, put-together gal) looked at me and said, "Ah, the joys of motherhood."

I looked up at her from the carpet, hair in my face (I couldn't very well brush it off my face, given what was on my hands), and replied without thinking, "It's truly a privilege to wipe this adorable tush." I know I was stressed. I know I was overwhelmed. And I know I wanted to be somewhere else—with clean hands. But I also knew that she had no idea how wonderful I had it and how lucky I was to have that precious little bottom in my hands. After all, my mother always said, "A little poop never hurt anyone." So I left there tired, embarrassed, dirty, and scared to have this new house. (Did I mention we couldn't really afford it?) I never forgot that moment of knowing that what I had in these children was more important than anything else, no matter if I could make that mortgage payment or not.

I've often felt discouraged and completely beaten, but with time even our largest challenges feel more manageable. No matter the level of stress, no matter the point of conflict you are experiencing with your child in the moment, and no matter the uncertainty you are feeling in your role as parent, always remember the privilege you have of being a parent. I guarantee this will not always be easy, but it is important.

## Character in Action

Ordinarily, the Character in Action sections in the following chapters will consist of vignettes for you to consider and reflect on. I will provide what I think is the best advice based on my experience as a parent, as a teacher, and as a researcher, bearing in mind that each parent, child, and family has specific needs and constraints.

These vignettes are designed as learning moments for parents. They can help you think about what you would do in each situation. Consider my suggestions and how they would work in your family, with your child, with your community. Throughout the book, I will remind you to use reflective practice: Consider your decisions, past and present, and let your experience inform your decisions going forward.

## To Summarize...

- Parenting is a job, and you should always strive for the next promotion.

- The best mistakes are the ones you learn from.

- Keep up with your mental training, and be ready to embrace the next new thing.

- Honor your role, and don't take it for granted.

# Chapter 2

## Acceptance: The Power of Yes

### In This Chapter...

- Making judgments and using them to move forward
- Go for it and take new risks, big and small
- Think big picture, even when invested in the small stuff
- Fly by the seat of your pants and work within the situation at hand

**M**y mother always says, "Never say never," and I've tried to remember that when I make snap judgments. Let's face it: Others make snap judgments about our parenting all the time. The criticisms begin with, "Your baby's hungry," and then they get harsher and the consequences more intense. "Your daughter is going to get a reputation if you don't do something about her appearance." Your rising anxiety only builds from there. In this chapter, you will learn to embrace acceptance as well as teach it to your child to support an open mind and flexible thinking.

# Acceptance Looks Different at Different Stages of Life

## Zero through Five Years Old

In the early years, children are generally accepting of the world around them. They adapt to new situations and pick up on new routines with a little support and encouragement (and sometimes without). Parents can introduce acceptance by offering new experiences, talking about changes in routine, and embracing change themselves. For very young kids, acceptance can include calming down from a tantrum without getting their way, being at ease with a variety of people, and going down a slide for the first time after being afraid of it.

## Six through Twelve Years Old

Acceptance is extremely important and most challenging in the elementary and middle years because children at these stages are rapidly balancing new routines in school and academics and are developing independent personalities while navigating an entirely new social scene. Parents can encourage acceptance by supporting new activities, nurturing interests, and offering a wide range of opportunities. Some of those opportunities include going with the flow with friends, trying a new food, or doing chores or homework when asked without complaint.

## Thirteen through Eighteen Years Old

The teen years are ideal for developing a sense of acceptance. Adolescents by nature have a knack for both demonstrating unique identities and fitting in. They are able to adapt like chameleons and enjoy the challenge (though they don't let on). Acceptance at this stage might include trying a new after-school activity or sport, selecting a new elective, or supporting a friend in the midst of adversity.

I recall seeing parents who used Pull-Ups and thinking, "Why would you buy those? You're either in a diaper or underwear. When *my* son is ready, he'll wear underwear. Until then, he'll wear a diaper." Well, then came baby number two. At age two, my daughter decided she was going to wear underwear. The only problem: She had not yet decided to use the toilet. You can imagine what ensued. It took many loads of laundry and several days of frustration and the worst stink, but I finally realized that she was the prime candidate for Pull-Ups. Never say never! As our kids grow older, it is more important to acknowledge not only that, yes, we do judge—all parents do— but also that we as parents (and probably in our nonparenting lives too) need to use our judgments productively.

## Practicing "Yes, Let's!" in Small Doses

You won't always agree—with your spouse or partner, with your child, with your child's teacher. And the list goes on. You won't always agree, but you *can* try to accept some things without agreement. Have you ever heard of the expression, "Pick your fights"? It's very true. Not every disagreement is worth an argument. Sometimes giving in can be a form of protecting your relationships. When your daughter wants to go to school in an orange and pink ensemble that includes tights, shorts, and pants, let it happen. Embrace that she's getting herself dressed and making independent choices. When she's older and she wants to experiment with her hair, let her wear three ponytails or get a purple extension. Of course, when she's even older and her behind is hanging out of her jeans, that might be the time to pick the fight. At this point, you have nurtured her interest and ability to dress on her own and express her own style, so a suggestion that she keep it modest or at least keep it covered will be better received than if you had been arguing that she dress as you'd have her dress all along. Show her the respect she deserves, and you will be more likely to receive it back.

Saying yes is not always easy. At age seven, my daughter would ride to school once a week on a tandem attached to her father's bike. She desperately wanted the independence to ride her own bicycle, but living in San Francisco, we were very nervous, given all the street riding involved. Finally we gave in and made time on a Saturday morning for her to try it out. Sure enough, she made it all the way to school. (Mind you, three miles is no small feat when you're riding up and down San Francisco hills.) We were so proud!

I confessed to her I wasn't sure she could do it, but I was very proud because she knew her strength and advocated for herself. She looked back at me and said, "I wasn't sure if I could do it either, Mom, but I was sick of my friends asking why I was on the back of my dad's bike." Ah, the power of yes! She knew for her own reasons (peer pressure) that she had to try it, and given the opportunity, she did it. Even if she hadn't, she would have learned that on her own terms. Either way, it was important for me to listen and support her so that she knew she had me as a believer and an ally.

Practice acceptance with your spouse or partner as well. And if you can't accept, don't blame. I remember one time jumping in when my husband was doing the laundry. Instead of thanking him and moving on to do something else that needed doing, I felt compelled to refold our son's pants the way *I* like to fold them. Then I moved on to the towels (can't fold them in half—has to be a trifold). I remember the look of confusion on his face as I wasn't reaching for clean and unfolded clothes but redoing the task he had embarked on. How rude! Sometimes you have to accept that your spouse or partner will do things differently and love that instead of find fault with it. Of course, little tasks like laundry are simply a practice round for you for when you embark on the harder areas where you're bound to find some disagreement. Acceptance in small doses will help you embrace your spouse's idiosyncrasies. If you generally go with the flow, your attitude and respect will provide a strong foundation for the conversations you will have when you can't go with the flow.

# No Judgments without Realization

We all do it. Judging is human nature. We need to acknowledge that we judge and that we need to be better than our judgments. We see people and immediately take in their appearance (what we like and what turns us off). But we can train ourselves to look beyond those judgments. After all, don't you preach to your child that it's not how you look but what's inside that matters? If that's truly how you feel, then you should model that mentality for your child.

There was a mother who really got me. She was always dressed to the nines for a preschool tumblers class and talked about everything like she knew best. She bugged me, and I didn't even know her. I used to think to myself, "Why does she dress so nicely for this toddler class?" Once the class was over, I was so glad I wouldn't have to see her again. Of course, a few months later, we ended up in another class together with our kids. It was then and there I realized I'd have to give her a second chance. And when I did, I found she was a really interesting and fun person. Funny enough, I also realized that I really liked the way she dressed, and if I was being completely honest with myself, I was initially a bit envious of her because I couldn't pull off the cigarette pants at tumblers class. Over time, we became friends. I was embarrassed by how I had given in to my first impressions so quickly. That next January, I made a resolution to judge if I have to but not to act on my judgments and to give everyone a few chances. It was clear to me that living in a relatively small area, I would run into the same parents and families over and over again. Once you have children the same age, you're bound to end up in the same school, little league, gymnastics class, or drama class after school together. Without fail, I have run into the same set of parents again and again. Sometimes our own judgments tell us something about ourselves. We must find those moments in our lives so we can continue to better understand where we are coming from before we hope to share with our kids where we would like to go with them.

I encourage my children to do the same—be aware that we form opinions about others quickly, and use this knowledge to keep an open mind. In fact, your opinions and judgments are part of what makes you you and helps determine your likes, your dislikes, your instincts, and even your moral code at times. However, be aware of how they impact your decision making. You'll notice that children start off in life with very few judgments. Your toddler son might ask why you muttered about the cashier under your breath, and hopefully that will remind you of your snap judgments. When you first hear your child utter a negative comment or insult someone, you will be taken aback. You might even find yourself chastising your child for calling someone fat or ugly. But think about why your child is uttering these words and why you are so offended.

### Flip Your Judgment

The next time you find yourself judging someone or something, pause and change your attitude. Flip your thinking and embrace in your mind what you're criticizing.

**Perspiration**

Take a moment and talk through it. Perhaps the person is in fact fat. Maybe your child was simply identifying. Or maybe there is a negative connotation attached. Perhaps the person is ugly to your child. What's important here is to make sure that your child is polite to people and also that your child understands why these things matter or don't matter. Be sure to talk about the comment and not simply punish and move on.

One time, my six-year-old son boasted that he was better than his friend because my son had beaten him at a game of chess. He said it right there, in front of his friend. At first, I was appalled. I quickly checked to make sure his friend wasn't crying. I was humiliated that my son would brag about his skills and put his friend down. I gave him "the look" and took him aside to let him know how rude he was being. In talking about it, we uncovered something. My son was confident! Wait a minute. It was time to celebrate—and still teach! I let him know that, yes, he should celebrate his win and he should be proud. This conversation will last a lot longer (read: years), but there *is* a difference between *better at* (chess) and *better* (generally speaking). We talked about how we are all good at different things and about how, in fact, his friend may one day be able to beat him, so he should be careful about coasting on confidence. We had to dissect the nuance of better. *And* I had to recognize that I was grateful he was proud of himself and developing self-confidence.

## Improvise, Improvise, Improvise

The best-laid plans… Sometimes life doesn't go as we plan, and it's important to be able to fly by the seat of your pants. Read any parenting book, especially one geared toward parents of younger children, and you'll hear a lot about the importance of routine—and with good reason. Kids (and many adults) thrive with routines. It's good to know where you're headed and how you'll get there. Routines provide safety and comfort. That said, even the best-laid plans sometimes fall apart. You cannot always rely on a routine, so it's important to practice flexible thinking, which begins with you. To have a flexible child, you need to be a flexible parent.

We have institutionalized "choice days" in my family. It began when our eldest got to travel with his father out of town and our daughter was home alone with me, envious of her brother. She asked why she couldn't go on the trip. Instead of explaining it again, I asked her what she wanted to do, thereby

•••••••••••••••••••••••••••••••••• Chapter 2—Acceptance: The Power of Yes  **17**

**Words to Parent By**

*If you don't like something, change it; if you can't change it, change the way you think about it.*

Mary Engelbreit

**Quote**

redirecting her energy and introducing our first official choice day where we did meals and activities of her choice within reason. She had so much fun (and who wouldn't, with dessert before lunch?) that we repeated it on another free day. It was such a screaming success that the other two children began requesting it. Now we have occasional choice days for each child.

Your child will take cues from you. If you think flexibly, *generally* your child will try to do that too. Of course, this can be harder than it seems. Picture yourself in the carpool line at school. You are there to pick up your two children and two others for a carpool. Your daughter gets in the car and sits in the least convenient seat. You try to welcome her, get the other kids you need, and hurry along so you don't inconvenience the line of people also waiting to get their kids. Not to mention you have to be super, über careful, as there are lots of children and idling cars.

It's tempting to look back and ask your daughter to take the more convenient seat. However, look at it from your daughter's perspective. She's likely getting in the car after a full day at school where she's been making compromises all day with group projects, PE class, and recess. What she needs most from you right now is a big smile and hug—or at least a "hello." Your daughter might be thinking about homework or something a friend said. Making room for someone else is not likely at the front of her mind.

In this scenario, you and/or your child might get flustered and frustrated. How can you work it so that your daughter gets what she needs so that you can get through carpool without bickering children and honking horns? It's not always easy, but try to remember that this is the small stuff, and express that to your daughter. If you can roll with it, so can she. Ask her nicely to change seats. If she just can't see it happening today, make sure she understands that this is an opportunity to do some flexible thinking and that you'd like her to remember this situation so that she might feel more open to

### Flexible Thinking in Baby Steps

Encourage your child to practice thinking flexibly with small decisions (like splitting a turkey sandwich instead of a tuna sandwich with Mom), and then build up to bigger decisions (like which instrument to pursue).

**Perspiration**

it in the future. Let her win this one if she really needs it. You can make it through.

With enough practice, your daughter will hopefully practice flexible thinking when you are not there to help her think it through. For example, if she goes off to a birthday party and doesn't get the corner piece of cake she wanted, can she deal with it rather than throw a fit? As she grows, you'll want her to be able to handle even more difficult situations with a flexible mind. She will no doubt encounter social and academic challenges that will unfold more smoothly with an open and resourceful mind.

## Remember the Big Picture

My father always said, "Life isn't fair." Kids are going to struggle sometimes. That is part of what childhood is about. They are going to be sad, or angry, or frustrated. When this happens, try not to lose sight of the big picture. Remember that each challenge and struggle will contribute to your child's character. It's how you deal with those obstacles that makes the difference. Accept that there will be good days and bad days. Accept that your child won't be the best of the best at everything. Accept that your child will throw an occasional fit, be selfish at times, make mistakes, get hurt, and make bad decisions. Once you've accepted that your child is human, you can move forward to help your child understand how to step back and refocus on the big picture.

In order for kids to grow and develop, sometimes they need to feel uncomfortable, which can be - frankly - uncomfortable for parents, too. Nobody wants to see their kid uneasy. However, kids need to feel discomfort (emotionally and physically) for them to understand and appreciate what they have and learn how to deal with it as discomfort of all sorts is inevitable in life. We wouldn't enjoy our good days if we didn't have bad ones to compare them to. It's not always a fun way to think, but it's true. So, when your child experiences discomfort, remind yourself and your child about the big picture.

It's easy for parents and kids to get wrapped up in something that really isn't a big deal at all and lose sight of the big picture. Have you ever tasked three siblings with choosing a movie to stream on a Friday Family Movie Night? Well, I am not too proud to admit that on more than one occasion like that, we've ended up bickering and canceling movie night because "never the Twains shall meet!" Sadly, the kids were actually well mannered while they were discussing options, and I was the one who got frustrated that they couldn't agree. Instead of helping the kids collaborate or simply making the decision for them, I let things get to the point where I came down too hard and canceled the whole evening, not realizing that I was losing out on my fun night too! I lost sight of the big picture.

I remember that when I would call my grandmother with my troubles as a new mom, she would often say, "This should be your biggest problem." That always helped me put things in perspective. Truthfully, _____ (fill in the blank) is rarely ever your biggest problem, whatever *it* is. When it concerns our kids, it often feels like our biggest problem. I find that repeating my grandmother's mantra to myself does help.

## Go for It!

Try new things. This advice is as much for you as an individual as it is for you as a parent. Sometimes we hesitate out of

### This Should Be Your Biggest Problem

Picture your car breaking down. You're late for your child's piano lessons. Your AAA membership has expired. You're hungry. And one of your kids has to use the bathroom. Let's not forget that you're looking at a hefty bill between the tow (should the truck ever arrive) and the actual fix (assuming it's fixable). This makes for a very stressful situation. Try to remember—this should be your biggest problem. You've made it off the road safely, there is a truck on the way, and at least everyone is healthy. So your wallet is slimmer than you'd like, but all in all, this is not the end of the world. Repeating this mantra—and thinking back to even more difficult situations—will help you keep the big picture in mind. And if you think flexibly, your kids will learn from your example.

**Pure Genius!**

### Let Go of Control

Accept help and be open to suggestions. You might be surprised by what you can learn from others and how your child might respond when someone else is in charge for a short time.

**Inspiration**

fear. We need to parent with a sense of adventure and seize the moment, the task, the opportunity. It's important for us, as parents, to step into new situations that will benefit our families.

We often don't try new things because we are comfortable or afraid of the unknown. Research suggests that continually trying new things in life correlates with a positive attitude. We want our kids to try new things because we want to offer them a variety of experiences so they can choose what they like and want to pursue in life. Generally, this is a great attitude for your parenting (as long as you offer those experiences in moderation). And if you try new things yourself, you provide an opportunity for your children to learn through your example.

You may be completely surprised to see that your child is suddenly an on-stage performer. She may have your eyes and your spouse's ears, but where on earth did she come by this keen desire to sing and dance in front of people. And why the heck do you now have to schlep her across the state for auditions and rehearsals? Embrace it. Love your daughter and admire her enthusiasm for performance art. Support her to the best of your ability. Maybe even try her new hobby yourself. Who knows? You might find a new interest, but even more importantly, you'll show your daughter you aren't afraid to take risks and try new things.

Often religion can present issues in family life. Sometimes the parents come in with a religion they hold deeply as a part of their identity, and more and more, parents these days come into a marriage or relationship with conflicted or mixed feelings about religion, multiple religions, or no religion at all. It's a great idea to talk about religion before having children simply because religion is such an important aspect of many parts of life. But there is no reason to think you cannot come to a compromise or accept it as a manageable and exciting challenge for your relationship and family. Parents can find comfort and guidance in religion.

# Character in Action

### Zero through Five Years Old: Mother-in-Law in Town

Your mother-in-law has offered to watch your toddler for the weekend so you and your partner can get away for a few nights. You're nervous because the two of you rarely see eye to eye. She seems critical of your parenting (thinks you read too many parenting books and think too hard about small decisions). She lets your daughter drink juice, which you don't allow.

She may be critical, and you may not agree on the small decisions, but if she has a relatively sane head on her shoulders and your daughter's best interests at heart, say yes to the weekend and enjoy yourself. So your daughter will be exposed to some high fructose corn syrup. She'll also know it's something she does with Grandma. You're a strong enough parent to let this happen. Now be a grateful daughter-in-law and enjoy the weekend!

### Six through Twelve Years Old: Bat Mitzvah Brouhaha

Your wife wants your eleven-year-old daughter to become a bat mitzvah, and you don't. You entered into your marriage essentially as an atheist. Religion has not been a huge part of your adult life. You believed the same of your wife, but as you raise your daughter, she is reminded of how big a part of her life Judaism was and would like to share the experience with your daughter.

Take some time to talk with your wife about why this religious ceremony is important to her. Talk with your daughter to see if there is interest. The good news is that your daughter can become a bat mitzvah at any point in her life, so there is no need to rush or feel pressure by her upcoming thirteenth birthday. If your daughter has a keen interest, try to compromise on the beginning stages. Allow her to go to Hebrew school to check it out. Maybe you could attend some services or classes at the temple and see for yourself what it's all about. There are many options out there for mixed-religion families. Rabbis are teachers, and they are usually happy to talk with parents about these kinds of decisions. Start with an open mind, and ask your wife to also tread lightly so you can get comfortable with the idea.

### Thirteen through Eighteen Years Old: Road Trip

Your seventeen-year-old son saved money from babysitting and odd jobs in the neighborhood. He's just secured a job waiting tables over the summer and would like to spend his money on a road trip with some friends. His friend has access to a car, and they've planned out a route. You're nervous. You worry he's too young to travel on his own, that he will make poor decisions, that he might experiment with drugs or sex and get into trouble, that the drivers are too young and, therefore, the driving could be dangerous. The list goes on. Your son has demonstrated his ability to take responsibility in his work. He has made a plan with his friends and presented it to you with some maturity (a route, financial savings, etc.).

Take a chance on your son. This is a relatively easy way to show you believe in him. Make him aware that this is an opportunity for him to earn your trust and show you that he can handle this. Make sure he has a phone or some way to contact you. Let him know he can contact you about *anything*. He will hopefully deal with minor discomforts and challenges and contact you only should he have to.

## To Summarize...

- Judge if you must judge, and use your judgments to learn about yourself and to help you grow.

- Try new things, and you'll be surprised by how happy you will be if you begin to say yes!

- Flexible thinking is a great key phrase for you and your child. Be willing to bend.

- It's good to be mindful of the day-to-day, but don't dwell too deeply because it's the person your child is and will be that is the most important.

# Chapter 3

## Empathy: Understanding and Experiencing

### In This Chapter...

- How to keep your child's perspective in mind
- Understanding empathy through care of others
- How demonstrating gratitude can build empathy
- Practicing and maintaining relationships

You won't always understand your child's motivations, but you can try. And you can try to help your child understand others. In our society's race to achieve and perform, empathy is frequently overlooked. People generally appreciate the effort and feel safe and comfortable approaching you when you've shown them you can be empathetic. It doesn't mean you have to agree or believe what they believe, but soul searching shows that you are making an attempt to understand. In this chapter, you will learn about using empathy to parent as well as developing empathy in your child to help nurture a lifetime of connection and caring.

It takes time to develop true empathy. Young children cannot be expected to "imagine how it feels to be your friend when you say that." Developmentally, kids from birth through much of their elementary years are very self-centered. They are seeing the world through their own eyes and figuring out how the external factors of the world affect them. As children develop into their elementary and adolescent years (some sooner than later), they will naturally begin to understand the world does not belong to them alone. You can teach your child about empathy, model it, and expect it, but don't be disappointed if it takes time for your child to really demonstrate it.

I recall my daughter in her toddler years. She was, and still thankfully is, very willful and set in her opinion. She knew what she wanted and would go for it. This, mind you, is something to be admired in a young woman! Because this sometimes included pushing people out of her way, physically, I was worried about her being polite and appropriate. In addition, she was a real deep thinker (another wonderful asset for a young woman), so when I would talk to her about her behavior in these situations, she would look at me long and hard and not respond verbally right away, if at all. In the moment, I worried that she was without regret or empathy because I wasn't hearing, "Sorry." I would come to learn that not only was she a deep thinker, but she was incredibly empathetic as well. In one moment where she was upset about how a friend was treating her, she said, "Well, [my friend] *did* hurt me, and I want to talk to her about it, but even if she did mean to hurt me, she *is* my friend and I don't want to make *her* feel bad." Can you imagine feeling so selflessly for someone who had hurt you in that very week? I was amazed by her ability to step back to understand the situation, see things from another's perspective, *and* care for that person's feelings before her own.

## A Mile in Their Sneakers

What better way to develop empathy and the ability to really understand and even identify with the experiences of others than to practice walking a mile in their shoes? Before we help our children practice shifting perspective, we need to practice it ourselves. Try this mental exercise. Imagine you are now your five-year-old. You wake up in the morning to a bustling house and may or may not feel like getting up and dressed. What noises or smells or sights bombard your senses? How about your adolescent who is naturally programmed to sleep late and yet has to wake up early for school? What

## Empathy Check

Stop at least once during the day today or tomorrow when you are not with your child. Think about what your child is doing at that moment and imagine how your child feels. Check in at the end of the day and talk about it. What's going right? What can you help adjust?

**Perspiration**

kinds of social conflicts or adventures are in store for the day, and what about academic challenges or boredom?

Breakfast, backpack, school… are you thinking through the entire day? How might it feel to move from space to space hoping you understand what each adult and every peer wants from you but not having the developmental skills to accurately predict consequences? How often, even as an adult, have you come to a sudden realization that you are tired or hungry or just need a self-imposed time-out? It is no wonder that our kids sometimes feel bewildered! The capacities to forecast the future and to link actions to possible reactions develop with age and experience.

Now replay the exercise by thinking through your child's entire day. Are there consistent times when your child has to rush from one activity to another? Have you noticed patterns in your child's mood on particular days or at specific times? Examine the high points as closely as you examine the low points. You might be able to identify the time or type of transition to which your child does or doesn't respond well. If your child has consistent meltdown moments during the week, try to incorporate elements from more successful transitions into the rough days. You might shift the schedule and pick your child up a few minutes early from one activity to create a mini-snack-and-decompress session. You might decide to change a music lesson to the weekend to create more space on a weekday. You might offer more time with nothing planned. Try to understand where your child is coming from and what would best serve your child. And when you can't make things more comfortable (and that happens), try to understand that frustration and help your child deal with it.

Model empathy by admitting that you are imagining a day in your child's life. Offer your own feelings about the array of people and tasks in a given day, and then ask questions. You might start a conversation such as, "Wow, we woke up really late this morning and had to rush through breakfast. I felt really frazzled for the first part of the morning! How did you feel?" Your child will feel valued and will also practice articulating feelings. These conversations will also build empathy as your child sees you reflect on someone else's feelings.

## Pets (No, You Do Not *Really* Need a Dwarf Hamster)

Having a pet is like no other experience in the world. Of course, the level of responsibility changes with the type of pet, but caring for a pet creates a bond that cannot be replicated. If it is feasible, consider letting your child care for a pet. Depending on your child's age, temperament, and experience, you may need to help with the transition from partial to full responsibility. If your child is seven or younger, the buck will have to stop with you, meaning you are ultimately responsible for the pet. However, a child as young as eight is able to care for most family animals. It's a great shared responsibility for siblings and parents too.

When caring for an animal, a child begins to understand a new kind of love for another being and what it is like to empathize with someone else. If the animal is scared or nervous about going to the vet, riding in the car, or being around other animals, the child can usually pick up on those emotions. Children often volunteer to protect their pets—sometimes even more than they need to... Remind you of anyone—yourself, perhaps?

In the event that having a pet is not an option for your family, you can help your child learn to be empathetic with animals by volunteering at an animal rescue organization or shelter, attending a camp focused on animal care, or pet sitting for a friend or neighbor. You might also take advantage of foster situations, which can mean a short-term commitment.

## Thank-You Notes

Your mother was right about this one: Send a thank-you note! Composing such a message, no matter how short, reinforces gratitude and your child's memory of the gift giver. Depending on the age, your child might dictate the note, write only "Dear Grandma" and "Love, Stephanie," or be capable of drafting the entire note. No matter what the developmental stage, your child can draw or write some part of the note. Thank-you notes can (and

should) become an important ritual after any celebration involving gifts as well as unique and special experiences.

A couple I know throws magical and large birthday parties for their daughter. The rule in their family is that she may not play with any birthday gift until she has written a thank-you note for it. I have other friends who use the week before the party to address envelopes and write the beginning part of the notes so that the final part of the process is easier. Find a routine that works for your child and your family, and make thank-you notes an essential part of your schedule. The handwritten note is so lovely and possibly a lost art. It's okay to use email for your older kids. Think of it as practice with typing. The important part is communicating thanks to help build empathy.

In addition to fostering gratitude, writing thank-you notes and acknowledging gratitude triggers empathetic behavior. Empathy, or understanding how another person feels, is key to writing a thoughtful note. Sit with your child during the writing process and ask probing questions that help get at why the giver chose that gift, how much time the person might have invested in the process, and what the gift reveals about how well the giver knows your child.

For a friend who lives far away, a grandparent who does not walk easily, or an aunt who is working eighty hours a week, thinking about and then purchasing a meaningful gift might involve a lot of care and planning. The more our children think about the experience of others, the more they develop empathy.

## Role Playing: How to Counteract the "Mean Girls" or 'Bully" Behavior... Before It Starts

Role playing is a very useful tool in much of parenting. When in doubt, offer to play out challenging situations with your child. Role playing can help your child understand how someone else is feeling. Moreover, it provides rich and sometimes surprising insights into how your own child is interpreting social situations. Listen closely as your child acts out a part or predicts a peer's response. Offer to play multiple roles in scenarios as you act them through with your child so your child begins to understand the way someone else might feel. It also allows for both of you to explore new options in what may feel like a cut-and-dry situation.

It is easier to say "Imagine how she must feel" than it is to truly imagine it. So work with your child to act out situations through role playing. You cannot start too young. As your child grows and inevitably winds up in new and difficult situations, you will have a tried-and-true process for working through problems and challenges. The other nice thing about role playing difficult situations is that you don't have to provide the solutions—you can discover them together. We use role playing often in our own home to work out conflict-resolution issues that sometimes arise in school. Often these sessions begin in earnest, and a sibling will want to join in and help model good (or sometimes bad or funny) behavior.

## He Said, She Said

Make role playing a natural go-to when you're talking with your child about difficult or new situations. It can feel funny at first, but if you get in the habit, it will become a very simple way for you and your child to work through problems that will occur throughout life. Use the words you think might be said in a situation and go from there. Try it out a few times with different starts and outcomes.

**Perspiration**

## Authentic Connections

We want our kids to have authentic connections with us, extended family, friends, teachers, coaches, and leaders in our community. It's important that they make these connections because it strengthens their sense of worth in a community and helps them see how they fit in. It affords them multiple outlets to share ideas, ask advice, and express disappointment. Some children form many connections across different groups. Others create a few deep links with one or two valued mentors. You can foster these connections through simple socializing (like playdates and neighborhood potluck dinners) and also through more intentional participation (like donating time to a local charity or participating

## Providing Opportunities for Authentic Connections

You cannot make authentic connections just happen; you must develop them. To start, offer your child multiple opportunities to meet and be with other individuals. In addition, help your child understand others' feelings, which inspires positive social behaviors and deeper relationships.

**Inspiration**

in a community event). For more ideas about selecting an extracurricular activity and coach or educator who fits with your family's values, see **Chapter 10** for a discussion on exploration and **Chapter 22** for a discussion on competition. For more information on connecting with others, see **Chapter 23** and **Chapter 24** for a discussion on relating and socializing.

Talk about empathy, model it, and expect empathetic behavior. Even if your child is young and not yet able to empathize as much as you'd like, you can still set a high standard for your child. Consistently ask your child to think about others' feelings and offer opportunities for role playing. Share your own feelings in different situations. You don't always have to focus on hurt or pain. You can empathize with others' joy and excitement too. These practices will encourage empathy and, thus, deeper connections—between your child and others and between parent and child.

As important as it is to help your child foster strong relationships with others, you can feel good about letting go too. It's normal to feel threatened by an intimate relationship your child may share with someone else. Jealousy is a human trait and can rear its ugly head even when we know in our minds that it's not helping the situation.

Know that you are fulfilling your parental duty by letting your child demonstrate some social independence, even though it might lead to some hurt feelings from time to time. Those hurt feelings help teach your child how to navigate the space between bumpy and threatening relationships. You might also prepare yourself to share the role of confidant, as your child's new relationships stand to multiply the number of people in a young person's trusted inner circle.

With your newfound space, enjoy a moment with your own friend. By modeling good social interactions, your child will see firsthand both the work and the enjoyment that come from new relationships.

# Character in Action

Now let's apply the principles of nurturing empathy. Here are some real-life predicaments and suggested solutions.

### Zero through Five Years Old: Personal Space 101

You've got a hugger. What can you say? Your two-year-old boy barrels over to every Tom, Dick, or Harry and gives a hearty old hug. You think it's adorable, and many adults do too. However, the kids at the park are easily overwhelmed by your son's presence. Some push him away, some run away, and some just appear generally uncomfortable. What do you do?

You need to teach your toddler about personal space. It's hard at his age, but it's not too early to start. You can explain that some people love hugs (and you're one of them) and some don't. Younger children respond well to role playing, so find a couple of stuffed animals and explain that this bear loves to be greeted by a "squeezer hug," but this stuffed dog gets scared and worried when he is hugged. Ask "How might you approach the dog differently to help him feel safe?" You can talk about whom to hug and why. Maybe Aunt Anne is coming over, and she's a great person to hug because she is family. It might be best not to hug kids we don't know or kids we do know but we can see don't like it.

In addition to talking, help your toddler read facial expressions and react to physical cues (like a child pushing him away). Talk about how he feels when he's pushed away, and let him know that the other child is likely feeling something similar when he is touched unexpectedly.

### Six through Twelve Years Old: Practice Makes Perfect

Your ten-year-old son comes home frustrated that a really annoying boy in the class is always hanging around him. Most recently, he reportedly won't leave your son alone during recess and insists on playing "all the same games" as your son. And while the situations he recalls may seem innocent

# Empathy Looks Different at Different Stages of Life

## Zero through Five Years Old

In the early years, a child is naturally egocentric—or, literally, self-centered. It is the job of the parent to introduce the concept of empathy by modeling, offering opportunities, and role playing. Empathy takes effort in extending oneself. In these early years, it can look like sharing toys in the sandbox, making a gift or card for someone, or comforting someone in pain.

## Six through Twelve Years Old

It is especially important to emphasize empathy in the elementary and middle years because this is a time when children naturally develop a sense of themselves as part of a larger community (for example, they are part of a family, school, or neighborhood). At this age, children can be expected to start reading social cues and body language on their own and begin responding appropriately. Empathy can be nurtured at this age through small-group work in school, community activities or service learning projects, or playdates that include compromise over activities or snacks.

## Thirteen through Eighteen Years Old

By adolescence, children understand they are part of something bigger than themselves and have the ability to extend themselves emotionally, intellectually, and physically. They are ready for more intimate relationships and can be encouraged to continually see life through different lenses, helping them understand others. Empathy can take shape at this age through independent social relationships, asking for advice, or steady volunteer work, as these experiences include interaction and understanding of others.

enough to you, you can tell they are bugging him because he talks about them every day. He declares that this other kid is a "total loser." You might explain that your son does not have to like everyone, but he does have to treat everyone with respect. Labeling anyone a "loser" is not okay.

Begin by asking your child to explain a specific behavior or incident that made him uncomfortable or angry or embarrassed. Assure your child that he does not have to hang out with this boy or become best friends, but he might think through how this boy feels and respond more kindly in the future. As you talk through it, write down phrases describing what the boy does or says and how your son feels in response. Remind your son what it is to be kind, and then role-play what he can do next time this kid is in his space. Use the examples from your list to play through a few scenarios. Offer multiple chances to play them out, as he may find himself stuck on what acceptable responses might be. Feeling unsure about next steps often provides a dangerous opportunity for kids to say mean things, so you can help your child make those unexpected situations more familiar.

### Thirteen through Eighteen Years Old: Doggone Hard Decision

Your family dog is very old and sick. And you've brought him to the veterinarian, who has told you it is time to let him go. Your sixteen-year-old daughter insists on taking the dog home. What do you do?

You can certainly ask for a second opinion, but assuming your veterinarian is a good one, it's time to let a professional guide your decision. That said, you do have some options. You can take your daughter and the dog to the veterinarian so she can hear the reality. By making the time (taking her out of school, taking time from work, using the all-important family dinner hour, whenever it is), you are showing your daughter that you are not taking this lightly and giving her the respect of being a part of the process. If after these conversations you stick with the professional decision, you could take the dog home for goodbyes. Keep in mind that taking the dog home is really to comfort your daughter (and maybe you) but may prolong the dog's suffering.

While it's hard to say goodbye, this is an opportunity for your daughter to extend herself and think of someone else. Allow your daughter room to express her feelings and offer any suggestions she might have—within the parameters set by the veterinarian. Some pet hospitals allow owners to be with the animal up until sedation, others might allow a beloved toy or pillow to be with the pet, and some vets will permit owners to spend a few minutes with the pet prior to a procedure.

When it's over, it's not over. Give your daughter space to grieve. People often overlook the loss of a pet, and it can be very painful. Talk with her about what will help. You might consider a memorial service, a day off of school, a favorite meal, a framed picture of the dog for her. Think of something to mark this moment, and let her be a part of it.

# To Summarize...

- Think things through from your child's viewpoint.

- Consider caring for a pet and fostering an out-of-self experience.

- Help your child thank others and be less egocentric.

- Encourage relationships that go beyond play and hanging out.

# Chapter 4

## Forgiveness: Apologies and Letting Go

### In This Chapter...

- How to allow yourself a little forgiveness
- Finding clarity in anger, frustration, or disappointment
- How to truly say you're sorry
- Expressing yourself

This chapter will focus on practicing forgiveness as a parent and teaching it to your child to support compassion and a life of learning rather than regretting. If you learn to forgive yourself for your mistakes, your child will sense that approach. It's detrimental to your confidence and future choices if you focus too hard on mistakes. Learn from them and try to move on. Most will seem less significant with time. Some will remain in your memory, and you might continue to feel shame or regret as you move forward, but it won't help you to fester. When you embrace forgiveness—of yourself and others—your child will likely be the greatest beneficiary.

It's hardest to forgive yourself. Just slightly easier, but not easy, is to forgive your children their bad choices, as parents often worry that bad choices are a reflection of our parenting. It is the job of parents to help their children learn from these mistakes. Yes, you can allow them to feel a little shame when it's really bad, but forgive them so they know they are safe and can come to you when the going gets tough. In this chapter, I will walk you through ways to practice forgiveness of yourself and your children so that you can learn to move forward through problems.

## A Little Bit Goes a Long Way

Before you can help your child forgive, it is important to understand how complex the process can be. It is also important to reflect on your own ability and willingness to forgive so that your child can learn the nuances by watching them in action.

Forgiveness is not conflict resolution (though sometimes that is involved in the process). Forgiveness is the ability to acknowledge feelings of anger, disappointment, resentment, pain, or frustration—and to let go. Holding on to a grudge can inspire a host of more bad feelings. To forgive is not to ignore the offense. In fact, the offense may continue to hurt for some time to come. But forgiveness is the act of deciding not to let these feelings fester and build. Making the decision to forgive must be sincere. And with it will come the ability to connect more deeply with other people and yourself. Disappointment, anger, frustration, and resentment can contribute to physical and emotional distress (increased blood pressure, headaches, anxiety, or stress). Forgiveness can help reduce these symptoms and can help you break free of the hold the offense had on you in the first place.

Often the first instinct is to either punish yourself or look for a place to lay the blame when you make a mistake. It's human nature to make mistakes and be averse to accepting responsibility for them. It's up to you to acknowledge the mistake *and* to forgive yourself. It's great to show your child you are willing to take responsibility and that you've forgiven yourself.

We were a relatively new family of five when I plumb forgot we were supposed to be meeting another family for dinner. They didn't live near us, so they had been in the car for over an hour at rush hour, then waited for us

# Forgiveness Looks Different at Different Stages of Life

## Zero through Five Years Old

Very young children are perhaps the most forgiving souls. After all, they don't care if we've combed our hair before leaving the house—so long as we remember their snacks. Forgiveness is best taught at this age through example and patience. Toddlers' forgiveness can include avoiding a fit when Mom left the crayons at home, getting buckled in the car easily when it's time to leave the park, or coming to snuggle with you after you've lost your cool.

## Six through Twelve Years Old

Elementary-aged children are at the perfect age to learn forgiveness because they understand mistakes and make very forgivable ones on a pretty consistent schedule (for example, breaking a glass or leaving a sweatshirt at school). Parents can support forgiveness at this stage by demonstrating patience and forgiveness when small mistakes happen rather than blowing them out of proportion. Forgiveness in children at this stage can include not kicking back when kicked, moving on after a friend or sibling apologizes, or writing a note to a special friend after a disagreement.

## Thirteen through Eighteen Years Old

Forgiveness can come easily in adolescence with fellow teens or younger children, but it can be a challenge with adults, especially parents. It's important to have patience and respect independence during your child's adolescence. You can't demand forgiveness, but you can nurture it by modeling it with your own friends and colleagues and keeping open lines of communication. Teenage forgiveness can include reaching out to a friend who cheated at your child's expense, hanging out with a group who previously excluded your child, or giving up a long-held grudge against a teacher.

at the restaurant for a while before calling. I didn't pick up the phone since we were having dinner with the kids. So I didn't realize what had happened until it was too late. It was a simple and honest mistake. No one was hurt, but my friends were not thrilled. I could've made up excuses (and, believe me, I almost went there), but I had to fess up: I had simply forgotten. The event was in my calendar, and we had confirmed it via email, but I was caught up in the moment. I felt terrible, and my friend gave me a hard time, which made it worse. But I reminded myself of all that had gone right that day, and in a few days' time, I managed to get over it. It did take a while. Ultimately, I thought about how I would feel if my friend had done the same to me. I would have had a nice dinner out with my family, been annoyed, given her trouble, and moved on. So I was able to put it in perspective, apologize, and continue living my life.

The same goes for your child. Give your child the benefit of the doubt and help your child through the process of forgiveness. Help your child learn confidence and self-awareness by acknowledging mistakes and moving through them. You can read more about owning blame in **Chapter 14**. Modeling and supporting this process with your child will help when the mistakes are made at other people's expense as well.

# Clarity

Did you ever watch the television show *Friday Night Lights?* One of the recurring sayings throughout the series is "clear eyes, full heart, can't lose." Clarity offers so much in any given situation. When a child disappoints you or you make a huge mistake, you respond physically and emotionally. It's best, as much as possible, to take a step back and get a clear vision of the events around you. Know when it's "my bad." You may have to say "sorry." And guess what? That's a good thing. It's good to be aware of when you're in the wrong and to model that behavior for your child.

I recall disciplining one of my children. My voice was raised, my finger was pointing accusingly, and I was physically clamped up (my fists, face, and stomach). I had a moment of clarity as I fell silent for a moment and processed what was happening. I almost laughed at the ridiculousness of the scene. Here was this child, my child, squirming and scared. And here I was, a raving lunatic. How did we get to that place? Children do get scared when they see their parents out of their minds, and it's especially scary when they are the reason. I stopped and announced that I was removing myself from the situation because I was too angry to think. That gave us both time to figure out what was happening. When we were both calm, I initiated a conversation.

Take a break when you need it. This is not always easy to do. It's very natural to react when you're angry, so it's a learned skill to step back and gather your thoughts. There are practices (like mindfulness and meditation) that can help if this is a particularly difficult skill for you. And I encourage you to ask your child to find you when ready to talk if it's your child who has lost control. I don't love time-outs, but time is great. My typical response to an angry child is, "Take some time and join us when you're ready."

Now, it's not the worst thing for you to lose your cool with your kid, and it's also not bad for your child to see you angry or disappointed. If your child does something to provoke these feelings, it's appropriate for you to show your frustration, so long as you reserve strong reactions for very select times and are not constantly losing your cool. Breaking a dish shouldn't send you over the edge, but lying is a big deal. Accidental damage to the house or car or other property can be costly, and you can show your concern about that. You can (and should) even require that your child take responsibility and help repair the item or even help pay for it. Don't forget that your child owes you an apology, even if it was an accident. There is still blame. Forgive your child—not just with an "okay"—but explain what it is you are forgiving and why you are willing to move on. Show that you are letting go so that your child learns how to do the same rather than hold in feelings. You can do this by stating your feelings and then not revisiting the issue over and over again. You can also show it through your mood and affect.

## How to Forgive

Forgiveness is a complex process that emerges through multiple stages:

- Accept the harm done.

- Don't dwell on feelings of hurt or anger.

- Make the decision to let go.

- Communicate your decision.

- Let go.

**Inspiration**

### Words to Parent By

*To err is human; to forgive, divine.*

Alexander Pope

**Quote**

To help gain clarity, consider what's behind the issue and the apology. If the incident was truly an accident, it's a problem that needs to be dealt with, but your reaction should remain within reason.

It would be surprising if you found out your child crashed the car and you reacted calmly and said, "Aha, I see. Thank you for being honest with me. Let's take the car to the shop." You're human and you should react. You might cry or yell. That said, make sure you can bring yourself back to a place where you can communicate. In other words, it's okay to lose your cool, but do your best not to. And in the event you do, make sure to find a time to talk calmly after the fact. If you lost your temper, it's likely that you owe your child an apology.

Focus your apology on losing your cool, not on being mad or scared. You're allowed to be mad and scared! Explain that you love your child, that you're grateful everyone who was in the car is okay, and that while the incident will cost money, you're willing to let go and move on. You might be (and should be) nervous about future driving. There might be new rules around lending the keys, but teach your child about forgiveness by forgiving. Show that you are willing to let go of the feelings of anger and disappointment.

Irresponsible and disrespectful behaviors are bigger issues than accidents. Here you're dealing with the symptom (a crashed car, for instance) and a larger issue of character. If your child was careless or thoughtless in intention, you have to deal with the behavior in addition to the physical problem. Talk about the reasons behind your child's decision making. When you can gain clarity on motivation, you will have a guide to lead the discussion.

No matter the problem, no matter the fault, walk your child through the process of apologizing, accepting an apology, and truly forgiving. This will not always be an easy thing to do, but if you start young, the practice will help. Don't worry if you didn't start young. Forgiveness teaches your child empathy and responsibility at any age. It takes work to truly forgive, and it's not too late to start with an adolescent.

## Sorry for What?

My mother-in-law taught me with my first child that sorry simply doesn't cut it. Saying sorry isn't enough; she told me that children should show they are sorry. So when your child apologizes, ask why: "Why are you apologizing?" Your child should be able to explain. And, if not, then your child needs to think about it, and you need to talk it through (when you're calm and ready to have a true conversation without raising your voice).

After explaining why, your child needs to come up with how to show a true apology. Again, this can be a discussion—and really should be with younger children. If your three-year-old daughter writes on the wall with her crayon, she can show you she is sorry by helping you clean it up. She can offer to continually put her crayons away and promise to sit at the desk or designated area when she uses her crayons. These are age-appropriate ways for her to take responsibility and make up for her mistake. If your seventeen-year-old son gets a ding in the car when he takes it out, he can show he is sorry by getting it fixed. If he cannot afford the body shop's bill, he can do something else: take care of car washes for the next few months, purchase gas for the week, or perhaps help with a home improvement he is able to do.

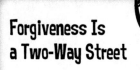

### Forgiveness Is a Two-Way Street

We worry so much about disciplining our kids and teaching them to be polite (and say they are sorry) that we sometimes forget that forgiveness is part of that equation. Help your child understand how to seek true forgiveness and how to offer it.

**Inspiration**

## Time Heals Many Wounds

Often people will suggest after something bad happens that time will help fade the memory as it fades a bruised knee. It's true. Whether you are a parent teaching your child or a parent modeling best practices for your child, keep in mind that time offers emotional space from feelings of anger or frustration. With a little distance, it's easier to think about what you wished you had said or done in the moment. Don't beat yourself up over this reflection, but use it to help you in the next difficult moment. You can't count on time to take care of everything, but it does help offer perspective.

And even a good night's sleep can help heal some of life's smaller troubles. I know that Mr. Brady said we should never go to bed angry, but sometimes it's okay. In an ideal world, you would problem-solve all issues before the dinner hour, but life is more practical than ideal. Time offers space to think about what's going on and to figure out solutions. Don't leave everything to time, but allow it to work its magic. Take a moment for reflection before jumping in to a discussion. And allow forgiveness to come. You don't have to forget, but try to forgive.

# Character in Action

### Zero through Five Years Old: Cut It Out

Your five-year-old son lied to you about cutting a picture out of your high school yearbook. It was an outright lie. He looked you in the face and said he didn't do it, but then later, when you find the slips of paper in his wastebasket, he cops to it. You're bummed about the picture, but you're devastated that your sweet baby who snuggles in bed with you and tells you he wants to marry you just stared you down and lied. This certainly calls for an ongoing conversation (brief conversations for a few days in a row). Talk about honesty and trust. He needs to know that you are very disappointed and have lost a little trust in him at this point. He has to earn it back. But also be sure he knows that he's not a bad person just because he did something bad and that you forgive him. It's a great opportunity to share stories and fables that might help show him the error of his ways. And, for a few days following, reinforce when he tells you something you know to be true and remind him how important that is.

### Six through Twelve Years Old: Failure is the New Success

Your twelve-year-old daughter failed a test and is convinced this is awful because it will be on her "permanent record." Of course, you'll want to read more about resilience in **Chapter 13** so you can let her know that this experience is an exercise in character building. Maybe she can learn from her mistake. But before she does, she needs to forgive herself. She won't be able to use this experience productively if she continues to beat herself up. And that's no good for her self-confidence either.

### Thirteen through Eighteen Years Old: Growing Up Fast

You find out your sixteen-year-old daughter had sex, and you are disappointed. You had hoped she'd wait longer, and you're not sure she's emotionally ready for this. You've had conversations about it, and you are especially surprised she didn't tell you.

First, forgive her. I don't say this to imply that she needs to be forgiven. You feel betrayed that she took such a big leap into adulthood without you, and you feel afraid for her because she has entered a world of intimacy where she can now be hurt much more than she could before. There's no use in holding this act against her. What she did was human. Sure, you'd rather she had waited. And you know that, in time, maybe she'll wish she had too. But at least you've talked with her, and she was somewhat prepared. Now you need to continue to be there for her. Just because she's having sex doesn't mean she's all grown up. You still have work to do. Love her as you always have, and let her know you do. She's growing up, and your job is to make sure she does that. Make yourself open to her for future conversations about sex. Offer her some other places and people to go to, because she may prefer not to talk to you. You can read more about this and other related topics in **Chapter 18**.

# To Summarize...

- Forgive yourself, and teach your child to do so.

- Get clear on the situation. It's usually not as bad as it seems.

- Ask your child to go beyond "sorry" and explain why an apology is needed.

- Offer forgiveness.

# Chapter 5

## Gratitude: Understanding and Appreciating What You Have

### In This Chapter...

- Why is gratitude important?
- Where and when can you find moments to show gratitude?
- How to spot appreciation even in a dark moment
- Sharing and receiving appreciation within your family

In our hectic, materialistic world, it can be a challenge to find time to appreciate the many things going well in our lives. Current research suggests that regularly incorporating gratitude into your life improves empathy. Additionally, the growing body of literature based on the science of happiness highlights gratitude as a key component to happiness, creativity, connection, religion, and beyond. This chapter includes information about how to practice gratitude as a parent and strategies to instill the practice in your child to help encourage a fulfilling life.

# Appreciation. What Is It Good For?

As it turns out, appreciation—both giving and receiving—is good for quite a bit. My family took a trip down to Santa Barbara for the weekend. The trip ended with a six-hour drive home that started at seven in the evening so that we could fully enjoy the day in that lovely paradise in Southern California. My husband did the lion's share of the driving while the rest of us read, watched movies, zoned out, snacked, and slept.

Once the car was parked in our garage, around one in the morning, my husband and I started the process of waking the kids so they could stumble into their beds. My oldest son, through very bleary eyes, looked at his father, gave him a hug, and said, "Thank you so much, Dad, for all the driving and the trip." That sleepy gesture perked my husband up enough to get everyone in the house and demonstrated that our son was learning the importance of gratitude in his own life.

It is not surprising that most of the empirical research around gratitude supports the idea that feeling appreciated makes people feel better. What might be surprising is that the research also suggests that we feel better when we appreciate others. People who regularly take time to think about and articulate what they appreciate are likely to feel a stronger sense of well-being and have a more positive outlook on life. Each time we tell someone we appreciate something about them, we strengthen a connection with that person. We are not only validating an effort on their part but also actively reminding ourselves that we are part of a larger community.

Gratitude makes us happier by helping us stay focused on the many tiny things (and, if we are lucky, the big things) for which we can be thankful each day. In times of challenge or distress, a practice of gratitude can act as a calming foundation from which to approach the difficult situation. And when we are content, gratitude helps solidify our feelings of comfort and joy. Try to find time in the day to offer gratitude to your child and to allow and encourage your child to offer it back to you. Be grateful that your child is in your life, and be sure to share that sentiment. This practice helps you remain grounded and also provides a model for your children to incorporate gratitude into their own lives.

# Gratitude Looks Different at Different Stages of Life

## Zero through Five Years Old

Gratitude is not a natural instinct for very young children, because their needs are usually met and they haven't yet been fully conditioned to want beyond their means. Of course, they have some exposure to worldly goods, and marketing companies have become ever so clever at targeting the young. But, generally speaking, young children move through life with expectation and don't think to be thankful for it. Parents can model and encourage gratitude by reminding young children about want versus need. Gratitude at this young stage can include thanking an aunt for a present, helping prepare or clean up a meal, or enjoying a goody bag without asking to trade for a different one.

## Six through Twelve Years Old

For elementary-aged children, gratitude is easily nurtured. They are beginning to understand the bigger world around them and relationships with other people. If parents practice gratitude in their own lives, it will become second nature to their children. At this stage, gratitude can include writing a thank-you note, thanking someone without prompting, and acknowledging want versus need when asking for a new toy.

## Thirteen through Eighteen Years Old

Ideally, gratitude is a natural practice by adolescence, but it's never too late to start. Teens are constantly creating their place in the world, and they understand that they are not alone in it. At this age, gratitude can include buying gas for the car after borrowing it, pitching in with housework without being asked, or organizing a special dinner or outing to thank you for supporting their schoolwork.

My son and I enjoyed a mother-son dance at his bar mitzvah. The day was full and flying by us fast. He did a wonderful job with his prayers and sermon. We were surrounded by friends and family. I recall taking a moment to be thankful amidst the busy day. What I didn't plan on was my son whispering in my ear a dear thank-you for the day to let me know that he was having a great time.

## Stopping to Smell the Roses

Robert Emmons and his research colleagues have been researching many facets of gratitude for decades. In addition to examining the positive relationship gratitude appears to have on well-being, they have also explored ways in which both adults and children can boost attention to this central emotion. One easy and powerful method involves keeping a small gratitude journal. Anyone who can draw or write can take part. This private diary is most effective if done each day, even if only for a few minutes. Imagine the record of gratitude you or your child would create after a month or a year, even if the entries are brief ones.

Some people like to express gratitude physically through yoga poses or other kinesthetic expression, musically through song, or artistically through some other medium. Like journaling, the practice fosters a stronger sense of well-being and connection if done regularly. In my own yoga practice, my teacher often prompts students to dedicate their practice to someone or something. I've taken to thinking about dedications as I get ready to leave the house and note things the kids have done that morning and often dedicate my practice to them or their actions as a reminder to myself of small things I am grateful for.

A note in a lunchbox or backpack, especially of an older child, is a great way to privately share your appreciation. Finding this spontaneously will add a lift in your child's day, and thinking about it will do the same for you. I try to remember to include a note in my children's lunches and backpacks. If I go on a business trip, I often leave notes by their beds. Now I find notes randomly in my own room. My insomniac daughter, girl of the night, will sometimes slip pieces of paper with sweet notes under my door, and I'll find them in the morning. One of my favorites reads, "I love you for hoo you are."

Don't forget to honor others in your community too: your spouse or partner, your friends, your colleagues, and your extended family. Write a note, a text, or a quick email. Take some time to make a call. Let people in your life know what they mean to you and that you are grateful to know them. Those actions will improve their day and contribute to your own sense of self and purpose.

## Crystal Clear

In the midst of writing this book, my coauthor left the project so she could spend time with her ailing father. She needed to be with her family. (She totally "gets" family, which is why I loved writing with her.) I was devastated and unsure if I would continue with the project. She was my sounding board when I had too much to say, my inspiration when I was lacking, and my voice when I ran out of words. I was debating at the dinner table whether I would finish the book when my daughter said, "I'm really glad it's not your dad that's sick, and I hope her father feels better soon." In that moment, I knew not only that this project was worth continuing but also that all my life had built to that moment of perspective and gratitude. I was, in turn, grateful to my daughter for her grounded perspective and her ability to see beyond the ordinary stress I was experiencing.

**Pure Genius!**

My next-door neighbor is a real sweetheart. Whenever I make even the smallest of neighborly gestures, such as taking in her garbage bins or lending her a cup of sugar, she writes a lovely thank-you note and slips it through my mail slot—sometimes days later. I know how busy she is (I see her packing her kids up in the car to run off to the next place, and her husband works long shifts), but she manages to make time for me. And when I do something really nice, like watch her children, my note is usually accompanied by a box of cookies or pastries from our neighborhood bakery. When my kids are enjoying the baked goods, it sends an especially strong message about doing favors for one another and the power of gratitude.

Sometimes appreciation can feel forced, such as the act of writing thank-you notes. By modeling and requiring these small acts, you instill an ongoing practice in yourself and in your child. It might feel like moving through the motions, but then gratitude will become a natural part of your perspective and you and your child will begin to appreciate more of what you have in life and think less about life's annoying details and frustrations.

# Honoring Moments

Taking time to record small moments on a regular basis is an excellent start to making gratitude a regular part of your life. It is also important to express appreciation as a family. We tend to focus on appreciation at certain times of the year, around holidays or special moments. It's good to implement a practice of gratitude on a regular basis and to truly feel it and not just pay it lip service.

Meals are a natural moment to offer thanks to the person or people who provided the food, set the table, and made an effort to be present. Some families enjoy the religious practice of saying grace. In addition to rituals, you might highlight the best or most challenging parts of the day or consider adding another gratitude-based ritual to your dinner or family meal.

Our youngest brought home the following snack song from preschool: "Thank you, thank you, my heart sings! Thank you, thank you, for everything." It was sung to the opening bars of the alphabet song—and the song stuck. We now begin our dinner routine by singing the thank-you song and then saying, at our youngest's insistence, what we are "thank you'd" (grateful) for. In addition to creating a family practice of appreciation, we have generated many interesting conversations about what we think should or perhaps should not be associated with gratitude. One family member may be thrilled that the Giants are heading to the World Series, but does that merit gratitude? Someone might appreciate a birthday present. How can that appreciation be deepened by thinking about the thought, time, and effort the giver put into giving the gift?

Another great time to consider offering gratitude, especially for younger children, is just before bedtime or during bath time. These tend to be calm and quiet moments when you can really dig deep if something else comes up. It's also great to go to bed, when possible, feeling positive. For

## Words to Parent By

*Gratitude is not only the greatest of virtues, but the parent of all others.*

Cicero

Quote

### A Not-So Random Act of Kindness

Commit a random or nonrandom act of kindness on the fly, and share with your family how it felt. Then plan an act of kindness with your family.

**Perspiration**

adolescents, it's often nice to find a quiet time where you can have an authentic conversation to share gratitude. It might be in the car on a routine drive to an activity, before or after sharing a television show together, or before bedtime.

You can also create mementos of kind acts through a kindness chain, which is sometimes done in classrooms. This involves recording an act of kindness you are grateful for on a strip of paper. Each strip is stapled or taped in a circle around another strip, making links, like a homemade construction paper chain decoration you might find on a Christmas tree. You can drape this around a common area in the home, or each person can keep personal kindnesses separately (unlinked). Our family's kindness chain often has to come down as it grows and overcomes the room, and we have to begin again. This is a good problem to have!

Most times, a simple thank-you is enough. Just the words themselves will brighten the heart of your child. The other day, I stopped in the hallway during the busy-morning routine of tooth brushing, breakfast, shoe tying, and lunch making and thanked my oldest son for helping my youngest find his show-and-tell item. He honestly looked stunned, like he was expecting me to ask him to do something like brush his hair or grab something from upstairs. He stopped and smiled. It didn't take much, and it came from my heart. I was honestly grateful. And it showed my son that his efforts were not in vain.

## Accentuate the Positive

It's much easier to be bogged down by the negative than to locate the positive. If something bad happens, we tend to focus on it. People often process their challenges through talking. But how often do you acknowledge what's going well in your life? Don't just acknowledge it. Focus on and accentuate it. Your children will see and hear you doing this and will begin to do it on their own as well. It will create an entire new outlook for the family. Accentuating the positive will help your child enjoy life and learn deep appreciation.

My husband and I suffered a very difficult loss with a child in utero at six months who had no kidneys. The loss was awful, and the process of overcoming it was a long one (a whole other chapter). But whenever my son wets his bed and I have to change the sheets (always great timing—right in the morning before we have to run off somewhere), I remember how grateful I am for his little kidneys that help him wet the bed. I know it sounds cheesy, but it's a reminder to me of all I have and that the trouble of changing sheets is really not all that horrible. I have shared this openly with my three children, and now my older kids remind me when I'm in a hurry and not thrilled to be doing laundry so early in the morning that it's a sign my son has healthy kidneys. They have learned to be grateful too!

# Don't Eliminate the Negative—Just Put It in Perspective

While appreciation and gratitude are essential, they are most powerful when they are grounded in truth. (Some researchers contend that they are powerful *only* when grounded in truth.) Being thankful does not mean creating self-affirmations that are false. It involves thinking deeply about what you truly appreciate. Even stellar practitioners of gratitude experience frustration, loss, and negative feelings. It is okay to understand that a tough situation in the present might seem like a "growth experience" in the future, but it feels plain rotten in the moment. It is essential that we acknowledge and honor these feelings in our children as well. However, it is also possible to find something to appreciate in most situations. In particularly difficult situations, it might take some time and a lot of deep breathing, but a long-term view of the situation may illuminate something for which your child can feel grateful.

My youngest got into a phase of reporting his news at the dinner table or after school and dwelling on negative moments in his day—problems with sharing or kids not obeying rules, etc. No doubt, he was overwhelmed by these frustrating moments and needed to share. My husband and I would talk to him about these moments and how they made him feel. We would offer him the opportunity to role-play some ideas for similar issues that might arise in the future. What we found through deeper discussion was that typically these were isolated moments during his day and that he moved on without any real

## Count Your Blessings

When you find yourself stressed out and feeling defeated, remind yourself of one thing in your life for which you are grateful. You don't have to forget your troubles, but you can remember your blessings. If you talk through your feelings with your child, you will model gratitude in its purest form.

**Perspiration**

negative consequences. I wanted to honor his reflection and struggle with these challenges, but I also wanted to direct his mind toward the positive outcomes so that he would not interpret one bad moment as a bad day.

My daughter recently came to me with a problem with her friends. One said the other was saying mean things behind my daughter's back. My first thought was, "Oh no, girl drama." We talked for a while and even role-played how she might approach the two girls. I was distraught. You never want to think of someone talking poorly about your child, especially in the context of gossip. Regardless of the outcome and the sadness I was feeling, I was able (that evening, not in the moment exactly) to realize that my daughter had come to me with a problem. Not only had she shared this with me, but she wanted my input as well. And we were able to come up with a solution she was comfortable with. That's a lot of silver lining— for me and hopefully for her. We had decided that she would talk to the friend who had come to her. My daughter made it clear that talk behind her back was more hurtful than the comments themselves. She considered talking to the supposed originator of the gossip, and we practiced that conversation. In the end, when she was with that friend, she felt solid enough in the friendship that she didn't even have to broach the conversation. She had learned that sometimes it's enough to open up with your problems and talk through them.

# Character in Action

### Zero through Five Years Old: Count Your Blessings and Go to Bed

You're exhausted and your two-year-old daughter wants another story. You want to call it a night and collapse. Take the time to let your daughter know that you enjoy her company. Tell her how much you love to be with her and that you're glad she enjoys her books. Let her know she's lucky to have books, and help her say thank-you for the books. Then invite her to look through her books in your room while you get ready for bed—while being grateful yourself for the love of books your daughter has found.

### Six through Twelve Years Old: Dance Diva

You are driving your nine-year-old daughter to dance practice, and she complains she's tired: "Why do we have to go?" You automatically break into "We pay good money… You love to dance… Just go, and I'm sure you'll have fun…" Stop for a moment and help your daughter show some gratitude for the opportunity to dance. Without lecturing that she's made the commitment or reminding her how much she enjoys it, let her find the joy in dance. Ask her what she appreciates about the opportunity, and give her a chance to share her gratitude.

### Thirteen through Eighteen Years Old: Stop and Smell the Dirty Socks

Your fifteen-year-old son's room looks atrocious. His bed is unmade, and the floor is littered with stuff. You walk in and are about to nag him (as regularly programmed each evening) to clean his room. Before you start (and it's okay to ask him to do this), acknowledge something he's done that you're proud of or appreciate. Let him know you are grateful he helped with the dinner dishes or the dog walking. Let him know how proud you are of him for studying hard or how excited you are that he had a good time hanging out with friends. Your appreciation will show him there is more to your relationship than the nagging, and he might surprise you with a conversation.

## To Summarize…

- Gratitude will improve you as a human.

- Taking time to appreciate makes a difference.

- Show your child your appreciation.

- Understand the negative and underscore the positive.

# Chapter 6

## Integrity: Developing Your Child's Inner Voice

### In This Chapter...

- Modeling decision making
- Making the most of opportunities to develop character
- What makes a choice a good one?
- Talking with your child about issues and choices

Integrity is arguably the deepest and most personal facet of responsibility. Developing a system of values by which to live can take a lifetime and is often done in exactly the way humans learn most things—through mistakes. This chapter will explore ways for you to analyze and develop your own integrity as well as support that of your child through ongoing conversations (sometimes earlier than you anticipate). This will encourage your child to come to you with moral dilemmas.

The more you arm your kids with information, create a safe place, and honor them as individuals, the stronger they will be when it is time for them to chart their own course. Think of these early conversations as laying a foundation for future conversations and decision making. Being able to tap into and use a strong value system doesn't look the same at three as it does at thirteen. At three, your toddler might climb the slide at the park and go down without you watching. At thirteen, your teen might be trying out a new style that reveals more skin than you would prefer. This chapter will discuss the importance of giving your kids the independence to develop their own character, even when it feels scary.

# Intentionally Model Good Decision Making

That old saying "The apple doesn't fall far from the tree" gets to the heart of parenting. For better or worse, your child is consciously and subconsciously observing everything you do and say—and often imitates your behavior. More than any discussion, exercise, or experience, parents play the most important role in modeling strong integrity.

Whether being careful to recycle or throw away trash (or, the teacher in me would suggest, even picking up trash) or taking a breath instead of yelling at the driver who just cut you off on the highway, your actions speak volumes to your child about how to behave when faced with decisions. If your child hears you making excuses or lying frequently, that behavior becomes the norm.

We're all human, and life is complicated. When faced with an opportunity to take a shortcut or get involved in a conflict, there may not be one "right" decision. Use dinnertime or drive time to have a conversation with your child about how you think you might have reacted differently or maybe should have reacted differently in a given situation. Depending on the circumstance and your child's age, ask your child's opinion. What would your child have done? Reflecting and predicting are potent tools for fostering your child's inner voice. First, you are overtly signaling that you know your child has his or her own inner moral compass and that you value it. Second, you are helping your child think through scenarios in advance, a practice that will be invaluable when faced with a real-time decision point.

# Opportunities for Character Independence

One key to helping children develop their inner compass is allowing them to make mistakes on a small scale so they can appropriately gauge risks as the stakes get increasingly important. When children are toddlers, it is easy to encourage them to take small risks in development and to applaud their efforts. However, as time goes on, the risks children take have increasingly important consequences both for themselves and for others. When toddlers say they do not know who ate the last cookie, it might seem endearing. However, a young adult not telling the truth is a different matter. A preschooler may not feel any anxiety about leaving a sharing item at home, but a seventh grader may struggle with confessing to leaving the math homework at home.

It is imperative to keep the larger view in mind when you struggle with allowing your child to make those little mistakes. As with all parenting, there is no set of milestones for independence that fits all children. However, there are some basic questions that can help guide your decisions. Is it really the end of the world if the math homework comes in a day late? If your child has worked hard on an assignment, has not established a pattern of forgetting items, and might feel temporarily devastated by this one instance, you might consider bringing the item to your child—if you are able! If this has happened before, consider your response carefully before dropping everything to rush in and rescue your child. By allowing your child to make this mistake and to realize that the world will not end, you are setting your child up for both resilience and better moral decision making. If children are shown that they are trusted to navigate their world, they will understand implicitly that they are still loved, mistakes and all. Your child will build competence and confidence through both failures and successes. Finally, your

## Earning Trust

Offer your child opportunities for character building each day. If you sense your child is lying, talk it through and make sure you don't presume it to be true. Show a little trust, and if your child abuses it, take it away. Lack of trust speaks much louder than lack of a toy or television privileges.

**Perspiration**

child will have a strong grounding in handling small, manageable failures, which will support decisions, such as whether to give up after a tough basketball quarter, cheat on a difficult assignment, or cave to peer pressure in fear of a friend's anger.

## Success Is Being Left Behind

Poor decisions about integrity—cheating, lying, using illegal substances—can often be seen as a means to a desired end. Due to a host of parental, media, community, peer, and self-imposed pressures, children often believe there is one particular desired outcome in a challenging situation. Your child might believe there is only one way to solve it. If you become upset about a spelling test, your child may become increasingly anxious about the next test. Your child might think that cheating to get a good grade is more important than really mastering the material or even just going through the process of trying. As the stakes for each challenge seem more important, a child may decide that the risk of being caught cheating is worth the possible benefit of "making Mom and Dad happy."

You can work against this idea by reminding your child how important effort is. It's important to praise effort, and it sends a much better message than praising products, such as grades or trophies. If your child plays hard in a soccer game, compliment the play and effort. Winning sure feels good, but the truth is that the game can often go either way, and it's important to consider the point of playing. I am not suggesting an everyone-wins approach. (In fact, I can't stand that.) But I am suggesting that praising effort will remind your child of the time and energy invested. In the long run, perseverance and determination pay off. Encourage those traits over the end product.

### Words to Parent By

*Character is how one acts when no one or everyone is watching.*

Ed DeRoche

**Quote**

The media, for better or worse, offers a rich opportunity to discuss cheating as a means to getting ahead. The news is filled with examples of politicians, sports stars, and business people who have lied or cheated and eventually been caught.

Rather than using each incident as a lecture, use it as an opportunity to pose questions to your child: What do you think about this particular case? Do you think the individual still should keep the awards/job/office now that this has been exposed? How do you think the person feels right now? How do you think you would feel if you were that person's best friend? Each question you pose can help your child construct a personal understanding of what good character and true integrity might mean.

Carol Dweck's research suggests that students who are praised on their performance (versus effort) actually seek fewer challenges than students who are praised on their effort. As you parent, focus your praise and attention on effort. A heavy focus on performance (i.e., winning, grades, or test scores) will not only pressure your child but will also deter intrinsic motivation and an authentic desire to learn.

## "Good" Choices

Developing values is a lifelong process by which each individual determines her or his own framework for making decisions. In times of challenge or risky decision making, an individual needs the ability to either acknowledge or move past the uncomfortable feelings that accompany the situation. Is your child anxious about a test? Worried about letting an adult or a friend down? Desperate to have an item to better "fit in" with a particular group? If one's emotions are completely overwhelming, it is not possible to clearly evaluate a decision and check how it fits into a moral framework.

As children develop, they become more skilled at consciously acknowledging those feelings to better analyze them. It is well worth remembering that children are born with very different emotional temperaments. What may seem like an emotionally neutral decision to one child might paralyze another. You can help your child build that framework by reminding early and often that many (hopefully most) mistakes in life can be overcome. Using books, media, or peer experiences, you can gently and naturally open a conversation about the feelings around disappointment or anxiety. Questions like "How did that make you feel?" or "What was your thinking there?" or "Looking forward, what would you do differently?" or "Is there anything you can do to improve the situation at this point?" may help mitigate the feelings. As your child gets older, you can (and should) work

## Using Examples

Find examples in your community, in the media, or from history to illustrate strong integrity. It's much easier to identify key decisions in retrospect or from afar. Analyzing the process of making choices from a distance will help your child understand integrity before being faced with difficult decisions.

**Perspiration**

actively to foster that inner voice that asks, "Is this a good decision?" Continue to prompt with the above questions but also encourage your child to begin asking these questions internally.

We cannot be with our children every moment, so we must nurture the filter in their minds so that we can trust them and they can trust themselves. Talk to your child about choice making. At the toddler stage, this looks like choosing between carrots and celery, staying home if you cannot control your volume, or making the decision about whether or not to go to the park. Your child may be off on a playdate and offered something that is discouraged in your home. Will your child eat it anyhow? Will the words "My mother prefers I don't eat that" emerge, or will your child tell you that said food was consumed?

Your elementary-aged child may need to make choices about pretend games at school. Is it appropriate in your family to use a pretend gun, for example? If others in class are talking out of turn or goofing off, will your child join in the fun? Will your tween get distracted by a cell phone if it's at school? Will your tween cheat on a test he or she forgot to study for? And will your teen engage in sexual intercourse, use alcohol or drugs, or skip school? The scary but real answer is that you don't know, and you may never know. The bigger answer is that your child will likely say yes to at least one of these, but you know that and have prepared your child for what it means to stray from your family's moral compass.

Your children will surely falter, but will they know they have faltered? When your son goes to the movies and starts to speak out in a loud voice along with his friends, or when your daughter slips something in her purse while at the drugstore with her friends, will they know they are doing something wrong? That is the most important thing. Will they tell you? Maybe they will; maybe they won't. Even if you do have a great relationship, they will no doubt keep some secrets to themselves. So you want to be sure that when they do mess up, and they will, they will know it. The humiliation of someone in the movie theater shushing your son in front of his friends or the fear and anxiety your daughter experiences when faced with a store manager in the midst of a shoplifting incident will teach your children more than a wag of your finger will. You might even want them to get caught, and you can read more about responsibility in **Chapter 14**.

# Side by Side: The Art of Serious Conversation with Your Child

Part of setting up trusting future conversations with your child is building those bonds early—eating dinner together, driving carpool when you can, reading to and playing with your child, and simply being there. A second facet is practicing the delicate art of conversation. If the bonds are established, there is a much better chance that your child will talk to you when something serious comes up. However, negotiating a difficult conversation still takes incredible patience, listening skills, and the right questions. Especially in matters of integrity, questions are the most important tool we can use.

The end goal of helping your child create a robust set of values is the ability to access them independently. Depending on how verbal your toddler is, you can begin asking your child to think about value decisions as early as preschool. Rather than wait until your child has made a poor choice, use examples all around you to offer questions—*not* lectures.

Think back to a time you received a possibly brilliant but heavy-handed lecture about some important matter. Did you absorb every word? Or did you hear the parts that validated your own opinion and then tune out the rest and hope the lecturer wrapped it up? Rather than lecture, pose important questions for your child: How do you think that child felt when the other child grabbed the toy? Do you ever want to grab something that isn't yours? Why? And even though you have words of wisdom to convey on this subject, just let the questions sit. In some rare moments, your child may even ask for *your* opinion and, by virtue of having asked, may actually listen to your ideas.

Don't be afraid to admit when the conversation is too heavy for you. It's okay to react and even tell your child that you would like some time to think about the issue before talking again. You then give yourself time to grapple with the challenge and model good communication skills. The important thing is to be honest with yourself and your child. There will be times when you need to let your kids know that you are disappointed in their choices. Think carefully about how you let them know—they still need to know that you love them. However, we all make mistakes, and some can be serious. No matter how serious, there might be natural or even more structured consequences to poor decisions.

In the end, the actions and consequences will hopefully lead to a new or clarified understanding of one's values.

# Character in Action

### Zero through Five Years Old: Liar, Liar!

Your four-year-old was on a playdate at a friend's house. When you pick him up, the friend's mother mentions that your son cut her child's hair. She saw him doing it as she walked in the room. She acknowledges that it was all very playful but that she is very upset about the haircut. You confront your child and ask about it, and he flat out denies it. You want to believe him, but he was caught red handed.

Okay, so your son won't make his millions doing the hair of celebrities. Life moves on. But why won't he admit it, and what can you do about it? A lie is a wish. Your son wishes he hadn't done what he knows is wrong. He made a poor choice. The best option is to explain to him that lying is wrong. Take the time to define lying so he understands—or can at least begin to understand— what it means. Also explain that you would like to be able to trust him. He needs to know that he can share his shame with you and that you will still love him. The phrase I use with my own children is: "I want to know. Even the things I don't want to know, I want to know."

Finally, do some role playing. Let him practice. If you think of it, throughout the day and evening, throw in a lie for a minute and let it sink in. For example, at bedtime, if he asks you to read a story, say yes and then leave the room. Come back in and ask how it felt to be lied to. Of course, after the conversation, read the story!

# Integrity Looks Different at Different Stages of Life

## Zero through Five Years Old

The early years provide easy opportunities for conversations about integrity building because so much about it involves conversation, and at this age children, are developing language skills. Parents can encourage strong integrity by using and teaching the appropriate language. Integrity during these years can include helping to fix something after breaking it, confessing to taking something without asking, and recognizing poor behavior after the fact.

## Six through Twelve Years Old

Six- through twelve-year-old children are very open to conversations with their parents. Parents can help develop integrity by steering the conversation intentionally and looking for conversations about simple mistakes. Integrity in the elementary years can include coming clean after lying about something, acknowledging making pencil marks on the wall, or understanding the difference between an intentional bad choice and an honest mistake.

## Thirteen through Eighteen Years Old

While conversations about integrity can feel like a personal attack to your teenager, they are as crucial as they were before. Teens can be defensive, and parents can broach the discussion in a more universal way by using outside examples and talking about practical application. Integrity in the teen years can include admitting cheating on a paper without being caught first, confiding in you about using recreational drugs, or advocating for someone in need.

### Six through twelve Years Old: "I Cheated"

Your daughter comes to you and tells you she cheated on a chemistry test. She did not get caught, but she feels terrible and does not know what to do. No matter how tempting it might be to explode, the first thing you should do is give yourself a pat on the back! Whatever pattern of communication you have created with your daughter has worked. She has made a really poor decision and decided to share it with you, even though she has no external pressure to do so.

Here are some possible prompts you might use to start a conversation: I am really glad you are discussing this with me. How does it feel saying it out loud? Are you proud that you listened to that voice in your head, the voice that reminded you that this was wrong? Let's think of what the worst possible scenario is—a zero on the test, loss of respect from the teacher, other academic or social consequences? What is a best-case scenario? Five or ten years from now, what do you hope your adult self thinks about this incident?

You will have to consider how hard you want to push. The most important thing in following your own values is being able to hear your own voice of integrity. Encourage your daughter to share her offense with her teacher or a counselor. If she can't bring herself to do it, accompany her. On a first offense, the school will likely be understanding and have a consequence prepared. Continue the conversation at home, and consider a logical consequence of your own (doing homework with you present, checking all emails and texts before sending/receiving, or even tutoring a friend or other student).

### Thirteen through Eighteen Years Old: "We Have Your Child at the Security Station"

You receive a call that a security guard caught your son shoplifting and that the store may or may not press charges. Again, it may be tempting to begin yelling and/or lecturing immediately. After all, what in the world was he thinking? In a calm voice, begin asking questions: What did he take and why? Did he want it badly but have no money? Was he trying to impress a peer or just test a limit? Did he simply forget he had slipped it in a pocket?

No matter the answer to the above questions, your son still stole. As difficult as it might be, let your child face the consequences. Instead of demanding that he apologize, arguing on his behalf, or insisting it was a mistake, try to listen. If the store employees offer a chance for your child to be involved in setting the consequences, your ideas might be welcome. This may be an opportunity for your child to suffer consequences that involve work. Can he stack or break down cardboard or arrive early and stock shelves? Any activity that gives your child a different insight into the work involved in managing a store might help him develop a new appreciation for the people who work there.

Chances are, you and your child will be emotionally drained after the incident. Allow yourselves to reflect by letting him know you will discuss this after dinner or tomorrow. By setting a time but also giving some space, you can avoid uncertainty about when "the talk" will take place and can focus your energy on what you want to discuss. When you do discuss it, hopefully your child can articulate why he stole the item. If money was the issue, perhaps he can write a proposal to take on extra work at home or with neighbors to earn additional money. If peer pressure or limit testing was the reason, you will ask a different set of questions. Why did he want to impress that peer? Now that he did push that limit, how did it feel? If there is a legal ramification, how might that affect his future hopes? As with all tough conversations, remind your child before, during, and after that you love him.

# To Summarize...

- 🔦 Remember that you are the role model for decision making, so be intentional with your choices.

- 🔦 Find new opportunities to help your child understand and practice values.

- 🔦 Help your child make good choices, even when they're hard to make.

- 🔦 Don't be afraid of serious conversation. If you're not ready, take some time to prepare so you can make the most of it.

# Chapter 7

## Patience: How Often Have We Heard It's a Virtue?

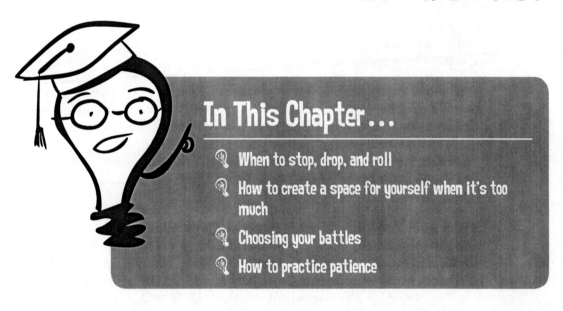

### In This Chapter...

- When to stop, drop, and roll
- How to create a space for yourself when it's too much
- Choosing your battles
- How to practice patience

It sounds easy, but patience takes practice, and you won't be patient with your child until you learn true patience with yourself. It's more than taking a moment—it's about understanding the moment. Children feel calm and more optimistic when their parents are tolerant, and that can open up space for them to share more with you. In this chapter, learn to practice the true virtue of patience as a parent and how to teach patience to your child to encourage tolerance and understanding.

## Yellow Light, Green Light

My driver's ed teacher began the class with the question, "What do you do at a green light?" I, being the good little student I was, raised my hand and proudly stated, "Go!" He told me, "No, it means you proceed with caution." That was embarrassing to get wrong, admittedly, but he had me pause and think. Much of parenting is about taking a deep breath before proceeding. And when parents do proceed, they must do so with caution rather than just jumping right in.

Throughout your life as an individual, as a member of your community, as a spouse, as a colleague, and in just about any role you play, you will be faced with situations that cause you confusion, anger, frustration, or disappointment. Parenting can bring all these (and a few more feelings) on at once. It's times like these, when you're overwhelmed with emotion, that you need to proceed with caution. Tread lightly until you've got your wits about you. Sometimes it will take place in a fleeting moment with your child, and sometimes it will be in the midst of a months-long situation.

Your babysitter arrives, and as you prepare to leave for a dinner, your four-year-old daughter starts to pull off all her clothes. You're tempted to stay and deal with this, but you don't want to be late for the dinner. Engaging with her in her mood is only going to ensure you will be late and end up even *more* frustrated. Try stepping in, and if reason doesn't work, model the break you and she both need to take from the situation. Leave this one to the sitter if it cannot be resolved quickly by you.

If your seventeen-year-old son is suspended from school after pulling a prank in the teachers' lounge, proceed each day, for at least the next few weeks, with caution. He will need reminders about what he's done, but he also needs space to recover and earn back some trust. Be patient with him, and don't expect everything to be perfectly resolved by bedtime on the night the offense occurred. It's so hard to go to bed angry and to feel let down by your child. But time will work its magic so long as you work to help him understand his digression and how to restore your trust in him.

## Find Your Happy Place

My favorite place is probably my bed. I love my bed. It's big, comfy, and warm. It fits my entire family of five when necessary. We can play a board game in it. (I keep a backgammon set in the room.) We can watch a movie curled up in it. I can fold laundry while my husband reads to my kids in it. Sometimes I can't wait till the end of the day to crawl into bed; I have to make time to get there before the going gets too hard. Beyond my bed, I can find great peace and joy in many spots: my backyard when the sun is out, my neighborhood for a walk, and almost anywhere with a good book.

Identify where you can go to get away, even if it's not very far. Because a beach vacation isn't always an option when you're at your wits' end, it's important to figure out where you can go that will give you the restoration you need. So find a few places you can go when you need some time and space away. Consider a walk in the park, a yoga class, a hike, a visit to the gym, a jog, a dinner out with a friend, a cup of coffee and a good book out at a cafe, a massage, a walk with a pet, a stop at the bakery, a drive on your favorite scenic route, or even just vegging out in front of the television or listening to a podcast. Sometimes physical exertion does the trick. Exercise can help stimulate your endorphins and get you into a better mood. But you don't have to break a sweat to give yourself the space you need to develop a practice of patience. Getting away (even if you don't travel afoot) will give you the space you need to process life's tougher moments.

You can't always slip away when you really want to most, even if it's just upstairs. Sometimes you find yourself in a difficult moment and must sustain your patience within it. In that case, it's important to create a mental place for yourself. This is where a count to ten can come in handy. Stop, count to ten calmly, and take a deep breath. Meditation is a surefire way to calm your nerves, but only if you've been in the business of doing it regularly. So if you are lacking a mental escape for yourself, try to create one. Work with some visualization techniques. Check out a meditation class (or a do-it-yourself book). Or just practice closing your eyes and put on a pair of headphones with some of your favorite music. Any of these tactics will enable patient parenting, and they will also teach your child the art of stepping away from vexing situations.

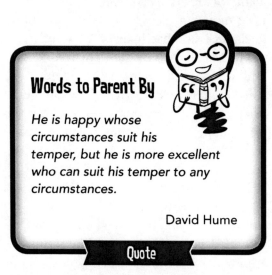

**Words to Parent By**

*He is happy whose circumstances suit his temper, but he is more excellent who can suit his temper to any circumstances.*

David Hume

**Quote**

I recall once when my son was throwing a fit in the car. I was on the highway in terrible traffic. There was nowhere for me to go. He was really crying hard. I wanted to console him, but I also needed to console myself if we were going to make it home safely. I opened the windows and turned up the music. The fresh air calmed me and dulled the noise coming from my child. The music helped me focus as I sang along. He didn't stop crying, and these quick fixes helped me through the moment. I needed a lot of "me" time and space once we got home.

## Reality Check

My friend once said to me that she considered any surgery she was having "major surgery." I've giggled through that phrase when I've gone in for a few "minor" procedures of my own. When your child's emotional or physical well-being is at stake, life tends to feel like major surgery because the situation is difficult on both you and your child. But just because it feels that way doesn't make it so. In fact, with so many *huge* decisions I've had to make concerning my kids, the element of time offers me a much clearer perspective than I had in the moment.

### Promise to Pause

The next time you are making a decision that has anything to do with the family— from where to go on a hike to what to make for dinner to which colleges to apply to—think about your response for at least fifteen minutes before sharing with your child, spouse, or partner. This will help you practice patience and encourage acceptance.

**Perspiration**

When I was sleep deprived and trying to help my first infant learn to fall asleep independently, my exhaustion and the sound of the crying alone made me think I was on the brink of the most important decision ever: I had to let him cry and put himself to sleep, right? If I caved and went into the room, he would never learn to sleep on his own and I would be sleepless for the rest of my life. If, on the other hand, I let him continue to cry, he'd resent me for the remainder of his life and suffer childhood trauma that would show up at the most important times of his life. Neither of my fears was really true. If I went into his room (which I did), he would eventually learn to sleep. This approach might have taken longer than if

## Keep Calm and Parent On

With each new challenge you face, remind yourself of how big the last one seemed at the time. That approach can lend some perspective to the current situation and remind you to have patience once again. You won't always have the time to take a moment or find a happy place. Sometimes you have to react right then and there. This is why it's important not to get bogged down by the small issues in life.

**IMPORTANT!**

I had just let him cry it out each night, but I had to do what I was comfortable doing. I knew that no matter what decision I made in my sleep-deprived stupor, my heart would overrule my mind when that helpless infant would cry at bedtime. I needed the patience to make the decision that worked for my child and me. I realized that when I heard him cry, I was anxious, so I had to make some decisions about sleeping when I wasn't in the moment (listening to his cries). I talked it through with my husband and read many books about sleep. We made up our minds, and then we tried our best to do what we felt was right and to support each other when we were exhausted.

So often when you are dealing with a conflict, a decision, or a challenge, you feel you are dealing with one of the biggest conflicts, decisions, or challenges you've ever faced. My son's sleep habits felt huge at the time, like the future of my own happiness and that of my son's was resting on decisions made during that very stressful period. With the right amount of space and time (and patience!), I was able to make good decisions and move on. There have been many more challenges with my children, and with each one, the decision can feel heavier. I laugh at how easy establishing a sleep routine seems now. And yet, if I were to do it again, I guarantee I would need to go back and find my patience.

You must find patience when it is hardest—in moments of anxiety, anger, embarrassment, or disappointment. Your first instinct will not always be right. Sometimes it's best to take a step back, even for a day or two if possible. However, it takes more than time to practice patience. Sometimes you need space, and sometimes the person you're dealing with needs space, and you need to respect that. If you're dealing with your child, take a moment before talking, because your emotions can sometimes cloud the conversation.

Remember, this isn't about you or what happened to you as a child. And the issue your child is facing does not define your child's personality or determine your child's fate. In these situations, patience pays off.

## It's Easier Than You Think

I was in my haggard-mother costume. I was rushing out the door, three children in tow. I was holding a toddler on my hip, and my oldest had run into the house to grab whatever it was he had forgotten. I had my pocketbook slung over one shoulder, a bag of snacks and supplies in one hand, and keys in my other hand. I was just off the phone and rushing to get the kids into the car and off to their after-school activities. You know the scene, right? I was talking to my daughter about goodness knows what. I noticed I had continued walking and she wasn't replying. I went back to the front steps of the house and said something like, "Why are you ignoring me? I'm talking to you!" She looked back at me intently with those beautiful blue eyes. I demanded, "Answer me!" She replied, "I'm thinking." In that moment, I was stunned not only by her ability to think before speaking (how I wish I did that more) but also by her ability to articulate her process while I was in the midst of what felt like a thousand things. I recall literally dropping everything, including my jaw, and taking a moment to pause and think too. What was my hurry? Wasn't relating to my child the most important thing in that moment?

So often, parents react without thinking. It's so easy to get caught in the moment. After all, if you spent your life thinking about the big picture, you wouldn't get much done. But that would be a nice problem to strive for, because it's so easy to focus on the details. Taking the time and energy to think before acting will improve your sense of purpose and allow you to reflect on your intention. Even with small decisions, take a moment to think before making up your mind. You'll surprise yourself with what you come up with. Compare your initial instinct with your final decision when you do stop to think, and see if there is a lot of variability.

## Practice Makes Perfect

If counting to ten helps, then by all means, take a moment and count to ten. Whether or not you actually count, find a way to create that space. It never

# Patience Looks Different at Different Stages of Life

## Zero through Five Years Old

In the early years, children have very little patience. If they are hungry or tired, they cry. Patience can be taught by offering time and space to make children wait for what they want or need in the moment. At this stage, patience can include resisting the urge to grab, talking through a problem, or waiting for a turn on a swing at the playground.

## Six through Twelve Years Old

From six through twelve, kids enjoy immediate gratification, but they are developmentally ready for delayed fulfillment. While they may be impatient for what they want, they are capable of waiting for it. In these years, patience can include asking once for a story (as opposed to asking three or four times), waiting for a parent to finish getting ready to go out, or proofreading an assignment.

## Thirteen through Eighteen Years Old

Patience for a teen can be difficult, especially with parents. Teens are anxious to move forward, try new things, and grow up quickly. Parents can help by offering space and time, allowing teens to express independence, and asking them to be patient with themselves. Patience in the teen years can include helping a friend with a tough homework assignment, listening to a younger sibling with a social dilemma, or taking time after soccer practice to work with a coach on a difficult skill.

hurts to give a second thought to your initial thoughts. Find moments in your day to practice being patient.

Some people find patience within their religious practice. If you are affiliated with a faith, you might consider turning to prayer or study groups at your church, temple, or other place of worship. Conversation is another natural way to debrief a day or specific problem. If you belong to a book club, can schedule a walk with a friend, or are able to simply relax with a glass of wine and your spouse, make the time to take time. Both you and your child will be the better for it.

# Character in Action

### Zero through Five Years Old: Do-It-Myself Mode

Your two-year-old son wants to do everything "by myself." The funny thing is, he can't yet tie his own shoes and rarely sees a need for sunscreen or a jacket before leaving the house. You want to encourage him to do things on his own, but it takes forever and you just get fed up. Take a moment to show him that his independence is worth the wait. Sure, when you're in a hurry, grab him and your bag and go. But, whenever you can, give him the space to do his own thing so that eventually he *can*. The patience you express now will pay off when he's a self-directed adolescent. It might be hard for you to actually give him the space and time he needs, so try to set it up ahead to support this effort on both your parts: Leave early so there's extra time for him to prep. Put him on a timer so he understands better what it means when you say you're in a hurry. Make him a list of items he needs to consider before leaving. These supports will help him be prepared and will help you to teach him how.

### Combat Road Rage with Road Kindness

When you're driving in a car, go ahead and wave someone ahead. Tell your child what you're doing. Make a big deal out of the fact that it's more important to help someone else out than to rush to your next destination.

**Perspiration**

### Six through Twelve Years Old: Partner Poop Out

Your twelve-year-old daughter is working on a school project with a classmate. She expresses frustration because her classmate is not pulling 50 percent of the weight. Rarely do these group projects work out with an even split of work. While that can be frustrating, it's also a reality that your daughter will have to learn to deal with. Sometimes it helps to think from a new perspective, so ask her to think about the work and effort her partner has put in. If that doesn't help, let her know that it's okay to be frustrated, but she has to move forward and get her project done. So suggest she talk things through with the partner, expressing concern about the project while focusing on school and not personal annoyances. The lessons learned will help with the next, inevitable, group project.

### Thirteen through Eighteen Years Old: Night Owl

Your fifteen-year-old daughter is a night owl. She does her own thing after school with friends and then comes home to veg out, be with family, and talk on the phone. Sometimes she listens to music. She doesn't want to start with homework until after dinner, and you're nervous that she won't have enough time, won't get enough sleep, and won't have parents who are awake to help her out. She's fifteen. She should be able to manage on her own and make these decisions. In a few years, she will be out of the house. Be glad that she's doing her homework, and let her face the consequences if she runs out of time. This is the time to let it go and let her learn from the experience. She may truly thrive in the evening and be unable to get it all done when the daytime distractions are at bay. If she's floundering, then talk with her about it, but let her be a part of the problem solving and come up with a solution.

# To Summarize...

- When enough is enough, take the time and make the space for your emotions so you don't react too quickly.

- Create a variety of places you can go, either in your mind or physically, when you need to get away and you can't really go far.

- As with so many other aspects of parenting, keep the long-term view in mind before losing your cool on something small.

- You still have to deal with the details, so honor each one as a practice of patience.

# Chapter 8

## Perspective: It's All about the Small Stuff

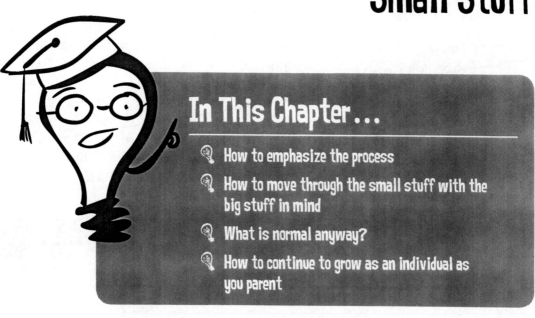

### In This Chapter...

- How to emphasize the process
- How to move through the small stuff with the big stuff in mind
- What is normal anyway?
- How to continue to grow as an individual as you parent

One of the difficult tasks of parenting is keeping perspective—about the moment and the lifelong process of nurturing another human. It's no wonder small joys get lost in the shuffle. We might be so busy with the minutiae of life that small hurdles sometimes seem enormous and daily joys disappear. Often, the best thing to do is step back and shift your viewpoint. In this chapter, you'll learn to keep perspective as a parent and help your child develop a sense of perspective to lead a balanced life.

The daily worry about a social issue, a schedule snafu, or a budget strain consumes many parents' attention and prevents us from appreciating both the magic of small moments with our family and the larger wonder of the decades-long process of parenting. Noted author and psychologist Madeline Levine remarks that knowing your child's schedule of activities is completely different from knowing your child. We get caught up in the daily hustle and bustle and forget about the big picture. In fact, think about the most recent holiday cards you received from families. Were they lists of accomplishments and activities, or were they about the people who make up the family? What we do does not define us; it merely helps shape us. While stepping back can be challenging, here are a few small practices that can help you keep your perspective.

## Record the Process

One easy way to celebrate the small moments is to keep a record. While there is little time for anything anymore, you can make time to record a few ordinary treasures. I'm not suggesting a journal where you write your child weekly love letters and progress reports—but a brief record of milestones, joys, and hurdles. A journal will help record these moments in a way that memory alone cannot. For me, it's an electronic document that I save and add to periodically. It's a simple table with the age on the left and the noteworthy items on the right, separated into two columns: physical milestones, and verbal and cognitive milestones.

| Age | Physical Milestones | Verbal/Cognitive Milestones |
|---|---|---|
| Two months | First smile | |
| Three months | Rolled over | |
| Nine months | | First word: "Da" |

In the beginning, there were so many, captured by the month. Rolled over to tummy, rolled over from tummy, first tooth, first word… anything I decided to record. Now the entries are much less frequent, but I have a place to keep them. I encourage you to consider recording these moments, no matter how simply. I began this because my mother was a researcher, and a colleague suggested she do it with our words. She found it fascinating to track our language development. I began with the same intention, but I have found

### Recording

Start by keeping a record of something simple. You'll never know if it helps you with the big picture until you try. Using a fun journal with a cute cover might help!

**Perspiration**

these documents have grown into so much more. And if I haven't convinced you yet, let me share with you the joy it brings my own children to read about their first words, their first thoughts, and their first lost teeth that are already fleeting moments to their young minds. One time my daughter asked what her first words were, so we went back to that document and found them— "uh oh" and "Ma Ma." We read farther down and found one comment that still makes me giggle— and still holds true: "We have to watch out for commercials, you and me, Mommy, because we like to buy new clothes and toys." In this quote, I can hear my own lessons to my daughter and her application of them.

Find a way that is easy for you to record meaningful moments. It might be a written document; it might be through drawings. Keep a small notepad, and find a time of day to regularly record a moment or two. This process will allow you to record memorable quotes or incidents and will also help nurture your process of gratitude. In reflecting on a highlight from the day, you will reinforce positive emotions. In time, the notebook or record will become a family treasure. And in this day and age, you can always digitally record and send yourself a reminder to add it to your collection of milestones.

Recording these small moments will remind you of how precious your time with your child is. Our lives move especially fast these days with all the expectations out there. And throughout your time together, you can look back together on meaningful moments, cherishing the memories.

## Keep Your Eye on the Prize

Though it may be easier said than done, try to remember the big picture as you move through the day-to-day. You are raising a family, and every decision matters, but not equally. Great things will happen, and bad things too. Both the good and the bad will help shape how you and your child roll with the punches.

Think about resilience (and read about it in **Chapter 13**) as you experience life's ups and downs. The good is fun and should be enjoyed. Enjoy the

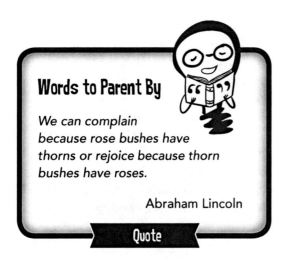

## Words to Parent By

*We can complain because rose bushes have thorns or rejoice because thorn bushes have roses.*

Abraham Lincoln

**Quote**

moments of laughter, connection, joy. Cherish the sparkle in your child's eye with new discoveries and special gifts. The bad can be powerful and productive. Don't ignore those times—learn from them. Examine them long enough to learn something for the next time and then move on. Work to trust yourself in the moment, and remember that all humans make mistakes, experience adversity, and face tough challenges. Also remember that we can all learn and grow—parents too!

Use your partner, a member of your trusted network, or even your child as a sounding board. Whenever you can, be explicit about your effort to keep a longer-term perspective. If you realize that you did lose your cool, take a deep breath and try to determine whether the incident was part of a larger pattern or an uncommon reaction. Acknowledge the incident and identify what you hope to do differently next time. Explain that you view the event as part of the larger process of growth, but feel free to admit that it might feel very important and negative at the moment. If you can share any part of this with your child, you will model a process of resilience and perspective that might help with your child's own feelings of discouragement.

Learn from your own mistakes as a parent, including how you deal with the mistakes of your children. After a hard day, help your child understand the big picture and how the day's events play a part in it. Your child may or may not have had any control over those events. Sometimes a child's day can boil down to one specific occurrence. Other times your child may simply be overwhelmed, overtired, hungry, or in a bad mood. Help your child see that we can all learn something for tomorrow and, most importantly, that tomorrow is another day. Again, keep the big picture in mind.

## Who Asked You?

When you were walking down the street with your brand-new baby girl bundled in the stroller, did anyone stop you and mention that her sock was missing? If she was crying, did anyone point out that she was probably hungry? When your two-year-old boy refused to wear his jacket (despite the fact that you suggested three times before leaving the house that he wear it), did anyone stop you and say he must be cold? These helpful people may not have known you or your children, and while it might have been annoying to listen to them, they were probably just trying to be helpful.

I remember being on an airplane with a screaming child. I tried the bottle, the pacifier, and singing (even though it totally embarrassed me to be singing "our songs" in front of these strangers). I knew that my baby was overtired and that my own anxiety was feeding into his reactions. A flight attendant came up to me and asked me to please quiet my baby. She made several suggestions about what I should do. I was mortified, furious, and near desperate. Of course, I hoped my baby could be calm, quiet, and comfortable. I knew I had tried everything in my bag of tricks and simply needed to relax to help my baby calm down. It was extremely difficult to remember that the flight attendant probably believed that she was being helpful.

When you receive unsolicited advice, take a deep breath. You may even learn a nugget of wisdom that you will use for years to come. If you can keep an open mind, you just might learn something valuable. You also may nod and smile and simply ignore the stranger's idea. Gathering ideas from others can allow you to shift or simply strengthen your own position, and you can actively seek opinions from your trusted network. (See **Chapter 21** for more on community.) You can evaluate other people's opinions and decide for yourself which ideas might work for your family and which will not.

### See It from Another View

The next time someone offers you advice on your parenting, consider it. Don't promise to implement it, but consider it. You never know—you might learn by doing something differently.

Perspiration

When you were a child, did you ever think, "When I'm a parent, I'll never do that to my kids"? When you were young, you likely wondered about, challenged, and begrudged some of the decisions (or what felt like decrees) your own parents made. As an adult, have you ever had an "aha" moment where you finally understood one of those decisions? Or, better yet, have you ever heard yourself utter something your mother or father "always" said? Your parenting is heavily influenced by your experience as a child. You want your child to share some experiences that created good memories for you and to be spared those that created bad memories. We must remember that our memories and experience can leave us vulnerable. It's important to notice when that vulnerability is clouding our judgment.

# Yes, It's Normal—or Not Abnormal

For the most part, what your child does, says, feels, and thinks is normal. You can pick up hundreds of books about what to do if your child bites, is a picky eater, doesn't sleep well—and the list goes on. You might worry about these issues, but most fall within the range of normal behaviors and issues kids face. Though you can find detailed information elsewhere about each of the following, what follows are a few of the most common issues that might seem large in the short term and are very normal from the perspective of child development:

- *Biting.* Kids satisfy a physical need by biting as their teeth grow in. They also develop communication skills in different ways and at different rates. Biting can be a defensive (or offensive) reaction to conflict, especially for toddlers. They might bite people out of a sheer physical urge or as a reaction to a perceived or real threat. Most kids grow out of this practice fairly quickly. You can teach your child not to bite by substituting a teething ring, using a stern voice to convey that biting is bad, or removing your child from a situation after biting. Depending on the age of your child, you might ask how the person being bitten feels. Even young children can understand when another person is hurt. One of the best ways to help your biting child's habits is to be proactive. Be aware of situations in which biting occurs and work to prevent conflicts or to provide space and safety.

- *Sharing.* A mother once told me that sharing is overrated. I agree wholeheartedly. It's a necessary skill in life, but not one you have to like at all times. Furthermore, sharing can be a concept that is very difficult for children to understand at some developmental stages. Model it and encourage it. You might start by having your child set some self-imposed parameters. Once a young person develops some feeling of control and ownership, sharing becomes easier. Maybe a friend can hold the truck for two minutes before your child gets it back for ten. Allow your child to *not* share sometimes, to feel disappointment, or to feel anger when someone does not share. Those are—guess what?—normal experiences! Of course, sharing will be crucial in many aspects of life, so don't dismiss the idea when it gets tough, but be sure to acknowledge how hard it can be.

*Friendship.* Being a good friend is not always easy, but it's a skill your child will use throughout life. Again, modeling is key here. Try role playing with different situations as your child develops. Something educators are seeing a lot of these days is kids who don't pick up easily on social cues. Our society encourages such autonomy and drive that we do not practice our skills of relating to others as frequently as we should. Refer to **Chapter 23** for more specifics on relating. And, if you are truly concerned about your child's social life, Michael Thompson wrote a wonderful book, *Best Friends, Worst Enemies: The Social Lives of Children.* In it, he discusses the range of normal behaviors and when it's time to start worrying.

*Moodiness.* Moodiness can affect the entire family in a negative way, and it is a very common facet of growing up. As children grow, their bodies change, and the balance in their hormones is not always there. Children need support through these difficult times. It's hard to see and feel your body changing. Sometimes children actually lose control of their moods and cannot rein them in. The important thing is for you to practice patience, insist on respect, and support your child through this. If your child is consistently moody, suggest shifting sleep and/or eating patterns. Sleep is an essential component of good health and positive mood, so you may start examining your child's bed and wake times. Is your child getting the recommended hours of sleep? Remember that recommended hours are an average. Your child might need above the average hours to feel well and balanced. Diet also plays an important part in hormone and mood regulation. Reflect on your child's meal and snack habits, and try to find a better formula for your child. Try offering almonds or edamame for a quick and healthful protein boost, or leave fresh fruit out as a snack option. Know that periodic moodiness is natural and normal, and look at other routines more deeply if moodiness becomes a persistent pattern.

*Defiance.* Do you want your child living at home at forty? I doubt it. Children are programmed to learn to be independent. And guess what? You want yours to be. However, it is this very drive for independence that can translate into direct defiance. Maria Montessori said, "Never help a child with a task at which they feel they can succeed." It can be frustrating to wait for kids to figure out how to do things—and sure it would be more efficient if you just did it—but by doing everything for your child, you take away the opportunity to learn autonomy. Defiance is an element of independence. Toddlers often defiantly claim, "I'll do it myself!" as they try to pour their own drink or use a step stool. Sure, they spill the drink or fall off the step stool at times, but if you consistently do these things for them, you stop them from learning to do them themselves. Adolescents often display defiance through questioning authority. Be consistent and clear about the rules that are firm in your family. At the same time, allow autonomy and mistakes when reasonable. As children grow, they need more and more independence.

# It's Not Normal, but That's Okay Too

There are times when your child experiences something that doesn't fall within the normal range. And that's okay too! Perspective can help you deal with the range of life's experiences. Know whom you can go to for help. Perhaps your mentor, a friend, or a trusted educator can make some discipline suggestions. Do you have a friend with a similar challenge? Maybe a friend of a friend? As the saying goes, knowledge is power. Get familiar with your situation and learn about the issue you are facing. Use written resources, and talk with your friends openly so you can share your own burden and find help.

Perhaps you have read about your predicament and asked friends but still feel unsure about how to proceed. Do you have a trusted pediatrician? Your pediatrician should be someone you are comfortable with and can go to with difficult questions. Whether it's a learning difference, a lack of social skills, or an issue with defiance, your pediatrician can help you weigh your options. Medications might be an option, if you are comfortable with them, but they are not a necessary option just because you are going to the doctor. Talk with

# Perspective Looks Different at Different Stages of Life

## Zero through Five Years Old

Infants and toddlers have trouble with perspective because, developmentally, they are focused on themselves and their needs and desires. Perspective can be introduced through conversation and modeling, but don't expect kids this age to master it. In these years, perspective can include cheering up a friend, being a good winner after a tough game of memory, or commenting on how a character in a storybook might feel.

## Six through Twelve Years Old

Perspective comes naturally to elementary-aged children because they are developing a sense of the world around them. Parents can help cultivate this value by reading stories with different points of view and talking about current events. During these years, perspective can include encouraging a teammate, questioning decisions, or understanding a historical event from two different angles.

## Thirteen through Eighteen Years Old

Teens can appreciate perspective because at this stage, attitudes and opinions are changing rapidly. Parents can foster perspective by asking questions and respecting answers. At this age, perspective can include correcting you when you say something narrow minded, writing a research paper presenting multiple points of view, or attending church with a friend for the first time.

## It's Not Negotiating with Terrorists

The next time your adolescent asks you to change your mind, change it. Is this issue worth fighting over, or is this something your adolescent can win? After all, your goal is to raise an independent-minded adult, so there's no time like the present to foster that independence.

**Perspiration**

your doctor about your ideas. There are social-skills groups out there for kids. There are support groups for depressed teens. There are learning specialists, and even full schools, that focus on specific disorders. Be thorough. Get to know the issue and all your options. Read, talk with specialists, and be sure to start with options you are most comfortable with—not just the popular options.

Once you have a plan of action and are working with your child on the issue, be sure to continually seek out support. Talking through your own experience will help calm you and allow you to be stronger for your child. It will also allow those around you to help support your process and respect your plan. If you are uncomfortable sharing with your friends, then find a trusted professional you can talk with. It's important that you feel supported in your efforts to nurture your child through a challenge.

In time, you will see that this, too, was just one more challenge that made your family what it is. Your calm and thoughtful approach will help nurture your child.

## Growth Is a Lifelong Process

Be glad for your family—in spite of any issues. The very word, issue, is so charged these days. Remember, everyone's got issues. Be proud of the efforts you make to know your child and yourself and the efforts you and your child make to grow and thrive. It can be easy to become frustrated by a negative behavior pattern and miss the small signs of slow improvement. Try to focus on the big picture and remember that growth and sustainable change take time. Use the resources you have—family, trusted friends, teachers, or professionals—to help you and your family acknowledge each small step toward a larger goal.

In psychologist Carol Dweck's work, she highlights the power of the word "yet." We might not be perfect at this conflict resolution, *yet*, but we are getting better every day. As parents, we might not react perfectly calmly to a situation, *yet*, but we are working to improve step by step.

When my son was a toddler and young child, he lied to me on occasion. (Heavens no!) We talked about trust, we role-played, and we enforced logical consequences. It was hard, and every time I would think, "Why would my sweet boy lie to me? Doesn't he trust me? Is he scared to tell the truth?" Of course his behavior was natural, but I had to put it in perspective every time. Now, as an adolescent, I am so grateful for those small moments. He understands honesty, and I am more keen to respect his privacy. With a little perspective, we are able to enjoy a more honest relationship.

# Character in Action

### Zero through Five Years Old: Attention, Everyone

Your five-year-old son's teacher has suggested he be tested for attention deficit disorder. She mentions he has trouble sitting during circle time and that he cannot stay focused on his desk work.

First things first. Most five-year-old boys have trouble sitting for a sustained period. Don't rush to conclusions or get nervous. Take the suggestion to heart and get some more information. Talk to other teachers or caretakers for more anecdotes. Start a journal about your own experience. And, yes, go ahead and make an appointment with your pediatrician (and/or an educational therapist or learning specialist). Just because you make an appointment does not mean you have to commit to drug therapy. He might not even have a disorder. Make sure you know and trust your pediatrician well. You will need to at times like these. In all likelihood, your doctor will discuss and have you think about sleep, diet, other activities, and a host of other things before recommending medication. Talk through the teacher's comments and anything else you've collected. Be as honest as you can, and your doctor can help you decide some of your next moves.

This is also a key time for your village. Your spouse or coparent should definitely be involved in all of the above. In addition, the two of you can talk through your emotions together to support one another. Confide in your friends, parents, and mentors. Once you've worked through more details, then you can make an informed decision about how to proceed. (For more about education, read **Chapter 17**.)

## Six through Twelve Years Old: Moody Ms. Tween

Your tween daughter comes home and is not interested in talking. When you push for a conversation, she barks something negative, goes to her room, slams the door, and doesn't come out till dinner.

Be thankful that she comes out for dinner. Her moods are completely normal. Her hormones are raging, her body is changing, and where to sit at lunch is the most important question she has to answer each day. On top of that, she has homework that challenges her and homework that bores her, and she's sick of playing soccer.

Give her space and understand that she will come through this. That doesn't mean she can treat you disrespectfully. When she is in a better place (likely after eating dinner), sit down with her. Do more listening than talking. And don't press her if she's not interested in chatting. Be with her.

At some point in your conversation, make it very clear she cannot hurt you (ignore, slam the door, etc.) but that, of course, she can have her space and time. Also explain to her that you hope your home can be a safe place for her but that there will be times she needs to push through and gather herself, like when she comes home just when you are heading out and she needs to watch her little brother.

Promise to try to understand as best you can, and urge her to talk to you whenever she can. Be open to her, and don't judge her comments harshly. If she opens up about how hard it is at lunchtime because she is being excluded, don't jump in and ask who is excluding her. Don't try to solve her problems. Listen to them and help her work through them. They are, after all, likely normal. She will make it through, and you will too!

## Thirteen through Eighteen Years Old: Lazy Bones

Your fifteen-year-old son simply won't do as he's told. He's supposed to take out the garbage every week, and yet he doesn't do it unless you nag him three times. He rarely helps clear the table. He was preoccupied with his friends when he was "watching" his younger sister. He sleeps late every morning, and he won't get out of bed until noon on Saturdays. He's not angry or mean. He just seems to be ignoring you and the family and seems, well, lazy.

He's actually not lazy—he's fifteen. He's got other things on his mind. You might not want to know what they are, but they are certainly normal. He's thinking about sex, his friends, after-school activities, and maybe homework (though it's likely low on the list).

To some degree, let him be to figure himself out. If the nagging is turning into fighting, be sure to take a breath and then find some time to talk to him. Find a compromise where he can grow up but also learn he cannot dismiss his responsibilities at home. Some of those might include assigning fewer chores in the morning so he can sleep in but scheduling more of them at night. You also might require that he be with the family for a certain time frame before returning to his room in the evening. Perhaps you limit the screen time during what you deem family time but allow more screen time after school or on the weekend mornings to encourage him to get up. Allow him some choice in the process so that he can gain ownership over more of the routine and still participate as a contributing family member.

# To Summarize...

- Enjoy the small moments while keeping your eye on the big picture.

- Your opinion matters most.

- Normal is overrated. Embrace your family's uniqueness!

- You're parenting for life. Go ahead and get comfortable.

# Promoting Independence

One of the goals of parenting is to raise a self-sufficient individual. A child who is encouraged to have an opinion and is honored for individuality is more likely to develop into a responsible, constructive member of society. This part, focused on promoting independence, will take a close look at why children need to think on their own and take responsibility and how to offer opportunities that allow for this growth.

Independence begins with confidence. Confidence comes from within, so if you model that trait, your child will likely adopt it. Exploration, moderation, perseverance, resilience, and responsibility also require you to take the reins yourself. I will walk you through ways to encourage and support these values in your parenting and with your child. These chapters will take a deep look at all the virtues associated with independence as well as how to develop them within yourself and your child as your child's identity emerges and grows.

# Chapter 9

## Confidence: Stick to Your Guns

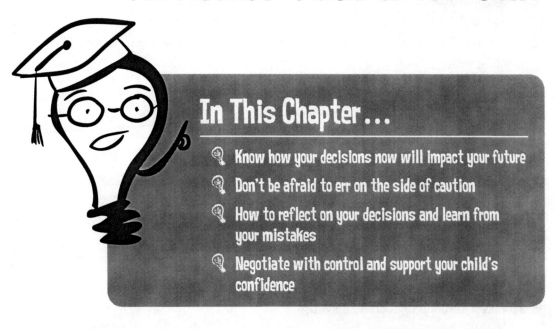

### In This Chapter...

- Know how your decisions now will impact your future
- Don't be afraid to err on the side of caution
- How to reflect on your decisions and learn from your mistakes
- Negotiate with control and support your child's confidence

Everyone's got an opinion about parenting, and many love to share it. While it's good to listen to understand other points of view, the trick in parenting is to make choices you can be proud of. You won't be able to please everyone, so do what you feel is best. I recommend a no-apologies approach (so long as you had best intentions). In this chapter, read about ways to reinforce your own confidence as a parent and cultivate confidence in your child to help support self-assurance and self-reliance.

Always use manners, but don't apologize for doing the best you can in your parenting. Confidence requires trust in yourself. Trust that you're doing

# Confidence Looks Different at Different Stages of Life

## Zero through Five Years Old

Very young children are naturally confident with their I-can-do-it-myself attitudes. Parents can help preserve this confidence in children with positive reinforcement and encouragement. At this stage, confidence can include taking a few steps, trying to use the toilet, or pouring a cup of milk.

## Six through Twelve Years Old

Children in this age group are susceptible to losing confidence as they interact more and more with other people and face academic, social, and physical challenges. It's crucial for parents to support confidence in these years by celebrating success, understanding failure, and offering praise when appropriate. However, false praise can be detrimental to confidence. At this stage, confidence can include spelling words inventively, singing a song in front of an audience, or joining a group of kids on the playground.

## Thirteen through Eighteen Years Old

Teens often volley from overconfidence to extreme insecurity. It's difficult to begin to nurture confidence at this age, but it's not too late if your teen doesn't have it. It can be encouraged with reality checks and by offering opportunities for success and failure. Remember, the child who fails is not a failure as the term is understood colloquially. In adolescence, confidence can include taking a shot at a goal or basket in PE class or on a school team, asking a boy out, or choosing to write on an original topic for a school assignment.

what you can to make good decisions, such as reading this book for starters. Trust that your instinct is generally right. And trust that you're going to make mistakes and own up to them. (See **Chapters 13** and **14** for more on learning from our mistakes.) And, seeing you act with confidence, your child is bound to follow suit.

# Go with Your Gut

Usually your gut instinct is something you can rely on. In spontaneous situations, your gut will serve you well. Go with it and see what happens: You're walking on the sidewalk, your daughter runs into the intersection, and you scream with terror, "*Stop*!" Okay, so you don't like to raise your voice and you're humiliated that you look like a terrible parent because your child is running free. What if some of the passersby think you're irresponsible for letting your child run ahead of you? What if they're saying to themselves, "My goodness, that poor child needs a parent who will hold her hand"? You did what you needed to do in the moment. Next time, you'll know to stick with her and discuss what to do at intersections. In the moment, go with your gut, scream your heart out, and be confident that you did what needed doing and that your daughter is safely on her way to the next errand.

Keep in mind that while your gut is often right, it is not perfect. Don't forget to reflect on your decisions. Sometimes, mid-decision, you'll realize it was too rash or not well thought out, and sometimes you won't know for sure until you see it through. Be sure to think back and consider your decision-making process too. When you reflect on your own actions, you teach your child truly invaluable lessons, which does not suggest a lack of confidence. Rather, having the confidence to acknowledge mistakes helps both of you learn from them and take responsibility in the future. When you discuss your actions, their consequences, and what you might do differently in the future, your child will be inspired to do the same.

## Words to Parent By

*No one can make you feel inferior without your consent.*

Eleanor Roosevelt

Quote

## Recognizing a Mistake and Learning from It

It's your job to call your child out on mistakes, and you will earn your child's respect if you do the same with yourself. We're human—we're imperfect. That's okay. And your child will learn to move forward by watching you have the confidence to do the same.

Your fifteen-year-old daughter's grades dropped, and you decided to punish her with no television, hoping that would motivate her to do better. A few weeks into the punishment, you realize that she's still overenjoying her downtime (sans television) and that she does not seem to be studying any differently. You realize that you've made a mistake—a ban on TV was not the right punishment. She needs help with her time management. You need to fess up. You need to acknowledge that, in fact, you made a mistake and are going to change direction. The two of you will begin by working together to devise a schedule. Think about whether this parenting decision had the desired outcome or not, and let that inform future decisions.

### Let Your Words Guide Your Way

If you're having trouble reflecting on your decisions, try keeping a journal. It's easier than ever with digital devices. You can start a word processing document, a spreadsheet of bulleted thoughts, a voice-recording memo program, a note form on a tablet, or an old-fashioned diary and pen. Whatever the medium, consider writing daily in the beginning. Note any parenting decisions you made that day and how you felt about them. See what kinds of patterns emerge and if you can use this information to help you with future decisions.

**Perspiration**

## You're the Parent!

I don't recommend the "Because I said so!" route. Not only is it futile, but it also will sound very cliché, and I can almost guarantee you'll want to take back your words the moment you hear them uttered from your lips. However, you are the parent and you're allowed to just say so. Hopefully you have reasons to back up your decisions, but truth be told, not enough parents take the responsibility of parenting to its logical end. Set limits and enforce them. Be as consistent as you can with enforcing the limits. When your child questions your choice, it's okay to justify it, but it's also okay to say you'd appreciate cooperation in the moment and you'd be happy to discuss it later. This offers you a chance to consider your decision, but at the same time, it allows you to move forward without harping on it.

Your five-year-old daughter is pitching a fit at the grocery store about some sort of cereal. You ask her to stop. If she doesn't, take her out of the situation. That might include leaving the cereal aisle or leaving the grocery store. When she is calm, then you can explain why Chocolate Covered Cookie Crumble Cereal isn't going to be stocked in your pantry. She will learn that sometimes your decisions stand simply because you said so. Yet there is no need to say those words: You said so for a good reason!

It's a good idea to work on "the look" for these kinds of situations. Usually, once a child understands that when you're dead serious and you give the look, it's time to shape up. Then you can discuss the details when it feels right. You don't have to practice the look in front of a mirror. Just let your child drive you to it, and it will come.

## Building Confidence in Your Choices

I have found myself at too many dinner parties where the conversation goes to television, computer, telephone habits, you name it, and the parents on the other side of the conversation begin to judge and justify: Does your daughter have a telephone yet? Isn't twelve too young for a phone? We got our son a phone because he really *needs* it. Well, we watch that show, but only when homework's done. We don't usually watch television, but... We don't allow the kids to use the computer at home. These are all claims and questions I have heard repeatedly.

Why do we feel pressured to justify our decisions to our friends? We talk about movies we've seen or parties we've been to freely, but when it comes to talking about our kids, we feel the need to explain why we let them
_____ (fill in the blank—play football, read a vampire book, surf the web, have a cell phone). Feel good about your parenting. It's fine—and even a good idea—to open yourself up a little, rethink some of your decisions, and take some tips. Feel free to imitate what seems appealing, but don't doubt yourself just because you shared something in the conversation that didn't

jive with another other parent's choices. Think about the content and treat it as you would any judgment, question, or advice you might get in another arena (at work or in a recreation league for example). Additionally, kids who hear all of the justifying and apologizing for their parents' decisions will then see and model that lack of confidence in their own decision making.

Our son and his friend desperately wanted cell phones. They were in fifth grade, eleven years old, and did not have any need. When asked what they would do with them, they replied, "Text, talk to friends." We told our son that if he had a need for one, we would consider it. This conversation came up multiple times with his friend's parents. They heard us say this and expressed the same reasoning to their child.

A few months after the last conversation about a phone, our son got a job escorting younger children to their soccer practice. He walked home from there just at dusk. We decided as a family that we would all feel more comfortable if he had a phone. It was a very simple decision. He paid for the phone and activation fee, and we added him to our service with the understanding that he would follow certain rules.

The moment his friend's parents got wind of this, they jokingly *accused* us of buckling. My first reaction was defensive: "But he has a job, he needs it to be safe, he paid for it…" I should have had more confidence in my own decision making to proudly say, "Indeed, he has a phone, and his father and I are very proud of him for showing such initiative." There is a balance between discussing your decisions with friends and feeling the need to justify decisions that others may not agree with.

Reading this book and others like it will help you know you are a good parent. You're doing the best you can, and you're trying to make informed decisions. Feel good about yourself and enjoy the fact that you're educating yourself and becoming a savvy parent. Remember, no one has ever parented your child before.

# Building Confidence in Your Child

I was talking with my mother and son, and the conversation went to how much a parent loves a child. It led to one of those moments where we were competing to love each other more: "I love you more than you'll ever know" and "Well, I

**Resolutions All Year-Round**

Make a resolution not to apologize for the next parenting tip or practice you share with a friend. Just say it with pride.

**Perspiration**

love you more than that and then a little more..." At one point, my son said, "Well, I love me more than anyone else does." I laughed at first. How egotistical! But then, upon reflection, I realized how healthy and wonderful that statement was.

You must learn to love yourself. How will others begin to appreciate all you have to offer if *you* don't see it? Of course, everyone needs fans in their corner cheering them on and reminding them of their worth, but you must be your own best advocate. What my son was demonstrating was a pride in himself that I couldn't give him. I could laugh, or I could celebrate. First I laughed, but then I went back and celebrated. I told him that I thought that was a wonderful way to feel about himself (but that, of course, I still loved him more!).

Be aware that you cannot give your child confidence, but you can support it and nurture it. Praise your child's efforts and ideas. Reflect together on decisions. Share your pride in your child regularly. Mention pride in effort, but also in accomplishments. Don't focus on accomplishments, but don't ignore them either.

We took our son to his first meeting with the cantor at the temple in preparation for his bar mitzvah. She was extremely gracious as we made our way through the small talk and basic introductions. Then she cut to the chase and had him begin reading his blessings to her. He had been in a class and had chosen to take the class twice the previous semester. It was clear his hard work had paid off, as he was familiar with all the blessings and read them with great ease. She was impressed, which in turn made me beam with pride. Later in the day, I mentioned, in passing, how proud I was of the way he read. He looked surprised and did a double take as he asked, "Really?" In his mind, he was expected to do a good job. This experience of becoming a bar mitzvah was a privilege for him (that he chose to undertake). He knew how hard it was for his father and me to get him to all his classes and extra tutorials, and he was working because he loved it and because he had the opportunity. He had no idea that I was proud, and it was a terrific moment of glory for both of us.

## Where to Go When You Need Help

Never forget about your village. You have friends, family, and professionals you can go to when you are in need. When the need for help gets bigger than you can handle, don't be afraid to reach out. Your child will make mistakes that are bigger than you can handle. You might make some of those too. When it gets to be too much, have the confidence in yourself to know you cannot (and are not meant or expected to) do this alone.

If your child is engaged in risky or harmful behavior, seek out the advice of your pediatrician. Your doctor can offer you some ideas and refer you to specialists who can work with your child. There are many family organizations, books, and other resources that are also there for the sole purpose of supporting children, parents, and families. (See the **Appendix** for some of these.) Having confidence in yourself means knowing when you can handle the parenting and when you can't.

## Character in Action

### Zero through Five Years Old: Sister Stress

Your sister-in-law is in town for three weeks to help you with your toddler while your husband is away on business. Your usual bedtime routine is to put your daughter down for the night and to leave her, even if she cries out. You have a strong relationship with your sister-in-law and are extremely grateful for her help. She is clearly trying to work within all your requirements (using the pacifier only in the stroller, glass bottles, and only organic formula), but she does express her concern about your daughter crying. Each night as you listen to your daughter cry, you also know your sister-in-law can hear her, and you can't get to sleep because you're so worried that she's judging you. Take a step back. Recall that this is not about you or your sister-in-law. She wouldn't come to help you out for this extended period and try to accommodate your preferences if she didn't already respect you as a parent. She also loves your girl. Acknowledge her concerns (and really listen and consider them). If you still feel you're making the right decision, let her know and ask her to let it go. Let her know that this is your decision. Do all this, and keep in mind that you're tired and sometimes you're being forced to respond in complete exhaustion (i.e., the middle of the night).

### Six through Twelve Years Old: Text Trauma

Your twelve-year-old son is texting friends inappropriate messages. You've uncovered this with a regular check of the phone and discussed how disappointed you are. What do you do? Express confidence in him first. Let your son know that you know he can do better and you expect better. The logical consequence is to require that you see all the texts he sends and receives for an extended period of time. Even after that, it's a good idea to continue to check his account (all accounts, actually, including email, Facebook, Instagram, and whatever else is popular when you are reading this). Let your child know that if he's ashamed to have you see it, he should be ashamed to be sending it.

### Thirteen through Eighteen Years Old: To Prep or Not to Prep

The sixteen-year-old sophomore in your carpool mentions he has SAT tutoring after school. In the midst of getting everyone buckled, driving, and figuring out dinner for the evening, your mind starts to wander all over the place. Is your daughter behind? Should she be in SAT tutoring? Go with your gut. If you weren't concerned about the SAT before, why should you be now just because someone else is? Your rider could have a history or trouble with test taking, be angling for a scholarship, or even be miseducated about the pros and cons of test prep. Whatever the case, have confidence in yourself for making that decision, and do not send your child to test prep simply because someone else is going. At the very most, let it spark a conversation about the idea without pushing it.

# To Summarize...

- Trust yourself and your parenting!

- Trust your child!

- Take your time when you can, but don't be afraid to act in the moment.

- Reflect and respond. Support your child's confidence by example.

# Chapter 10

## Exploration: How Will You Know If You Don't Try?

### In This Chapter...

- When and how to try new things
- What are the options out there for exploring?
- How can I join in the fun?
- When it's time to stop and reconsider

There's so much available for kids today, and knowing what to choose and when to choose it will help you make informed choices. The important areas to consider are: financial commitments, time commitments, and last but not least, your child's interests (as opposed to what *you* might want your child to do). In this chapter, you will read about new ways to explore and encourage your child to do the same in order to sustain curiosity and confidence throughout life. There are many experiences to investigate, including travel, relationships, and competitive sports, which are covered extensively throughout this book. The arts are a valuable outlet for children and families, and this chapter will look at exploration through exposure to art.

A balanced schedule of extracurricular activities helps model the importance of living a balanced life. And exploration of the arts, culture, and athletics contributes to a rich and vibrant life. However, there is a growing body of research supporting the necessity of free time in children's (and, frankly, adults') schedules. In creating a healthy and balanced schedule, listen to and observe your child closely and remain open to change. Allow your child to contribute to your family's active exploration of arts, culture, and food.

It's often easier to entertain the idea of exploration with younger children, but don't forget it's as important for adolescents as it is for elementary-aged kids. Parents often feel adolescents should have a passion or dedicated activity already clearly defined. This simply is not true. It's completely normal to continue exploring as an adolescent and to try new things without pursuing anything with a dedicated passion. Support your teen's interests, and don't be disappointed if they don't stick. Be sure to encourage commitment (see a season of soccer through or finish the semester of painting), but don't require a lifetime commitment.

As an adult, you too should be exploring. Trying new things will keep you engaged with life and help with your memory. Not to mention, you might have a little fun or find something to enjoy with your child. My tween daughter tries everything and refuses to focus on only one thing. It's terrific because she has a taste of so many experiences. Last year she opted for figure skating, and we signed up for a class together. The first few beginner-level classes were challenging for her and easy for me, as I had many years of recreational skating under my belt. That said, figure skating is certainly not what I would have chosen to spend my scarce free time on (I don't care to be cold), but I love going with her. I quickly moved through the classes, and as they got harder, I found I didn't really like them. And then one day, I got my T-stop! I did it! I mastered a skill. I was stoked, over the moon! I went home and shared the news proudly. Now she and I skate at the same level (goes to show how quickly kids can

## Words to Parent By

*The artist is nothing without the gift, but the gift is nothing without work.*

Emile Zola

**Quote**

pick things up), and we look forward to our time together. Not sure I'll ever get that spin, but hey, I'll try.

## See New Things through Dance

Try new activities formally or informally. A spontaneous dance party is one of our family's favorite evening activities. We turn on the music, and everyone dances around until we collapse, one by one, from laughter or shortness of breath. Free dancing is a vibrant and self-directed way of communicating with the entire body. Dance and music have traditionally been undervalued in our school system, yet they remain central features of many cultures. Dance can be a wonderful form of physical exercise and artistic expression and, depending on where you live, is often offered in a variety of modes. From hip-hop to ballet to folk dancing, your child can almost certainly find a type of music and movement that is interesting, challenging, and perhaps most importantly, fun. Just as you do with athletic extracurricular exploration, investigate the program and listen carefully to your child before beginning any longer-term commitment. Find recreational versions of the dance that promote love for the form, development of skill, and noncompetitive learning.

If your child remains consistently excited about the program and begins asking to participate at a higher level, then you and your child can examine the various possibilities that might work for your child's schedule and level of commitment and also for your family's schedule and value system. In some cases, it might be

### Dancing Disappointment

One of my students was forced to dance from a young age. She was a beautiful performer and had lovely posture, even in class. I was always so impressed with her dedication and poise. I always respected her parents for getting her in so young and giving her this gift. In one assignment, she wrote about the pressure of dance and how she'd like to quit but that it would devastate her parents. She was only twelve years old, spending hours each day on something she didn't love. I realized it wasn't her choice and she had no voice in the decision. Here she could do something so well. Imagine what she could do if she was truly driven.

Uninspired

that the next available level after a recreational experience is an intensive, year-round, competitive program. This may or may not be right for your child or for your family, and it is worth exploring the details carefully. Choosing to spend another year in the recreational system may be a perfect way to encourage skill development and love for dance without adding pressure. The key here, no matter how much enthusiasm your child's teacher or you feel for the program, is to wait until your *child* clearly asks to join the activity at a higher level.

## Cue the Music

No matter where you live, your child can have free dance time each day simply by playing some music. Instruments, on the other hand, can be expensive or bulky, and some can require a minimum of instruction simply to create a sound. As with most things, allow your child to help to direct any music learning. I desperately wanted a piano player among my children. I could never master it myself after years and years of lessons and always found it fascinating that people could read two lines of music at once and control their hands to play separately. My children weren't interested, though. I knew from their music teacher at school that they had the gift. I begged. (Yes, I begged.) They just didn't want to do it. They danced. They acted. They were good students. They had friends. I had to let it go because I did not want a fight on my hands every time they needed to practice or go to a lesson. Lo and behold, one summer, my teenage son said he wanted to try it. So far, he loves it and practices spontaneously on his own. His younger brother has been inspired and is also taking lessons.

Find an instructor or class that supports the values you endorse and that nurtures the skills you believe are important. There will be times when you need to encourage your child to practice, but it should not feel like a battle to get your child to play an instrument or prepare for a lesson. The more you can encourage joyful exploration in the early stages of learning an instrument, the more likely your child will persist when the learning becomes more challenging.

If your child is ready to take a break or quit altogether, please discuss and consider the relevant option. Your child might have good reason to quit (needs a break, has too much going on, isn't interested), and it's your job to

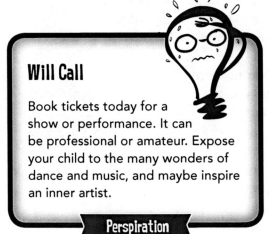

## Will Call

Book tickets today for a show or performance. It can be professional or amateur. Expose your child to the many wonders of dance and music, and maybe inspire an inner artist.

**Perspiration**

clarify. If the instrument is too hard, then encourage your child to push through this difficult time, possibly with a new instructor, new material, or some limited time off. Quitting may be nonnegotiable in your mind. If that's so, then at least consider offering a choice of instrument to your child. My daughter has tried violin, recorder, piano, drums, and guitar. I would love for her to stick with one and master it, but the true exploration is the beauty for her, so every time she's ready to quit another instrument, we have a long conversation (or three or four) about her reasons. I let her know she can always go back to it. I also insist she finish out any lessons that have been paid for or any commitment the teacher requires.

The easiest way to expose your child to the magic of dance and music is to watch or hear different performances. If possible, take your child to a live performance (amateurs or professionals) in a variety of settings. Use Internet videos or television broadcasts to interest your child in a variety of dance and music forms. Our children now beg to see if there is a new video posted by their favorite public school a cappella group. Before taking our kids to see *The Nutcracker* ballet in person, we showed them segments of the ballet and played music from the score. When we finally saw the ballet performed live, they were thrilled when they recognized the music and the story. Exposure and participation lead to increased understanding, appreciation, and enjoyment.

## Invite the Drama Queen

Imaginary play and self-directed reading are childhood staples and are wonderful introductions to more structured theater. Opportunities for children to participate in theater are more abundant in the middle and high school years, but some possibilities of exploring drama in earlier years exist. Many elementary schools produce plays at some time in the year, some cultural or religious institutions have plays associated with yearly rituals or celebrations, and many community centers offer drama programs. With many drama programs, the time commitment can be intense no matter how small a part your child plays. If your child decides to join a dramatic production, you will need to confirm that your family can commit to the rehearsal schedule to guarantee full participation.

As with dance and music, you can introduce your kids to the dramatic arts by watching a live or recorded performance. With younger children, focus your discussion after the performance on the story and the characters. Ask your child which part was the most interesting or which character faced the most difficult choice. Allow your child to generate ideas for what might happen next or to predict how your child might act in a similar situation. With older children, you can ask questions about both the story and the performance: What was it that an actor did to be so believable in that role? What about the portrayal resonated with an idea they might have had from reading the book before, and what was different from their imagination? Empower your children to be critical and appreciative consumers of the story and the performance. Above all, continue to share story and drama in some fashion as a family.

## Art Appreciation

Some families love visiting museums. For other families, a museum is the last place they would go on a free afternoon. Your family might have individuals who fall on both ends of the spectrum! No matter how you feel about visiting a museum, you can foster an appreciation of fine art in your children. While each person has his or her own taste and sensibility, art appreciation can be developed in everyone. The more you know about an artist or a style, the

### Go to the Library or Join a Museum

Visit the library with your child on a regular basis. Make this a natural place to go for entertainment and education. Set your child up with a library card—it's never too late—and make the library a place your child can go with you and explore independently. Younger children can participate in read-alouds, and teens can participate in reading programs and book clubs.

Museums are wonderful places to explore and learn new things. Usually they have special members' benefits and you can go back for multiple visits. Each time you go back, you will learn something new. You will also be teaching your child about multiple resources for information and entertainment.

**Perspiration**

stronger the understanding of the art and the greater the possibility of appreciating the piece.

One easy way to introduce fine art to children is through stories. Regardless of your family's background, mythological and religious art from all cultures can be a fascinating way to engage children in thinking about fine art. Origin legends from Central America and China, escapades of Indian or Greek gods, episodes from the Torah or the New Testament all contain dramatic and exciting stories and have been represented in fine arts. In beginning with the story or legend, you provide your child with a framework for identifying and eventually reflecting upon the elements in a piece of art. You might begin discussing Egyptian fine art through an exploration of mummies and the afterlife. You could initiate a discussion of Chinese fine art by showing a picture of the Terracotta Warriors as they stand in the archeological site. You might introduce Renaissance art by talking about the scandal of Michelangelo's painting of naked people in his wedding present to Agnolo Doni, called the *Doni Tondo*. Use your child's interests as entry points to any fine art exploration and build from there.

After sharing stories, try to find an exhibit or library book that shows art representing elements or segments of the stories and ask questions! What do you notice? How is the picture similar to what you were imagining in your mind when we shared this story? What part of the picture or sculpture is the most interesting? During one museum visit, our eight-year-old son was mesmerized by a series of small pictures of a man engaged in various exploits. His aunt asked him if he knew who the hero of the pictures might be, and he answered, "Well, it's either Jesus or Hercules. I get those two guys mixed up." Clearly, we had some more storytelling and explaining to do! However, he was absolutely engaged by the pictures and remains a fan of Renaissance art years later.

Another approach might be to allow your child to generate the story that might accompany a sculpture or a picture. Let imagination drive the story and foster a connection with a piece of fine art. Books and electronic images are usually easy sources to access fine art. In addition, they often contain stories about the artist and/or the piece that can serve as hooks in engaging learners with the art. As your children grow, expose them to multiple pieces from an artist and allow them to see patterns, different periods of work, or dramatic departures from earlier styles.

# Get Those Taste Buds Ready

Food exploration can appear to be daunting. The expense of going to a restaurant and the knowledge of your child's particular palate may make the expansion of your family's food appreciation seem burdensome. One small way to begin exploring new food of any type is through including your children in the shopping and the meal preparation. Children as young as preschool age can begin helping with fruit and vegetable selection and menu planning. Offer choices that are realistic—for instance, "Shall we try the cucumber or the bell pepper? You decide!" or "You get to choose if we buy cantaloupe or honeydew melon." As your child gets older, you can include budgeting. It is still appropriate to provide guidelines—for instance, you might let your child pick any leafy green vegetable from the produce section.

At all ages, it is easy to introduce new tastes. They may not all be home runs—the curry rice might work for some family members and not others—but each repeated introduction to a food or spice will improve the possibility that your family members might develop an appreciation for the taste. Though exposure to new food can be easier at earlier ages, do not despair if you are working to expand your adolescent's palate. It may require more patience and more direction from your child, but it can be done.

## Family Restaurant

For younger children, it can be great fun to draw up a menu, learn to set the table—inclusive of candles—and make a family meal together. Try it tonight. Ask older children to create the menu and cook the dinner (with or without your help as sous chef).

**Perspiration**

As with dance, music, and drama, you can expose your family to tastes of the culture at home before exploring the food in a more public setting. One of our kids decided he wanted to make sushi together as a family. The bamboo rolling mat was inexpensive and the grocery store carried short-grain rice, so he and I shopped for the ingredients he needed to help make the dinner. He decided he preferred cucumber and smoked fish and other random ingredients over raw fish, so we invented some very unique family rolls that evening. In addition, our poor sushi wrapping skills resulted in quite a few lopsided rolls of sushi and a lot of laughter. However, the next time we ordered sushi in a restaurant, we all had a new understanding of how difficult the art of sushi making is and were all more willing to try new rolls!

# Experiencing Culture

The idea of culture has a myriad of connotations. Your family might have an ethnic, religious, or family-centered culture. In most cases, families participate in a variety of social groups with explicit practices and activities. The groups in which your family actively participates will likely be well known to your child. However, you can also work to expose your child to other cultures in a variety of ways.

With children of all ages, the library is a rich source of information about different cultures. From picture and chapter books to films and audio recordings, there are resources explaining thousands of cultural rituals and practices. As you connect with people in your community, ask them about various cultural rituals if it seems appropriate. We have been fortunate to have been invited to Christmas dinners, Diwali celebrations, Chinese New Year feasts, and more. And, through our friends, we have been able to learn about other cultures with our children. As you experience the arts and food areas noted above, you and your kids will learn about important aspects of other cultures while also building your own family culture of inclusive exploration.

# Character in Action

## Zero through Five Years Old: Fickle for Food

Your seven-year-old son won't eat anything off a menu, and every time you go out, even for the usually coveted McDonald's, you end up having to bring something from home. This can be very challenging when you are traveling or when your son goes for a sleepover. He's always been picky, but with more independence, it's become a bigger challenge. (He's out more on his own and then grumpy when he gets back hungry.) Try exposing him to a new food each day. Make it a fun and playful exploration and let him pick the item he will try. In the beginning especially, this can include not-necessarily nutritious food. Talk about his food preferences, and be open to his response. There might be a number of reasons he won't eat other items, but coddling him and bringing his food everywhere will not help him explore one bit.

## Exploration Looks Different at Different Stages of Life

### Zero through Five Years Old

In the early years, exploration is fairly easy because parents have the strongest influence on a child's activities and surroundings. Parents can encourage exploration by introducing new activities and experiences. At this stage, exploration can include trying a new food, making a new friend, or doing a somersault.

### Six through Twelve Years Old

Exploration for elementary-aged children comes pretty naturally as confidence levels are generally high and they have a growing set of interests. Fear of failure does come into play at this stage, and it's important for parents to encourage discovery based on interest and in light of possible failure. During these years, exploration can include picking up a new instrument, sewing a new outfit, or inventing a new game.

### Thirteen through Eighteen Years Old

Adolescence can be a tricky time to try new things because teens love to stand out and fit in all at the same time. Parents can support exploration by offering room and space without judgment. Exploration at this age can include joining a school team, going on college visits, or applying for a job.

### Six through Twelve Years Old: Social Skater

Your eleven-year-old son wants to hang out at the skate park in the afternoons. You'd rather he be taking an instrument class or trying a team sport. You're concerned that skateboarding is a waste of time and that it won't allow him proper socialization. Try saying yes. See what happens. Let him go to the skate park. He will likely make friends if given the opportunity to do something that interests him. Maybe negotiate a little. Perhaps he can go to the skate park one or two days a week if he tries something *you'd* like him to try. But be available to listen to his feedback should he try something you suggest. Make sure he's truly trying and not just signing up for a yearlong commitment with no interest and wasting time and/or money.

### Thirteen through Eighteen Years Old: Culture Shock

You haven't encouraged your fifteen-year-old daughter to go to art museums or listen to classical music, and you fear you're too late to help nurture an appreciation of culture in her life. First, there's no sense in punishing yourself for something you cannot change. Acknowledge your frustration with yourself and commit to trying something new. If you share your feelings with her, it will offer two benefits: time with your adolescent who is quickly growing out of her home and the opportunity to see something new (and from two perspectives). Be honest about your intentions and hopes to broaden her horizons.

## To Summarize...

- Just jump in and get going!

- There's a lot out there, so find something that works for your family financially and interest-wise.

- Consider joining in and exploring with your child.

- Be cognizant of your child's interests and abilities. Be willing to let your child take a breather or even quit an activity.

# Chapter 11

## Moderation: When Enough's Enough

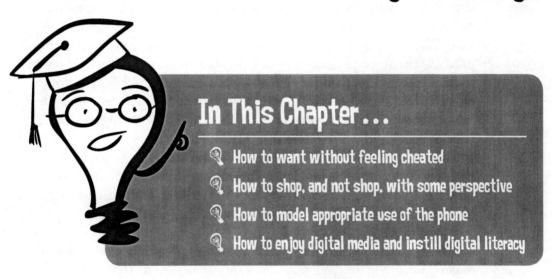

### In This Chapter...

- How to want without feeling cheated
- How to shop, and not shop, with some perspective
- How to model appropriate use of the phone
- How to enjoy digital media and instill digital literacy

**D**on't eat too much, don't stay in the sun too long, and don't watch too much television! These are just some of the "don'ts" we were told as children. It seems like the list has only grown over time. Too much of anything is liable to be correlated with disease or peril at this point. Moderation is key in just about all aspects of life. In this chapter, read about ways to moderate as a parent and to teach moderation to your child to encourage modesty, enjoyment, and gratitude in life.

In most of life, moderation can be a key guide for living and for parenting. Children will push our buttons and ask for more. It is our job to teach them the importance of understanding quantity, perspective, and priority. We might love to finish a family-size bag of Doritos, but the MSG would give me a headache and my daughter a belly ache, not to mention the acne it might stimulate on my teen, and the bag would offer well over the daily recommended serving of fat. Most of the chapters in this book speak to finding balance or moderation in some area, yet consumerism and media are two of the most challenging areas of moderation for kids and adults today.

## Want versus Need

One of the most valuable lessons I have taught my children is distinguishing between want and need. One way to teach this distinction is through modeling. You might start at the grocery store and explain that you want a particular item, yet purchasing it will mean you do not have the same money to spend on another item the family needs. If you are shopping for clothes or household items, you can be clear with your children about things you might want versus the things you really need. There is nothing sweeter than hearing your child in a toy store say, "I know I don't need this, but can I show you something I really want?" This implies your child knows the difference and may even apply that understanding during a moment of weakness and desire. It is completely normal for your child to want, and it can be a difficult lesson understanding the difference between want and need.

Sometimes a child is persistent about wanting a particular item. The child might discuss it at every meal, ask to look up the item on the Internet, or draw pictures of the item and leave the pictures in strategic locations. As you decide whether to purchase the item, you may want to ask some of the following questions: Is the item prohibitively expensive or large or time consuming? If so, is there a smaller or more affordable or less high-maintenance version? Is this an item that your child is likely to continue wanting for a year or more likely to grow out of? If it is something your child has wanted for a long time and seems unlikely

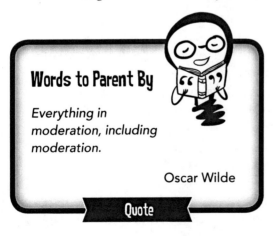

### Words to Parent By

*Everything in moderation, including moderation.*

Oscar Wilde

Quote

to disappear as your child develops, you may decide to purchase the item. Many teens express a keen interest in a car. A car isn't something you can just buy easily and be done with. There is insurance attached to it. It presents a considerable amount of danger. And on top of all that, even the cheapest car is a considerable amount of money, not to mention maintenance costs and potential parking tickets. Sometimes the answer must be no, and that's something your teen can live with, I promise. In fact, not getting a car will encourage your teen to work hard to earn the money for a car. It will also force your teen to learn public transportation, walk, bike, or—heaven forbid—ask you for a ride and spend some time with you!

Ask yourself about the core attraction for the desired item. Is it a creative product, such as a sewing machine or an art set or a construction kit? Is it an active item, such as a bike or ball or set of shoes? Even if it is unnecessary, does it promote values your family is working to support? Is there an option for your child to earn part or all of the money needed to purchase the item? Your child is much more likely to value the item if he or she has worked to earn it. Is this item part of a fad driven by peers? I can almost guarantee that your child's craving for the current set of cards or magnetic rollers or yo-yos will fade into a new "must-have" in short order.

Another practice that will help your kids reflect on wants and needs is the practice of gratitude. (Refer to **Chapter 5** for a deeper discussion of appreciation.) Being grateful for what you have, especially nonmaterial things such as health, a family, a great day, helps us put material things in perspective and might curb your child's desire for more.

## Consumerism

I'll admit right now that I am a recovering shopaholic. I don't spend money in a lot of other areas, so I used to rationalize that it was fine to spend a lot of money on clothes. Now with a larger family and a little more perspective, I've learned to budget for clothes just as I budget for other areas of our household. Though I still feel occasional pangs when I see an amazing new pair of shoes, it actually feels good to put a cap on spending. It helps me think about what I want to buy, decide how I can divide the money to clothe us all, and remember to appreciate what I have. This lesson has been hard for me to learn, but I am glad to see my children developing into smart consumers as a

## Budget Idea

Make a shopping rule that you and your child can honor. Consider a one-night-sleep-on-it rule for anything in the store you really, really want but didn't set out to buy that day. Once you go home and really weigh the need versus the want, you will have a better perspective. That practice also models good money sense for your child.

**Perspiration**

result. I still love clothes and shopping, but purchasing within reason has given me perspective and taught my children well.

Consumerism is a disturbing pattern in our world, especially as many things seem to be made to be disposable. I have my grandmother's hope chest from when she was married. It's a wooden chest with a cedar interior. The chest is in pristine condition, hinges and all. It was made to last. Nowadays, toys, books, school supplies, etc., are often fragile and made to be disposable. So not only are we wasteful in terms of our resources, but we also have a mentality that leads us to dispose, replace, and upgrade. Encouragingly, there seems to be a growing trend toward recycling, reuse, and maintenance.

It's wonderful to practice recycling—and not just with your waste bins. I'm talking about truly reusing. Try modeling good behavior, and then you can expect it from other members of your family. One of my favorite days of the year is my annual clothing swap. It's a night where I invite my friends who share my love of clothes, and we drink, dine, and swap! We each bring our castoffs and look through each other's skirts, pants, blouses, necklaces, purses—you name it. One woman's trash is another woman's treasure. Often I'll find something and rework it on the sewing machine to fit me or bring it up to date. I don't have a desire to shop for months after, and I love sporting my "new" clothes knowing they didn't cost me a dime. This has become such a staple in our home that my daughter now hosts one with her friends. With this party, we are able to proudly enjoy our love of fashion, and we don't have to spend or waste.

Moderation is very directly tied to responsibility. As noted in the "want versus need" section above, actively developing responsibility can decrease consumerism. Your child can earn money to make unnecessary (but strongly desired) purchases. A good habit to get into when your child is young is to approve all the child's extra purchases. Even though it is your child's money, you should still be involved in the decision making, and you can veto the purchase. Is this something you want? Is this something you will use? What happened to the _____ (fill in the blank) that you purchased? This thought process will model good purchase practices for your child's future independent spending.

As your child grows, it's important to teach about budgeting. Lessons in budgets will be lessons for life. The way you structure a budget for yourself can be a strong model for your child. And the source of your child's spending money may vary. You may choose to stay in control of the actual funds and simply allow some decision power for your child. Or your child may have a job or gift money. You might offer an allowance and have your child figure out how to divvy it up. No matter the fund, give your child choice in the spending and set limits. While it might be fun to shop for Air Jordans, a purchase your basketball player has been waiting for for months, you might set out a sneaker, or clothing, or other budget. And once that money is spent, it's gone, and there is less to be spent on the video games, telephone/texting service, other clothes, etc.

## Talking and Texting

Do people even use phones to talk anymore? In the event you might own a landline or use your cell phone as a phone, be sure to keep your conversations in check. It is usually rude to pick up when you are with another person, and there are many venues that specifically request you to turn your phone off when present. If you know you are expecting a critical call that cannot be missed, let your companion know before the phone rings. You might say, "I want to apologize in advance, but I am expecting a very important call that I might need to pick up while we are talking." Otherwise, let the call go to a message and respond when you have finished your conversation. If you do receive an urgent and unexpected text or call while you are engaged in another activity, explain to those around you that you are sorry but this might be an emergency. If upon answering you determine that the conversation is not an emergency, quickly excuse yourself and offer to return the call at a better time. This practice is good whether talking with a peer or with your family members. Model the behavior you expect from your child.

## You Should Be So Lucky to Have Just a Minute with Your Child

When your child is talking to you, make eye contact! Never wag the "just a minute" finger and continue to text when your child is talking to you. You may never have this opportunity to talk again. I know you're tempted to "just finish," but don't. Put down the phone! I mean it. Put it down.

**Perspiration**

Create electronic device rules for moderation in your home. Limit phone time to a reasonable period and try to carve out times when you will intentionally disconnect. You might have a charging station in the kitchen where all devices stay overnight. This is an excellent policy both for moderation and for supporting healthy sleep patterns. Screen time right before bed delays the body's production of melatonin, the sleep hormone. If you are not in a job that requires you to be on call, leave devices off when eating a family meal or playing a family game.

Using both explicit rules and clear modeling, you can enjoy your devices in moderation. Ask your device-owning child to observe the rules as well. It's easy for kids to fall victim to poor digital etiquette (and plenty of adults too, in fact), so be very forthcoming with the rules and help your child understand the reasons behind them.

## Internet

The Internet is an ever-growing presence in all of our lives. What things should parents be most concerned about? How can parents educate their kids on the importance of making good online choices? How can we, as adults, set positive examples when it comes to our own Internet use? Knowing your child's current interests will help you have conversations about responsible Internet use. Additionally, think carefully about creating guidelines *before* they become an issue when it comes to social networking and screen time in general.

Don't be afraid of the Internet. The best thing you can do is embrace it with your child. As you establish family rules around Internet use, you can also allow for growth and change as each child develops. If you allow your child to be on a social networking site, it is reasonable to insist that you be linked to the site as well. Note your child's usernames and passwords and create a contract with your child about expected behavior. Explain to your child, so it is not a surprise, that you will log in as your child and look through postings, emails, texts, and participation in games. Your child should engage in any electronic interactions as if they were in-person interactions. Your omniscient presence will help enforce this mentality. You do not have to check the sites every day. After all, you do want your child to learn independence. But the idea of your periodic presence will definitely help shape your child's electronic activity.

There are filters you can use to try to shelter your child from pornographic and other questionable material. There is no set of rules or filters that will fit every family, so you should feel confident in determining those that work for you. Note two cautions about filters. First, none are infallible. Be aware that some are very good but will still require your supervision. Even with protection from obviously inappropriate images and words, your child will still have access to at least a limited (and still large) amount of information that you will want to screen and teach your child to screen. Second, your child will experience an unsecured network at some point. It's important that you help your child develop a moral compass as a guide for questionable situations. When a pornographic picture shows up, it's natural for a child to be interested and look, but will your child also have a strong enough compass to know it is inappropriate and to click the window closed or, even better, discuss it with you?

## Spending Screen Time Together

As your child grows, consider spending your screen time as a family so you are all working or enjoying together. If you have a shared family computer, divide time appropriately and keep the computer in a public area.

**Pure Genius!**

Finally, there are online contracts and suggested guidelines that you can use to explicitly lay out your family's online rules. Your child's school might even endorse one in particular. Find something that works for you, your child, and your family—and live by it. Most importantly, know that there will be a time when your child will freely explore the Internet without you. Your child may see pornography, and you may never know. Do check-ins, talk about choice making, and constantly help develop that oh-so-important moral compass.

## Television, Movies, and Video Games

So your son likes video games? Play them together, especially online interactive ones, where he might "meet" questionable characters. Your daughter loves the television? Share this love with her and make sure you watch together. This will ensure she is watching appropriate material, and you can spend some time together. Not all television, movies, and video games are terrible! However, as with most things, moderation is the key to healthy enjoyment. It's okay to sit down and relax in front of the television with your children. Just make sure that you're not watching too much and that you feel comfortable using the shared screen time as an interesting conversation point for discussing family values. Enjoy the show while it is on, and then use the story to spark questions at the next family meal or while driving. How did that character react during the crisis? Do you think the choice was a good one? Have you ever had a friend do something similar? Using fictional events to discuss difficult topics will help build a conversational bond between you and your kids and will also provide the opportunity to practice talking about emotional things in a more neutral setting.

It may be that you don't even have time for the screen when all is said and done with today's world full of extracurricular activities. Young children (from newborn to three years old) really don't gain anything, including relaxation, out of television. It's fine to watch age-appropriate shows (e.g., Sesame Street), and they might offer you the break you need. While it might be optimal to keep the screen off, do not feel guilty about using a small amount of screen time as a resource. Try to make good decisions about content and set limits you can stick to. Judging exactly what's appropriate for your family is a very personal decision. The point here is to think about the limits ahead of time to create a reflective rather than reactive approach to media consumption. There are many resources in print and online, some of which are listed in the **Appendix**, available to help you create a family approach to television, movies, and video games.

## Character in Action

### Zero through Five Years Old: Screen Time-Out

Your three-year-old son loves to watch television, enjoys fiddling with your phone, and has his own portable Gameboy. You know you're "supposed" to

# Moderation Looks Different at Different Stages of Life

## Zero through Five Years Old

Because parents mostly control the environment and activities from birth through five years old, it's fairly simple to impart the principles of moderation, but it takes implementation and consistency on your part. Moderation at these early years can include eating just one scoop of ice cream after dinner, leaving the playground when asked, or thanking you after one bedtime story (as opposed to asking for another).

## Six through Twelve Years Old

Elementary-aged kids are impulsive and enjoy treats. They are also prime targets for marketing campaigns. Parents can best teach moderation at this stage by resisting temptation and encouraging children to do the same. Practice a waiting period (be it just minutes before dessert or a week before buying a new outfit). Moderation at this stage can include choosing just a few pieces of candy after trick-or-treating, turning off an iPad after a self-imposed time limit, or printing only necessary documents.

## Thirteen through Eighteen Years Old

It can be a challenge for an adolescent to practice moderation because we live in such a materialistic and disposable world. Parents can encourage moderation through conversation and limitations. Teen moderation can include choosing just one pair of shoes, enjoying a limited texting plan, or taking two AP classes instead of three.

limit screen time, but he loves it, he's easily entertained, and the shows he watches and games he plays are educational. In fact, he's even identifying letters and able to add small sums. Good for you for making sure the screen time he does enjoy is quality time. However, you need to make sure you do limit it. Large doses of screen time stifle creativity and physical development. Yes, these distractions are tempting (especially when you're waiting in a doctor's office or eating out at a nice restaurant), but try to think of other engaging activities you can do when you're with your child. There are many board games and small card games. And conversation never gets old. Kids do, in fact, say the darnedest things. There's enough time for the screen in his future. Help him develop some interpersonal skills first, and save the screen for a really desperate situation, such as a long plane ride when you cannot keep your eyes open any longer.

### Six through Twelve Years Old: Like All the Other Girls

Your seven-year-old daughter asks you, "Can I have an American Girl doll? A lot of the girls in my class have Julie, and they say they're in the Julie club. Can I get one?" Okay, a lot is at play here. American Girl dolls are expensive. Would your daughter be as happy with a similar doll that is more affordable? Furthermore, do you want to support (emotionally and financially) her desire to join this club? Talk with her about why she wants the doll. Does she truly want one? Will she play with it? Does she have other dolls? Is she good with her toys, or does she lose interest easily? Can you afford it? Can she afford it? There are a lot of possible answers here. You do not need to cringe just because your daughter wants to belong. You also do not need to feel compelled to buy her way into the club. Acknowledge that it feels good to belong. Kids learn from their peers and a sense of belonging is positive. You can read more about socializing in **Chapter 24**. Talk about the friends and other ways to connect. Try to separate the purchase of the doll from the social interaction to see if a special playdate or group activity might be in order or if she really wants the doll. It's fine to go for it if you feel good about it, she demonstrates enthusiasm, and you can afford it. I'll admit that when my daughter asked, I felt an immediate pang for her to have what she wanted. The price shocked me, so our solution was to make it a birthday gift from her aunts, grandparents, and parents. This solution helped her see how special the item was when she received one singular present as opposed to several.

### Thirteen through Eighteen Years Old: Designer Dos or Don'ts

Your fourteen-year-old is dying for a pair of designer jeans that cost $200. What to do? Can you or she afford them? Why does she want them? Will she wear them? What else does she own in her closet? Does she regularly ask for trendy items? Kids grow and change their style, so it's smart to invest in a small wardrobe and allow for changes. If she rarely asks for new items, this is an unusual request, she seems sincerely yearning, you enjoy shopping together, and you can afford the jeans—go for it! That is a lot of ifs. Even if all the previous are true, it's also okay to say no if you believe that is a ridiculous amount to spend on a pair of jeans or you simply do not endorse the purchase. You are the parent, and you get to decide. If she asks for new and trendy items on a regular basis, you can create a system: Do you have a budget for clothes? It's pretty easy to track all your spending using budget software or a simple spreadsheet. Think about your budget and let her know what you can afford. You can make this public to your daughter and suggest she earn her clothing money if she wants to spend more than what you can afford. She may choose to spend her entire year's budget on the jeans. One family we know has decided to purchase the basics for their girls (jeans, sweatshirts, pajamas, underwear) and insists the girls earn money on their own to purchase any luxury items.

# To Summarize...

- It's okay to say, "I want," so long as you focus on what you have.

- Purchase with thought, and be transparent with your child about the thought process.

- Be a model digital citizen.

- Support digital literacy in your home, and help your child develop a sensible moral compass.

# Chapter 12

## Perseverance: Pushing Through and Sticking with It

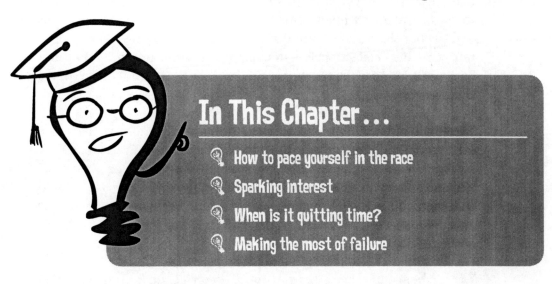

### In This Chapter...

- How to pace yourself in the race
- Sparking interest
- When is it quitting time?
- Making the most of failure

**N**ever give up on yourself or on your child! Children will learn to persevere through your modeling. In tackling a tough cleanup situation, a thorny work issue, or a family budget analysis, giving up is just not an option. As researchers have discovered, the ability to persist can be nurtured and is key to resilience and lifelong achievement. This chapter explores how to persevere in your parenting and how to nurture resolve in your child to inspire a lifetime of exploration and independence.

# It's a Marathon, Not a Sprint

Though many researchers are delving into persistence and grit right now, studies linking perseverance to high achievement have been around since the 1940s. From empirical research to popular nonfiction, support for the importance of persisting, practicing, and putting in time abounds. It is so easy to mark interim milestones with more significance than they ought to have. Life is a marathon and not a sprint!

One way you can set the stage for perseverance in the face of difficult challenges is by carefully gauging your reactions in times of achievement. When your child experiences success—a terrific grade, a victorious game, a magical performance—celebration comes naturally. It might seem intuitive to mirror and even amplify some of your child's elation. Enjoy the moment and let your child enjoy it, then think carefully about how you can help reflect on this satisfaction: Is your child proud because of the gratification of hard work, because the sports team had a lucky break, or because your child is seeking approval?

There is an old technique that advises parents to count to ten when frustrated. Try doing the same thing in times of success. Even though celebration is a positive emotion, the strength of a parent's or teacher's reaction influences a child's understanding of the event. If you leap for joy with each quiz or recital or game, your child will begin seeking that reaction after every success. Furthermore, that child will fear the converse when a challenge does not go well.

You can help make the celebration more powerful and intrinsically motivating in the long run if you emphasize the effort that contributed to the result. Smile, offer congratulations and a hug, and try to keep your emotions as neutral as possible. When the moment is right, and this might happen hours or even days later, ask what your child was most excited about or proud of in regard to the last success.

In addition to focusing attention on self-assessment and process (as opposed to external approval and an end product), you will create a framework for persistence and even resilience during times of failure. Your supportive and loving, yet emotionally neutral, reaction will focus energy toward your child's effort and feelings. Successes may seem to diminish a bit in stature, but so will failures! You can discuss challenges in light of the quantity and quality of effort put into the process. Your growing child will hopefully be able to use this framework during future successes and, perhaps more importantly, failures, in the larger world.

## Triggering Intrinsic Motivation

Wouldn't it be wonderful if your child began spontaneously cleaning the house, working as hard as possible in school, and preferring family time to time with friends? Actually, it would be a little strange! Some tasks need to be done, motivation or not. As covered in other chapters, it is very important to have family rituals, chores, and rules—and to stick to them when possible. At the same time, one essential trigger to perseverance is intrinsic motivation. So pay close attention to your child's interests and try to value and nurture them.

### Intrinsic Is on the Inside

I was once asked by a parent at one of my talks, "How can I motivate my child intrinsically?" There are some things you just can't control. You can support, nurture, and foster motivation in your child, but you cannot create it innately. That's why it's important to listen to your child and give your child some independence to find what's interesting in this world.

**Uninspired**

Intrinsic motivation is the incentive generated from one's own interests and is usually compared with incentive driven by external motivators. Grades are almost always an external motivator. Students want to earn good grades to earn approval from teachers and family. Free-choice reading is almost always intrinsically motivated. Children pick up books and continue reading simply because they are interested. Practicing persistence is a much easier task when intrinsic motivation is present. If you encourage your child to try something one more time or to concentrate more closely on something inherently uninteresting at a young age, that same encouragement can lead to discontent, unhappiness, and all-out rebellion by adolescence.

Stimulating or even identifying intrinsic motivation can be tricky. Parents expose children to new activities for many reasons: We want them to have some physical or artistic exposure, we know their friends have signed up, we think they might enjoy themselves, we do it for scheduling purposes, or some combination of those four. Some kids say yes to everything, some kids say no, and most kids move back and forth between the two. Knowing your child is key to understanding whether no means "I really do not want to try that activity" or "I am interested but a little nervous because I will not know anyone there." Set your child up to be perseverant by getting buy-in before signing up and really listening to how your child feels about the experience.

Your child's level of activity also affects motivation. And overscheduled kids may not have the time to reflect on what really interests them. Free time is essential to intrinsic motivation—especially for adolescents. Unscheduled time allows your child to imagine, ponder, reflect, and just daydream. Daydreaming allows the mind to wander and make connections or have insights that might not otherwise surface. It can help your child think about possibilities and envision possible goals.

## When They Want to Quit

We have all found ourselves in situations where we would just like to quit. For our overachieving society, the next bit of news may come as a surprise, but sometimes, quitting is the right choice.

After weeks of observing your child's resistance to putting on the cleats or practicing the flute, examine the reasons for the behavior. You might find that your child is experiencing some natural "stretching" while working to master new skills. Ask how your child is feeling, let your child know you value his or her experience, and brainstorm a strategy for the near future. Is it important to finish the season? Is it feasible to work toward a next recital or milestone and then evaluate whether to continue with the activity? If you feel very deeply that your child needs to continue the activity, try to be as honest as possible about why. Maybe you are regretting how you felt when you quit team sports and are trying to spare your child that regret.

On the other hand, you might discover that there is something more serious going on, such as a toxic relationship with a coach or peers, an inappropriate

### Words to Parent By

*I have not failed. I've just found 10,000 ways that won't work.*

Thomas Alva Edison

**Quote**

combination of skill building and competition, or an unsafe environment. Listen and communicate with your child. You might also choose to drop in on a practice or rehearsal. Try to observe as much of the activity as possible to get a deeper sense of what might be going on. And if your child is feeling emotionally or physically unsafe, stop the activity! My daughter wanted to quit ballet. She was an engaged dancer and suddenly started to complain about going to her lessons. Her older brother loved the studio when he danced there, so I was particularly surprised by her decision. I decided to talk with her teacher. It turns out she was always well behaved and on task in class. So I observed a session. I was bored out of my mind. It took all of one class for me to see that she wasn't truly engaged. Sure, she knew how to behave and look like an active participant because she was eager to please, but she was not truly enjoying or interacting. It was time to quit that class. My husband and I asked that she finish out the semester, as it was paid for. We decided to let her have a break if she wanted. And on her own, she came to the decision to try dance somewhere else.

## The Little Engine That Couldn't

Recent research suggests that a certain amount of perseverance is simply innate. Some humans just may be born with a stronger tendency to persist than others. However, there is a concurrently growing body of research that suggests perseverance can be cultivated through practice and a supportive environment.

If your child seems to give up easily or wants to quit every task (assuming you cannot uncover any good reasons for wanting to quit), it is time to think of strategies that will nurture perseverance. Oftentimes, children who give up easily do so because they do not think they can be successful at the task or they believe the effort they will need to invest may not be worth the end result. The next time your child gives up quickly, ask, "What were you hoping to do?" Remind your child about a previously learned complicated

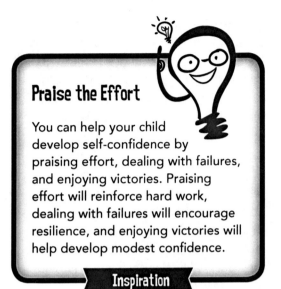

### Praise the Effort

You can help your child develop self-confidence by praising effort, dealing with failures, and enjoying victories. Praising effort will reinforce hard work, dealing with failures will encourage resilience, and enjoying victories will help develop modest confidence.

**Inspiration**

task—tying shoes, learning to read, hitting a baseball. Could your child do those perfectly the first time? Probably not! Children learn in steps, practice quite a bit, and then one day, they can do it. Remind your child that facing the challenge is not easy, but it can be conquered with effort and practice.

Help your child break each task into realistic, attainable goals. Depending on whether your child is practicing persistence on an academic, artistic, athletic, or another task, the small goals will vary. Ask your child how it feels to master each step and focus on praising effort. Each step will bring the end goal closer and, more importantly, will reinforce tenacious behavior. A student of mine was moved into an advanced English class. She was used to being the best in her class and found it frustrating to be confused and challenged. It took patience, trust in the teacher's decision, and perseverance on the young girl's behalf. Lo and behold, she was able to keep up with the group and proud of her accomplishments. It's important to introduce and seize the opportunity for a challenge, and it's okay to lean on someone (a teacher, a parent, a friend, a counselor) to see it through.

## Failure—It's the New Success

Failure has gotten a lot of popular press lately. School, jobs, health, relationships... No matter how carefully we plan, life will surprise and sometimes disappoint. It makes perfect sense, then, that children need a lot of practice with failure. Hopefully, your child will not need too many of what my middle schooler would call "epic fails" but will have a steady stream of manageable or, in the words of author and Stanford researcher Denise Pope, "successful failures." Disappointment is critical to resilience, integrity, and responsibility. It can't be overemphasized: Your child's development of persistence *depends* on facing small challenges and persisting through them!

Failures come in big and small sizes. It's important to help your child embrace them as a learning experience. That doesn't mean they have to be fun. You'll find that if you refer to failures as learning opportunities, your child will begin to see them that way too. Nobody is born able to do everything perfectly.

When your child was born, that infant was perfect in your eyes. Babies have done no wrong and have a clean slate. As they learn to walk and talk, they inevitably fail. They fall down, say the wrong things. And as they do, they develop a sense of self—and parents support them willingly through these failures. (Our daughter said, "mo" instead of "morning.") In fact, new parents wouldn't even call them failures—we'd call them developmental benchmarks or learning steps. So why do we react more strongly to bad grades or an athletic loss? The stakes, as your child grows, become higher and higher and can create anxiety for you and often for your child. If you let your child sense your anxiety, you stand to show that you are focused on the outcome more than the process.

# Character in Action

### Zero through Five Years Old: Pitching Practice

Your three-year-old seems to be pitching a fit every day about the smallest stuff (going to the park, what's for dinner, bedtime routine). Nothing seems that different to you, but you are getting frustrated, and he won't let up. This is a good time to take a look at **Chapter 7** for more on patience. Also keep in mind that you need to persevere as much as you need to nurture that drive in your child. Stick to your routine as best you can, and keep your patience as you muddle through this phase. It will pass. Do not give in to the whims of a three-year-old and switch the dinner menu. Trust me, he'll just think of something else to pitch a fit about. This is a great opportunity for role playing. Model how you might ask for a different food idea or suggest one. And then try to reinforce any positive behavior and cater to requests (as best you can) made in a constructive and polite manner.

### Six through Twelve Years Old: Kickin' It Up a Notch

Your eleven-year-old daughter plays recreational soccer, and her friends are moving to a travel team where the play is more competitive and there is a heavier time and financial commitment. She plays well and could make

# Perseverance Looks Different at Different Stages of Life

## Zero through Five Years Old

Very young children don't get discouraged easily and usually require fairly simple comfort in the face of frustration. Parents can encourage perseverance through encouragement and praise. For a very young child, perseverance can include learning to crawl, arranging a Lego structure, or buckling a seat belt.

## Six through Twelve Years Old

Elementary-aged kids enjoy a challenge. Parents can encourage perseverance by pushing children outside their comfort zones, using failure as a learning experience, and expressing encouragement. Perseverance at this stage in life can include showing up for a baseball game after three straight losses, figuring out an origami design, or learning to study hard for a test.

## Thirteen through Eighteen Years Old

Teens are susceptible to disappointment and self-doubt. Perseverance is important in developing independence and self-reliance. Parents should comfort disappointment but disallow wallowing. Perseverance for a teen might include persisting in an argument with you, failing a class and sticking with it, or finishing a college application.

the team with a little effort and wants to stay with her friends. She's nervous about the competition and fears she won't have a lot of playing time since there's not a rule that every player has to play. Naturally, if you cannot afford the time or financial commitment, the answer will have to be no. That said, if you're game, then push her to go for it if she's truly interested. This will be a nice opportunity to bond with her team, and she shouldn't pass on an opportunity out of fear. She can always go back to a recreational team!

### Thirteen through Eighteen Years Old: Accepting Rejection

Your eighteen-year-old son has applied to college. He was not accepted to any of his first choices, but he did get into a four-year college. He says that he doesn't want to go and will try again next year for his top choices. What do you encourage him to do? At this stage, it can feel like he will lose time if he doesn't keep up with his peers. Don't panic, and don't let him panic. Take a moment to be proud that he's pursued his dream and worked hard to get there. Assuming you can afford it and the four-year school is one he is willing to attend, encourage him to go. If he's disappointed and doesn't want to attend, acknowledge his disappointment and talk to him about enrolling him at a local community college so he can start earning college credit to apply to the four-year school he wants to go to. Then he can look at transferring (which is sometimes easier than being accepted as a freshman). Remind him that no matter if it is a community college, a backup school, or his first choice, it's a college education and he's lucky to have the chance at one!

## To Summarize...

- Life requires a long-term view.

- Nurture your child's interests, no matter the challenge.

- Quitting is okay for the right reasons. Don't let your child quit because the task is too hard.

- Find the success in your child's failure.

# Chapter 13

## Resilience: Bouncing Back

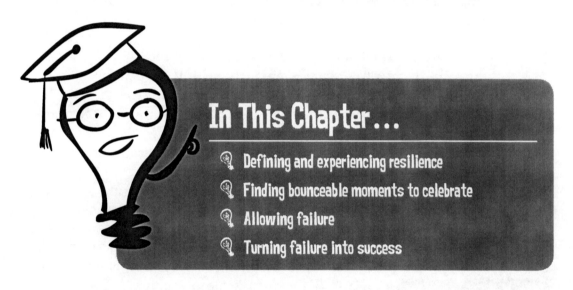

### In This Chapter...

- Defining and experiencing resilience
- Finding bounceable moments to celebrate
- Allowing failure
- Turning failure into success

**W**e all want resilient kids, but it's hard to see them fail, and our first instinct is often to help them up. But that's not always what we should do. Teaching resilience is about offering support in the face of failure and then weaning the support so your child learns to self-soothe. In this chapter, you will learn to build your own resilience as a parent and to instill it in your child to set the tone for a lifetime of practicality and strength.

Noted author and psychologist Madeline Levine reminds us that when toddlers are learning to walk and fall, no one says, "Get up, you failure! You'll never get into college if you fall like that." We applaud the effort and encourage them to get back up and try again. It may seem easy to do this so long as nothing major—college acceptance, earning potential, popularity—is at risk. However, we need to do the same *even* when major stakes are involved.

When you have a frustrating day or make a major mistake, what do you do? My first reaction is to tell someone and likely complain. Then what? Do I give up and crawl into bed? Maybe, for that night. But I know I must get up the next morning and face it, whatever it is. I don't have to do so happily, but I have to do so openly. Otherwise, "it" festers. We must model resilience if we have any hope of our children developing it. Whether your coping strategy includes a walk, a bubble bath, a personal time-out, or something else, let your child know. Explain that you are feeling disappointed or upset and need to take care of yourself to face the challenge again tomorrow.

Your child will try many things in life, recreationally, socially, academically, and more. There will be many bumps in the road. At that point, your child could (1) give up, (2) move on, or (3) try again until mastering the task. The latter two options are good examples of resilience. Giving up is okay. Quitting a sport or an art form is perfectly normal through life. Heck, we may find ourselves quitting jobs because we simply don't have the job satisfaction we need in life to do a good job.

Be sure that your child chooses the first option for the right reasons and not just because something got hard. The second option, moving on, is more about giving yourself space to fail, learning a lesson, and pushing through. It might mean stopping for a moment, trying from a new perspective. The third option, trying again, is about not giving up. Perseverance is a great virtue and should be applauded, especially when the going gets particularly tough.

The truth is that we don't have to be able to be expert at everything—but we do have to be able to identify what we like, what we enjoy, what we need to do, and what we can let go of.

### Words to Parent By

*When one door of happiness closes, another opens; but often we look so long at the closed door that we do not see the one which has been opened for us.*

Helen Keller

Quote

# What Does it Mean to Be Resilient?

Our daughter demonstrated resilience at a dance competition when she was eight years old. The schedule changed at the last minute, which meant she'd have to compete in the older age category. My husband and I praised her attitude and willingness to compete up a level and prepared her for the disappointment we thought was inevitable. She got up there on the stage and danced her heart out. I guess our words of comfort were words of inspiration because she danced beautifully. All of a sudden, my husband squeezed my hand and looked at me with horror in his eyes. I looked at him, confused, and then realized what he had noticed seconds before: She was dancing to the wrong version of her music. It was a longer variation than the one she had practiced for months. Not only did she persevere, but she continued to dance, improvising with heart and precision. We watched her so proudly. Would you believe she won first place in her category?

Resilience is the ability to cope and change course based on your experience. Your child will be teased and hurt in life. Your child will fail and be frustrated. Rather than protect your child from these challenges, teach your child to deal with them productively. It's okay and normal to feel bad, but it's also important to understand how to pick yourself up by your bootstraps. Being resilient means being able to process a situation without being crushed by it.

Resilience is required in every aspect of your life and your child's. When you cared for your child as an infant, you were so careful and possibly berated yourself for the slightest misstep. (You forgot to change the diaper, and now there's a rash.) But you realized you had to move on at some point. (The rash cleared up with a bit of cream, and now you know to change diapers more frequently.) When your toddler throws fits, you may have to change your schedule, shift expectations, and think of a new strategy for the next instance. You need to show resilience and flexibility both in how you handle the tough situation and in how you learn from it.

When faced with your own failings—real or perceived—rather than obsess about the cause and punish yourself for it, you might explain how upset you are and create new practices to try out next time. When your tween is yelling at you because you forgot to remind her to take a math book to school,

# Resilience Looks Different at Different Stages of Life

## Zero through Five Years Old

Very young children are naturally resilient. They are constantly learning new things and not yet expert at any. Parents can promote resilience with words of encouragement and support. For an infant or toddler, resilience can include self-soothing with a pacifier or thumb, rebuilding a Lincoln Log structure when it falls, or playing Parcheesi again after losing a game.

## Six through Twelve Years Old

In the elementary years, resilience can be a lifesaver as children learn to navigate school and new social settings. This skill can make or break these new experiences. Parents can offer support by talking about their own strength in difficult situations. At this stage, resilience can include going to school after being humiliated, trying out for the basketball team after not making it the prior year, or learning to read.

## Thirteen through Eighteen Years Old

Adolescents can help develop their confidence by practicing resilience. It's tough to face adversity when also trying to fit in, but parents can encourage it by waiting before jumping to conclusions, resisting the urge to problem-solve, and supporting a teen's choice. Resilience in the teen years can include getting behind the wheel after a recent car accident, reapplying to college after not getting in, or dating after a hard breakup.

allow her some room to develop resilience by reminding her that this is her responsibility and an opportunity to learn from her mistake. Follow up with a discussion about respectful communication too.

On the flip side, don't forget to praise your child. Parents should focus their praise on effort and not product. Yes, it's wonderful that your son earned a first-place trophy, but wasn't it the practices on days he had a headache or didn't feel like going that led up to the trophy? And what if he hadn't earned the trophy? Wouldn't you still want to encourage regular practice and sustained effort? It's easy to praise results because winning, good grades, and the like are enjoyable and easy to celebrate. But it's actually the process of getting to those points, or not, that builds character and future success.

Responsibility is important, and you can refer to **Chapter 14** for more details, but resilience is the ability to move past the blame game (whether the finger points at you or someone else). It's not always easy, and that is why it is a value to be nourished within yourself and to be taught to your child. Resilience also looks different depending on the situation and age. But, in any case, we can all encourage our children to be more flexible in their thinking.

## Resilience in Small Doses

Parents who rush in to rescue their child in times of challenge or crisis most often do so out of love. It can be excruciating to watch your child be disappointed, hurt, chastised, passed over... The list goes on. We swoop in to offer love and comfort. Luckily, young people can fail most of

### Get Over It, Mom!

We had purchased season passes for a local amusement park. We were preparing for our final trip of the summer. As we were packing, I was proud of myself for remembering the passes. The passes! Where were they? They were not where they were supposed to be—or anywhere else. Organization is one of my defining characteristics, so the loss of these passes was a personal humiliation. The kids helped me tear apart the house looking, and then finally, after packing everything else, I went to bed, completely defeated. When I awoke the next morning, my eldest said to me, "Mom, I know you want to kick yourself about the passes, because I do that too. But once we get in the car, I want you to just forget about them."

**Pure Genius!**

childhood's challenges without dire consequences. Small losses, forgotten items, and poor effort all may create uncomfortable situations but are safe opportunities to learn.

As a teacher, I have seen the drawbacks of untested resilience. Each year, I had one or two middle-school students who consistently left materials at home. The reaction would be to call home for a rescue without even a thank-you to a parent or caregiver for rushing the item to school. Over the long term, children who miss chances to overcome small hurdles in their everyday lives can become paralyzed when facing more complicated challenges. If they believe they can count on a parent or caregiver to rush in and bring a forgotten lunch, lie to excuse missed homework, or phone a friend's parent to insist on an invitation, they have no reason to develop and practice handling those challenges on their own. Unfortunately, when they do face their first serious setback, children who have never overcome disappointment can feel devastated. This leads to adolescents and young adults who are unable to manage the day-to-day requirements of independent living and who turn off peers and colleagues with their entitled attitudes.

Keeping the big picture in mind is key here, as it is with most parenting decisions. Do you really want to go to college with your child to help smooth any possible troubles? Will you need to be there when your child's first serious relationship breaks up? Do you expect that your child will never earn a poor grade? Can you imagine writing an excuse note to your child's boss upon failure to complete a task on time? In light of the independence you hope your child will have, it is imperative that you allow your child multiple opportunities to make mistakes and safely deal with the consequences—and then try again.

## Falling Off the Horse

Like the old saying goes, when you fall off the horse, get back on again. The important thing when you fall off that horse is not to punish yourself and decide that you are worthless just because you haven't mastered the art of riding. Improvement in any skill set requires some amount of patience and time. If your child becomes really upset from a small setback, offer a reminder about an activity that was difficult at first and now is easy. Once upon a time, tying a shoe or climbing stairs or reading were all challenges that your

## So You Fell Off Your Horse, You Say?

What the saying doesn't include is that it's also okay to acknowledge horseback riding might not be your thing. So when your child tries something and fails, encourage trying again, but even more so, encourage understanding the failure and whether or not trying again is worth it to your child, to you, or in general.

**Inspiration**

child worked to master. Remembering accomplishments can help build confidence in approaching new challenges.

My son decided to join an after-school chess group. After the second meeting, he came home and declared that he was done with chess and did not want to go back. Ever. After talking a bit, he explained that he lost every match and could not remember any of the special moves. The discussion was made easier, as he had chosen the activity in the first place. My husband and I let him know that he did not need to enroll in chess for the next session but that he had committed to attending for this session. We came up with some ideas for how he might engage his peers and his chess mentor, and then he role-played, asking for a chance to observe a match or two. By the end of the semester, he felt much more comfortable playing chess, was able to explain the pieces to his sibling, yet confidently chose to avoid the next session! He got past the initial barrier of difficulty and was able to make a decision knowing that he could choose to try again another time.

## Just Like Riding a Bicycle

Your child is destined to fail. In fact, this failure will make your child stronger. Imagine if you were coasting through life and never hit a bump. Life would be boring, and you would probably lack the initiative and motivation to try anything new. Challenge is what makes life engaging. It also makes life frustrating. When your child experiences frustration, it is your job to help illuminate the value of the frustration. Try to help your child understand where that feeling is coming from. Was there sufficient effort or planning leading up to the activity? Were there unforeseen circumstances that could not be avoided? You are your child's cheerleader, foundation and, hopefully, sounding board. With each fall, you can work to help your child handle it.

In our home, we frequently use the term flexible thinking. It's a term used often by teachers to support collaboration and cooperation. Being a flexible thinker includes thinking outside the box, going with the flow, not getting hung up on what you thought the project should look like. It's great to have vision and persistence, but it's also great to have listening skills and to be able to reconcile new ideas with your own. Flexible thinking is key to resilience, as it can allow you to see both the success within a failure and the opportunities for change. When things don't go your way, think flexibly.

## Defining Success and Failure on Your Terms

What is success? When I ask groups of parents and teachers this question, they often respond, "Self-fulfillment, strong relationships, financial independence." The number-one response? Happiness. Yes, there is more to life than an Ivy League degree and the title after your name. There's even more to life than money. Hard to believe, and money sure does make life easier, but it doesn't make it richer in the true sense. Interestingly, when I ask parents to define failure for their children, the most common response is, "Living at home at age forty!" Though this comment often provokes laughs, it contains an important truth about our deepest hopes as parents. We all have hopes for our children. And at the core, we likely want for them to be personally and professionally engaged, self-sufficient, and happy adults.

It's important as a parent to define success on your own terms. Challenge Success, a research organization founded in the School of Education at Stanford University, proposes that families define success on their own terms to help in setting expectations. Once you validate your own definition and stop worrying about a societal perception of success, you and your family can make choices that will support your own values. Walk proudly in your own shoes in order to help your child comfortably define success independently.

### Celebrate Success in Small Doses

Find little moments of success to celebrate, such as when your child demonstrates a moment of flexible thinking and tries broccoli or a movie that you suggest. Acknowledging this moment of resilience will encourage more like it.

**Perspiration**

Your child's resiliency will be the underpinning of future success. We live in a world where relationships can be difficult, sickness and accidents occur, and the global economic marketplace is unpredictable. In fact, the only thing we can predict with certainty is that surprises—good and bad—will happen. The small steps you and your child build toward creating a healthy response to failure will be the foundation of future resiliency. Once you have defined success, you can share that definition with your child. Your child will likely have a definition similar to yours (at least until middle school when all bets are off). Encourage your child to share in creating personal success with you and as a family. Your child will need to make some important decisions, and these will impact personal success. Honor what success means to your child, and help support decisions that will foster it.

# Character in Action

### Zero through Five Years Old: Playdate Don't

Your four-year-old daughter is invited on a playdate, and the host child tells your daughter she wishes your child had never come, goes in her room, and closes the door. The parent calls and tells you she found your child crying in the hallway and asks you to come pick her up. The most important thing is to get your child and assure her that her feelings are legitimate, whatever those feelings are. Behavior and coping are another story.

She should be as polite as possible when she leaves, and it's important for you to talk with her about what happened and why it may have happened. The situation was undoubtedly hurtful, and the pain might have been provoked or may be unknown. Talk with your child about what happened and how it made her feel.

At her age, this conversation should be brief and to the point. Explain your expectations for her behavior (no matter how someone else is acting). Encourage an open mind to the friendship, and move on. You may begin to feel hurt, angry, frustrated, and even scared yourself—that's okay—but you must not let those feelings intrude on the lesson your child needs to learn. You need to move on and not hold it against your daughter's friend or her family. Everyone makes mistakes, and your kid will too.

### Six through Twelve Years Old: Science (Un)Fair

Your twelve-year-old son worked on his science fair project for two weeks. He was adamant about doing it on his own and didn't ask for much help from you. The teacher has been clear that she would like students to do their own work. You send him off to school without seeing the final product. He is excited for the big day.

Three days later, he comes home with his grade, a B–. "It's so unfair! I worked really hard on that, and it was good!" he declares. Emphasize to your son that his effort does matter. Be as neutral as you can when he reports his grade, as hard as that might be to do. After all, the grade defines how he was evaluated on one assignment and has almost no other meaning in the grand scheme of things. Not only did he earn that B– on his own, but he also learned a lot from the project. He still has more to learn.

Find a teachable moment after he has cooled down and had some time to regroup, though you might be tempted to talk to him right as he walks in the door. Allow him to find some balance, and then try to help your son look at the high and low points of the project. Talk about what was good and what could have been better, and find out if he understands the deficits. Ask him what part of the project makes him feel the most proud. Which part did he feel was the least understood by his teacher or peers? What are some ideas he has for making that aspect of the project more like the successful part of the project? Talk about different ways to approach the next big project (ask for help proofreading, check the scientific process with the teacher, get peer feedback, work in a group, etc.).

If he just can't get past it, encourage him to talk with the teacher. You may need to offer to be a backup participant, but try to help your son ask for the meeting. This can be an open discussion, and he needs to be able to hear about what he needs to improve on. Most importantly, don't judge him based on his grade, and let him know it's just one disappointment in life. He can learn from this and move forward!

### Thirteen through Eighteen Years Old: Breakup Bummer

Your seventeen-year-old son was dating a girl in his class. The two of them were inseparable. You notice he is home more often and not as animated as usual. When you inquire how his girlfriend is doing, he tells you they are no longer dating. At this point, it's best to support him and not let your disappointment or celebration (depending on what you thought of the relationship) show. Though you might have questions, try to keep them to a minimum. You may be dying to know who dumped whom and want all the gory details, but the best thing you can do at this point is listen and follow your son's lead. Try to give him space to process his feelings, be available and present, and think of unobtrusive ways to show you love him. Many boys talk more openly when working side by side on a task, so you might offer to help him do his laundry or simply work nearby as he reads or completes homework. Hopefully he will talk with you and share when he is ready. The only way to develop resilience in the face of a breakup is to experience a breakup. When he is ready, you can share things that you do when facing disappointment and be sure to remind him that you love him and you know some or all of the hurt will fade.

## To Summarize...

- Roll with experiences; don't let fear rule your decisions.

- Praise effort more than product.

- Celebrate the process.

- Embrace failure as a means to success.

# Chapter 14

## Responsibility: Raising a Self-Respecting Adult

### In This Chapter...

- Teaching children to care for themselves
- Encouraging children to care for others
- Caring for the home
- Time management, money sense, and charity

When I talk to parent groups and ask what they want for their children long term, the number-one response is: "to be happy." This raises some questions: How do we achieve happiness? What does happy look like? Too many of us overvalue grades, athletic performance, and college admissions. With such a focus on performance, it's easy to lose the value of compassion, collaboration, and kindness. In this chapter, you will learn about modeling responsibility as a parent and expecting it of your child to promote independence and productivity.

**Words to Parent By**

*Character—the willingness to accept responsibility for one's own life—is the source from which self-respect springs.*

Joan Didion

Quote

Rather than worry about each performance as your child grows, think about the long-term development of your child. What will make your child happy as a high schooler, as a college student, as a twenty- or thirty-something? Will your child still be trying to achieve good grades or make money, or will your child be satisfied with other things in life? There are many ways to demonstrate responsibility, and this chapter will highlight ways to develop it.

Your toddler is taking responsibility with the declaration, "I do it myself!" (of which I am often reminded I did as a young girl by my own mother). Your tween is taking responsibility with the response, "I chose to do it that way; what's the big deal?" And your teen is accepting responsibility with the statement, "I'm sorry for not being perfect—so the car's a wreck, but aren't you happy I'm okay?" Whenever possible, try to include and teach the element of responsibility in your children's decision making.

Responsibility is ownership with pride—in the context of a community. Being responsible involves knowing you have contributed (either positively or negatively) to something that affects those around you. Your child will learn more from accepting responsibility for a "failure" than enjoyment from an unearned "success."

Your child should own decision making proudly. Decision making itself is a learned art, and by owning the decisions we make, we learn more from the mistakes than we would if we didn't take responsibility for them.

When my son was in fifth grade, he brought home a science fair project that involved significant and intricate building with toothpicks. I advised him that his concept might not be feasible, but he was sure that he had made the right choice, so I let him proceed. After an hour of trying to build it with his father, with increasing frustrations from both of them, he admitted that it wasn't going to work. He then, after a few deep breaths, reengineered his concept to a more feasible toothpick-based project. By experiencing the failure of his first concept, he was able to think more clearly about how to create a project and the steps needed to accomplish what he wanted.

Frankly, it annoys me when someone does not accept responsibility for poor actions and decisions. While it's not always easy to admit when you're wrong, it's much more attractive than denying or placing the blame on someone else. It's your job to teach your child to make good choices—and to accept responsibility otherwise. You can do this best by living this model. That goes for mistakes you make as a parent and as a citizen of the world.

So how can you best model the act of admitting mistakes so your kids can see it without damaging your "perfect-parent" image? Well, the truth is, the best parents aren't perfect. In fact, they are filled with imperfections. The best parents reflect on their own lives and model strong values in real time. So the best way to admit mistakes is to do it honestly and openly. If you lost the car keys, rather than lash out at your spouse or kids about how, if the house were more organized… own up to the problem and ask for help. Isn't that, after all, what you want your child to do in the same situation?

I recall once making a big mistake at work. I was so disappointed in myself and embarrassed to tell my boss. My children overheard a conversation about it with my husband, which led to a full-family discussion about it. We decided that I had to be honest, and we practiced how I should break the news. At dinner later that day, my daughter asked me how it went. I shared my humiliation, but I acknowledged that my boss was really reasonable about it and that we were able to troubleshoot the problem together. This was a great moment for me to share because it reflected the relief of being honest and owning my mistake. It also reminded me that my own kids might be scared in similar situations and that I should react reasonably even when I am disappointed or angry.

## Care of Self

Parents all make mistakes, and it's how you respond to them that will teach your kids the most about taking responsibility. If you are quick to lay the blame elsewhere or divert attention, your child will learn to do the same. If, on the other hand, you step up, even when it's really embarrassing or difficult, your child will learn to do so as well.

## Responsibility Looks Different at Different Stages of Life

### Zero through Five Years Old

At this young stage, children don't have a lot of responsibility, but it's a prime time to start setting the expectation. Parents can teach responsibility by asking children to clean up toys and do daily chores. Responsibility at this stage can include making a bed every morning, helping sweep the floor, or fixing a broken toy.

### Six through Twelve Years Old

In the elementary years, there is ample opportunity to practice responsibility. Parents can set a high bar for household chores and self-care at this stage. Children at this age can demonstrate responsibility by taking care of pets, doing homework, or practicing instruments.

### Thirteen through Eighteen Years Old

By adolescence, teens should have a strong understanding of responsibility and should be taking care of themselves in many ways. Parents can encourage responsibility by offering decisions and respecting them and by consistently increasing opportunities for independence. Teens can show responsibility by having friends over without parents home, returning the car in good condition, or managing homework without prompting.

Eighteen months is not too young to start. A toddler can help clean up the living space, comb hair, select snacks, and clean hands. You probably cannot rely on a child at this age to remember to do these things, but you can certainly expect some participation. Toddlers or young children can begin to partake in regular chores that express caring for themselves and independence, such as picking up toys, brushing teeth, dressing, and putting away laundry.

By age seven or eight, children can take responsibility for their own rooms, any messes they make in the general living space of the home, and their teeth, hair, baths/showers, and dressing. They can do much more than that, so feel free to experiment with what works well for your child and family.

At ten or twelve years old, your child is probably okay to stay home alone and possibly watch younger siblings. Again, the exact age is hard to nail. Check with your local police department about any age minimums the department may enforce or suggest. Of course, you and your child need to be comfortable with this situation. Make sure your child knows all the safety go-tos (what to do in case of fire, who to call if you can't be reached, what the exit routes of the home are, in which situations to answer the door). Start small; leave your child alone for just a few minutes while you run a quick errand. Leave instructions: "A package may arrive while I'm gone." "Tell anyone who calls that I'm busy." "Make sure you work on your homework before you play." "No television." These instructions are, of course, up to you and should reflect the rules of your home.

Your child will learn to make a quick and easy snack, work on a puzzle for entertainment, or work on homework. I was surprised when I returned home from a late night out and my son had used his school-issued iPad to make a movie with

## Just Do It

Try giving your child a single responsibility at a time. Make a point to enforce it daily with a gentle question—"Did you remember to _____?"—and then offer the time for your child to actually do it. Don't punish or do it yourself; make sure you're allowing time in the day. It will take more time in the beginning, but offer the opportunity for your child to take on the responsibility for life.

Perspiration

his siblings and cousins. I hadn't thought to restrict his use of the iPad, and lo and behold, he had used it appropriately and creatively while collaborating with his siblings and cousins. Incidentally, the movies were really fun, and I am sure we will enjoy them for years to come (and pull them out for my children's future spouses).

You can expect teens to care for themselves in many ways. They are away from their parents for such a significant amount of time during the day, so be sure they are handling themselves appropriately. Make sure your expectations are clear (e.g., what is and is not okay to wear outside of the house), and also allow for independence as it's earned: "I see you taking your curfew seriously, so let's extend it and see how you do." Adolescents are nearly adults and can earn adult privileges. For example, if you are okay with your sixteen-year-old daughter driving and you have a car, go ahead and let her borrow the car. If she uses the car appropriately and appreciates the privilege by, say, refilling the gas tank upon return, she can continue to enjoy it when it works with the family schedule. Teens can also contribute to their financial needs (clothes, transportation, books, music). This is a time in life when kids really want to express themselves, which often "requires" different accessories or material goods. It's fun to shop together when time and budget allow, but the responsibility of purchase can be a great lesson for a teen who really wants something. Believe me, a kid will take much better care of products purchased independently than with Mom's money.

## Care of Others (Siblings, Pets, Friends)

Now you can start saving all your babysitting money. Let your kids pitch in. There is no one right age for babysitting, but you'll know when you child is ready. And if you miss the cue, your child will likely tell you directly. Encourage your kid to start venturing out independently. At eight or nine years old, kids can easily navigate their close-to-home neighborhood. Is there a local library or playground that is in walking distance and easy to find (i.e., relatively few turns)? Is there a friend who lives just a few houses away? Let your child explore some independence. If going to the park feels like too much, offer a head start and meet up there together. With this independence, children can take on more by watching others or hanging out with friends. There are first-aid and CPR courses and babysitting courses offered to kids around ten or eleven years old. Our kids paid for their own training as an

## Researching a Pet

Following are good questions to ask when you're researching a pet:

- What is the feeding schedule for the animal?

- Are you really going to take the pet back if we choose not to keep it?

- What is the cleaning schedule for the animal?

- What does play look like with a _____ (fill in the blank—rabbit, guinea pig, dog, goldfish)?

- What are the costs involved with day-to-day care of the animal?

- Does the animal require anything special or unique?

- What are typical options for this animal when we are travelling? Any recommendations?

- Is my child the appropriate age for the animal we are considering?

**Perspiration**

investment in future earning potential, since they can charge more if they are certified.

Pets offer a wonderful opportunity for learning and practicing responsibility. Has your child been asking for a pet? Are you resistant? Try fostering at first. Fostering offers a wonderful chance to care for a pet and enjoy its company without the long-term commitment. It also offers your child a trial period to demonstrate responsibility. Oftentimes, you can find postings in neighborhood listserves or on Craigslist. Once you are ready for that commitment, be it fostering or long-term adoption, make sure you research the pet carefully. Some good people to talk to during your research phase are the owner or an employee of a local pet store, a representative at a local pet shelter, or pet owners you know or have been referred to.

## The True Homework: Work of the Home, a.k.a. Chores

Along with responsibility comes pride. You have pride in your home and your belongings, and so should your child. It's important that your whole family cares for your home, including the items in the home. If you constantly pick up after everyone, your child will not understand the work that goes into keeping the home organized. The same goes for care of specific items. If the general policy is for you to replace broken items, your child will not learn the value of those possessions. If something breaks, ask your child to help you fix it or pay for the repair. If it has to be replaced, talk about it. Things happen, and it's okay, of course, if glasses, toys, etc., occasionally break. Worse has surely happened. What's key here is talking about an item's value and whether or not it should be fixed or replaced. When your daughter breaks a cheap, plastic toy, it's a good opportunity to make a statement about taking care of things. You can try gluing it and show her that it simply won't work and that the toy is now trash (or hopefully recycling). If it's a more expensive or consistently used item, you might discuss the value of fixing versus replacing. If it's an instrument, for example, it might need to be fixed professionally. Who will pay for that? If your child cannot afford it, perhaps your child can work it off with chores or other work.

Your home should be a safe and happy place for your family members. Everyone who lives there can participate in its upkeep. That's a stretch for infants, but every other-aged person can contribute productively. For a toddler, this might include picking up toys and placing them in designated boxes, baskets, or shelves. For a kid or tween, this can include taking out the garbage, loading the dishwasher, putting away laundry, vacuuming after dinner, and making a bed. Tweens and adolescents can take on more, including laundry.

Chores are so much more fun when you do them together. Turn on some music; set aside time to help each other. Cleaning

## The Real Homework

The work of the home will depend on your home and your family, but here are some ways your child can help take care of the home:

- Helping out with spring cleaning (can include a garage sale with anything your child is willing to donate)

- Breaking down items for the garbage, recycling

- Helping out with maintenance of the home (painting, cleaning, weeding)

- Grocery shopping (go together and split the list, or send your child to a local store and encourage some decision making)

- Preparing breakfast or lunches on especially fast-paced days in the home

- Babysitting or watching a sibling

**Perspiration**

a bedroom can feel daunting to a child of any age, so help out, show how, and you'll be surprised at how much it helps in terms of long-term care. When kids are used to keeping a tidy room, they will naturally begin to tidy it daily, and they will also be more independent as they grow up and be able to do a big cleanup on their own.

And, once your child is used to helping with the challenging responsibilities like cleaning, food prep, and maintaining the home, your child can enjoy some fun responsibilities:

- Choosing a movie for family movie night

- Picking the ice cream flavor for dessert

- Weighing in on a vacation destination

- Deciding a color to paint a room in the house

- Shopping for a new family computer or television

- Deciding which radio station to listen to in the car

## Homework

Homework is your child's responsibility. When you hear yourself say, "*We have a lot of homework to get through tonight,*" you've stepped over the line. It's fine to help out with the homework when asked for help, but try to limit yourself to suggestions, minor proofing, and help with clarifying directions. That does not include holding pencil to paper or typing directly into an assignment. It does not include leading questions. It does not include taking the mouse from your child and "just doing it." Your child's teacher will not know what your child understands and does not understand if the work is not that of your child.

Allow your child the room to do homework and to learn from the process. The biggest help you can provide is a place conducive to work, supplies, time, and reminders. An appropriate environment might be a quiet place with a desk and shelf full of supplies, or it might be the kitchen counter with music on in the background and siblings running around. Talk with your child to figure out what works best. If you don't have the appropriate supplies, talk to the teacher to get a list. The school can often provide you with supplies if you cannot afford them or find them. And finally, check in with your child. Reminders such as "Have you done your homework yet?" or "Have you finished your homework?" are terrific. If your child asks you to review a homework assignment and you find a mistake, have your child take a second look. Maybe point out an error, but don't help too much.

## Jobs and Allowance

"But Peter gets an allowance!" is not a reason to start giving your child an allowance. Before you institute an allowance, think about your rationale: What is it you hope your child will get out of it?

### Never Too Young to Help

Your child is ready and able to help with a lot more around the house than you might think. Work together to determine what would be useful, and express yourself when you are impressed by the results. Kids as young as eighteen months can help with preparations for meals and even with menu planning. A child aged six and up can clean and set the table area, clean dishes, or clear the table after dinner. Your home will have unique needs, but scheduled chores (feeding pets, cleaning gutters, etc.) are completely age appropriate for your tween.

**Perspiration**

An allowance is a prime opportunity to teach your child about saving and spending. You can offer your child a budget for clothes, entertainment, or toys. If you do this, try to avoid spending money on these items from your own wallet. Of course, a special event may require a new suit or outfit, but generally speaking, stick to the allowance. If your daughter is hankering for a designer pair of jeans and it takes three months to save the money for them, she will enjoy those jeans and take better care of them. If your son regularly blows his allowance in one fell swoop at the corner candy store, it might be time to talk about spending wisely.

Some families choose not to offer an allowance to kids. This is a fine choice, and you still have opportunities to develop thoughtful spending habits in your children. Try to be clear about how you spend money and, when appropriate, explain your choices. For example, what determines the budget for clothing, toys, and entertainment outings and items? Discuss this up front and take the opportunity to model wise spending.

My family has an annual budget for clothing for the entire family. At the end of one year, we still had one hundred dollars left over. Our youngest needed a jacket, our daughter wanted anything we'd buy her, and our oldest wanted a few T-shirts. We spent an hour online as a family choosing the items our kids wanted and needed. Once we had everything in the virtual shopping cart, we were over budget and had to pare it down. This was a prime opportunity to share our family's decision making and model sticking to the budget (even though we could have just spent a little extra—after all, it was the holiday season).

A Jewish tradition is the tzedakah box. Families use it in different ways, but the idea is to put a bit of money in it every now and then or on a routine basis. No matter your religious background, you can teach your child at a young age the importance of charitable giving. Once you have collected a sum (either predetermined or perhaps after a set period of time), you can donate the amount to a cause or charity. You might like to choose an organization or cause together or alternate deciding. The idea is to show that it's good to share wealth and think about others. The lessons learned are numerous and special. You can learn about all different organizations in need, share interests, build collaboration, and instill lifelong giving.

# Character in Action

## Zero through Five Years Old: Toddler Toys

Yes, your toddler can take responsibility. It looks a little different, of course, and will take more reminding. But if you start young, you'll be glad you did. Your toddler pulls out his sixth toy of the afternoon as you are beginning to get ready for carpool pickup of your older children. It's a prime opportunity to teach him to take responsibility for the toy area while you get snacks ready. You can even say, "As I prepare a snack for you and the other kids, you can help by cleaning up." It's a bonus to have a special place for everything (clear bins are easy for toddlers to identify), but whatever your organizational system, your toddler can learn it and help out. He will be proud to help out, and it will make your life easier. This teaches him care of his own space and his own belongings (and others' belongings if it's a shared play space).

### Six through Twelve Years Old: Being Neighborly

Your tween is asked to run across the street in a pinch as your neighbor has to run out and leave her napping child. Send her over! This is a great way to get some independent experience. She may be nervous. Remind her you are there and she can call. If your tween is excited about babysitting, there are courses she can attend (at the Red Cross and other community centers) to learn more and become certified.

### Thirteen through Eighteen Years Old: Joy Ride

Your son wants to borrow the car to go out with friends. This is a prime opportunity to teach your son responsibility. He can borrow the car if _____ (fill in the blank—he does his chores, is back by ten o'clock, fills it with gas, etc.). If any of the stipulations are not met, then he will not get to borrow the car until he has taken responsibility. That might mean doubling up on the chores or making it up in another way.

## To Summarize...

- Responsibility starts with caring for oneself.

- Taking care of others can improve oneself.

- Help kids manage responsibility of self, others, home, schoolwork, and jobs.

- Share and enjoy financial success.

# Part 3

# Nurturing Well-Being

Our own safety and health, as well as that of our children and our families, is paramount in our child rearing. We cannot be expected to help model and mold character, offer and promote independence, or take an active part in our community if we have not cared for ourselves and our family. It's simply impossible to function as a parent (or much else) without a sense of security and without the intellectual and concrete ability to navigate the world. In this section, we will focus on physical and emotional health and well-being.

We will take a close look at virtues involved in developing good habits and physical safety, such as health and care. We will dig deep into education in an effort to build and sustain lifelong skills for learning as well as a love of learning. We will also take a close look at elements that encourage a shift in attitude, such as balance, play, and transitions. The discussions around these values will help you gain perspective on the well-being of yourself, your child, and your family.

# Chapter 15

## Balance: The Teeter-Totter of Life

### In This Chapter...

- How to attain the unattainable: balance in life and in family
- When and how to say no when yes is easier
- How you can help or hinder your search for balance
- How and where we can make room for family

**W**hether you're home with your child, working part time, or working full time, you must search for the balance in life. The trick of the balance is that there is no perfect balance between work and life. It's not about 50 percent work/50 percent personal. It's a combination of perspective and practice. This chapter will help you understand your short- and long-term priorities and decision making and help you help your child strike a balance for a life of achievement and enjoyment.

Who are you anyway? You're not *just* a parent. Get out and about: date night, exercise, book club, knitting group, bar, volunteering. Celebrate you with your family. Find time for your own flow. And have no guilt (well, maybe a little, but not enough to stop you from being you). Working at home or not, humans crave stimulation and satisfaction in their daily lives. If you're home with your child full time, you likely crave adult interaction or intellectual stimulation. If you're working full time, you likely crave more time with your partner, spouse, friends, and child, as well as more time on your own. The part-timers also have a struggle—how and when can you turn work or parenting off when you're trying to keep a leg in both worlds?

My favorite job, hands down, was that of a full-time mother. I enjoyed it on a daily basis, I knew I was making a difference, and I was challenged with each new adventure and stage. Did I get frustrated? Sure. Did I worry I should be looking for something more professional? Absolutely. Did I need money? Eventually, which is why I retired from that position. The only thing is, you never stop being a full-time parent, even if you've never taken a day off work in your life.

## Stop Worrying about Decisions You Made in the Past

I had a fitness trainer once say to me that each morning, you have a chance to make good decisions for a new day. You don't have to feel guilty about the dessert last night or justify the afternoon pick-me-up brownie. He reinforced that while you need to be mindful both of what you've done and how you want to move forward, you also need to let it go and move on. I encourage that with parenting. Don't worry about the decisions of the past, but keep them in mind. The day-to-day is about reinventing and revisioning your family. Each day is a new one with new decisions, new opportunities for family time, and new chances to take care of yourself. You have the chance to make good decisions, to spend time with your family, and to take care of yourself.

Life gets very busy, so find pockets of time for your family in between the busy. Carve out special moments, like family dinner, Saturday hikes, or Friday morning breakfast scramble. Beyond that, take an impromptu moment with your family. Sometimes homework can wait. You don't have to make dinner every night just to eat dinner. If it's a nice night, grab the family and head out for a restaurant or picnic of unhealthy snacks you can easily grab. Naps are fun. Create these moments together. If the weather is nice, encourage your child to postpone the homework and go with you on a walk to the park or for an ice cream. Who knows? Maybe you'll even get some information on the down-low about the upcoming dance.

A lot of parenting books talk about the importance of routine. Experts stress that kids thrive with routines because they know what to expect and have something to count on. This is true. Many adults benefit from this too. All that said, never be so strict with your routine that it paralyzes time with family. Don't be mistaken: When you are striking your balance, if there is ever a choice, let it be heavier on family time than work.

## Model a Strong Work Ethic, but Don't Live to Work

There are some people out there who literally live to work. They eat, breathe, and sleep their jobs. That's fine, but likely it's not you. I hope you do enjoy your work, but it's okay to have boundaries. With the adoption of smartphones, tablets, and whatever else is out there while you're reading this, employees are expected to be accessible 24/7. And, even if they aren't expected to, many employees feel like they should be. Work hard. Model a strong work ethic, but don't live to work.

If you find you are living to work and are never really at home with your family, it's time to find something new. If you truly cannot afford to leave your job (finances, professional goals, time—whatever the restriction is), then re-create it for yourself in a way that allows you put it in its place so that when you are home, you are truly present. Make sure your employer knows that you are dedicated to the job and that when it's time to go home, you are home and not on the job any longer. This is not an easy conversation to have, but muster the confidence to have it and know it is for the best cause out there. If you're doing shift work, then do your shift and be present when your shift is over. If you have an office job, don't take the work home. Talk with other employees who appear to be managing the work-life balance and get some tips for your specific area or field.

### Words to Parent By

*There's no secret to balance. You just have to feel the waves.*

Frank Herbert

Quote

### Dessert before Dinner

We were experiencing atypically hot weather in the Bay Area and had some time between our after-school activities and dinner. My family spontaneously took a long walk to the ice cream store. Instant family time, and we got to eat dessert before dinner— an unheard of treat in our family.

**Pure Genius!**

If you work from home, set up a clear schedule and physical space for the work.

Working a flex schedule or from home is one of the most tricky jobs a parent can have because the work is always there and waiting to be done. If you can, create a place for the work to happen and leave it when you've put in your hours. There's always more to do, but it's not your job to get it all done now. When you're with your family, really be with your family.

Your job is a means to supporting your family. Love what you do as best you can, and definitely take pride in your work. Know that what you're doing is meaningful because if nothing else about it is enjoyable, you are supporting your family. I had a job that I liked in theory, but my boss made very difficult. It seemed that on good days I was able to get my job done in spite of him. On bad days, well, let's not go to that dark place. I pushed through and tried to emphasize the positives of the work. (I could leave the office and be with my kids in time to get them from school, I was doing good work, I was making a difference in the world.) I tried not to dwell on the annoyance and frustration of my relationship with my boss. It didn't make the job easier or more fun, but it reminded me of the reason I was there, and that made all the difference.

## The Power of No (and How to Phrase It)

Always make sure you have time with your family, no matter how busy life gets. It's hard to say no with all the things life has to offer. We want our kids to be social, so we set up playdates, join parenting groups, and RSVP yes to every birthday party we're invited to. We want our kids to be cultured, so we buy tickets to shows, pay large entrance fees to museums, and travel the state, the country, or even the world with them. We want our kids to have a strong education, so we sign them up for religious school, language classes, and tutoring. We want our kids to be artistic, so we commit them to art classes, piano lessons, and band practice. We want our kids to be athletic, so we sign them up for soccer by age four, join a travel team by eight, and have twenty participation trophies by age twelve. Social, cultured, intelligent, artistic, and athletic are all great assets to want for your child—but, honestly, who is amazing in all those arenas? And for those adults who are, who had amassed them all by age eighteen?

Consider a new perspective when it comes to carving out time for yourself and your family. Brownies for the school bake sale? Sorry, not today. Playdate with Thomas? Sure thing, but why don't you stay just till five so we have time for family dinner? Homecoming dance falls on the same day as Dad's birthday? Let's pick out a terrific outfit for the *next* dance and enjoy some cake together. Or how about Dad and I celebrate with a romantic dinner and you attend that dance? I am reminded of a family that never schedules anything on Sundays so the parents and children are sure to have a day together. Things come up (read: soccer because that always comes up), but for the most part, this family has carved out a special time to be together. And before you roll your eyes and say, "Well, that could just never be us, they must have young children," I will tell you that both parents work and they have children in middle and high school. It's not easy, and it doesn't happen every Sunday, but it's a goal, and the family counts on this time to connect because Monday through Saturday are quite full.

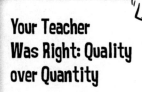

## Your Teacher Was Right: Quality over Quantity

Time with kids is truly about quality over quantity. My sister is a full-time professional. When she is at work, she's all in. When she's home, she's all about her husband and kids. This is not an easy achievement, but she truly makes where she is and what she is doing the priority, and her kids and husband (and those of us around her) can all see it very clearly.

**Pure Genius!**

## You Matter!

You do matter, and don't forget it. Don't get lost in the shuffle. Not only do you need to understand that, but your partner, your community, and your children need to understand it as well. They will not value you as an individual unless *you* value you as an individual.

A former colleague once quoted his grandmother as saying, "If you don't toot your own horn, no one else will." That has lived with me well beyond my colleague's name. She was absolutely right. You must love yourself and share that with the world. This will help others see your value. It doesn't mean you have to run around talking about all your newest accomplishments, but it does mean you should share them with your family and friends in a proud and celebratory way.

Once your child is grown and living an independent life, you will need to do the same. Of course, you will still worry and want to keep in touch, but the reality is that your baby simply won't need you in the same immediate and significant way. Honoring yourself in the here and now has many benefits. First of all, you will be a better parent, spouse, friend, employee, and contributing member of society if you have self-respect and know that your family respects you too. Secondly, by putting yourself first every now and then, your child will begin to recognize that you are more than just a parent (even though we all know that's the most important role you'll ever have). Finally, as your child grows into an adult, this will impact your child's perception of you and your relationship together.

# Family Rituals

Family rituals, big and small, will help remind you of your true priorities in life. It doesn't matter what the rituals are so long as you honor them. I've talked about the importance of family dinners. These are a wonderful tradition to instill in your home. Believe me, there are times when I just want to leave dinner on the counter and head to bed early. But I never regret sitting down at the table with my family and sharing our day. You can try creating rituals in any routine part of your day, including after school, at bedtime, or even bright and early. Waking up is a hard task in our house. When the kids were younger, I would blast fun music and have a wake-up dance party to help lighten the mood. After school once a week, we would go to the park and the kids could unwind and share about their day. As they got older, we continued to have a free time directly after school that created a space for unwinding from all the pressure of school and preparing for

# Acceptance Looks Different at Different Stages of Life

## Zero through Five Years Old

Balance for a very young child is determined by stability in family life. Parents can encourage balance by modeling it and honoring it. Balance for a young child can include a bedtime routine, small introductions to structured play, or dedicated time with family.

## Six through Twelve Years Old

Elementary-aged kids are developmentally ready to find balance in certain aspects of their lives. Parents can support balance by offering choice of activities, opportunities for exploration, and plenty of downtime for unstructured play or relaxation. At this stage, balance can include choosing to skip soccer practice to finish a homework assignment, opting for free play, or attending a cast party after a big production.

## Thirteen through Eighteen Years Old

Balance is important for adolescents because they are exposed to a variety of stressors (academic, social, and physical). And as they move toward adulthood, they need to be able to cope with even more. Parents can help teens develop a sense of balance by modeling it and by offering choice when appropriate. Balance in the teen years can include working a job, vegging out, or staying up all night to study for an important midterm.

homework or after-school activities. Sometimes that time is short, and some days we carve out extra time (maybe even for an ice cream cone). This time and space—away from school, away from homework, just with family—creates an opportunity in the day to relax and recharge.

Take joy in your child's interests. Join a class together. My daughter's friend is a figure skater, and she was interested in taking lessons. I signed up with her, and it became our thing on Saturday mornings. We spend our Saturday mornings together, and I better understand the activity she is so committed to. My younger child noted that he'd like to take art classes with me, "like how you do figure skating with my sister." He saw it as his turn to get to have some mommy time doing something that interested him. So we signed up and now have masterpieces to frame! Maybe you don't want to sign up for a class, and that's okay. Go to sports games and cheer from the sidelines, find a good book to read together and make time to do it daily, play tennis at the park, discover all the ice cream shops in town . . . the sky is the limit on things you can do with your kids.

A friend of mine enjoys International Night in her home every Sunday night. The family spins the globe, and whatever country a finger lands on becomes the inspiration for dinner. They make and eat food from that country and read about it in their atlas. They've enjoyed cuisine from Brazil, Tahiti, Germany—and the list goes on. It's a fantastic opportunity to explore food, enjoy each other, and learn about new cultures.

## Carving Out Time

Take a moment, right now, to consider your family calendar. Do you have something you do regularly with your family—with each member of your family? If not, take this very moment to identify at least one way to start implementing family time.

**Perspiration**

Once you have rituals in place, you will be surprised by how much everyone depends on them. For example, maybe you forgot to share news of your day at dinner one night—your child will remind you. Say you had a wedding to attend and missed your Saturday morning activity—your child will remind you. That's not to say you can't ever depart from the routine, but make note to maintain the norm as best you can as you are creating a community of trust and enjoyment within your family.

# Character in Action

### Zero through Five Years Old: Overtime Over Family

Your babysitter is scheduled to be with your five-year-old until six every evening, at which point either your spouse or you are able to get home. You usually eat by six thirty as a family. Your boss says you have to stay late to work on a project. You enjoy your work and you want to push through, but this is the third night in a row, and you miss your daughter and know that family dinner should be a constant. That said, your wife will be home for dinner and has been the previous nights you've been out. What do you do? Your daughter will survive without you three nights in a row. Dinner with her mother will suffice as a family dinner. Go ahead and stay if you feel it will make a difference and you aren't setting a precedent. Be clear when the project is done that you're taking some comp time to spend extra time with your child. (And don't save it up. Use it now!) If this is becoming a pattern, talk with your boss about your schedule and clarify that you have family responsibilities. You can stay and help with this project through the deadline, but moving forward you need to set limits. This will demonstrate your commitment to your job without compromising your family time in the long term. This is not easy to do, but it's important nonetheless.

### Six through Twelve Years Old: Birthday Tournament

Your twelve-year-old son plays competitive ice hockey and has a big travel tournament coming up that conflicts with your birthday celebration. Ordinarily, you'd suggest celebrating on another day, but you have a party scheduled and friends and family are coming from out of town. Your son insists he has a commitment to his team and wants to honor that even though he knows it hurts your feelings. What do you do? Start with a conversation. Is there an alternative way and day to celebrate your birthday with your son? Can he travel with another family if you decide to let him go? Is there a way for him to join the team late or leave early and still make it to your celebration? Assuming it is a direct conflict, you simply have to decide together. You're the parent, so you get to make the final call, but make sure he knows you're listening to his input and weighing his opinion seriously. If a compromise feels okay to you (there will be other family and friends there, and you're glad you'll have company to keep you busy), then great. Talk about ways for him to make you feel special and to thank you for being flexible. If you feel adamant he needs to put family first in this situation, remind him that it is your job to teach him about the importance of family and that you understand he's disappointed, but this is the decision. Ask him if there is a way you can show him how grateful you are for the compromise. Don't reward him, but see if there is a way to honor his love of hockey or the fact that he missed an important tournament. (Maybe go to another game you might have missed or watch a game together.)

### Thirteen through Eighteen Years Old: Pick a Kid

Your fifteen-year-old daughter has a softball game on the same day and at the same time as your seventeen-year-old son's soccer game. Of course, the games are at fields across town from one another. What do you do? The easy answer is to alternate, and if you have two children who are actively involved in athletic ventures, this is likely an available solution. That said, your own schedule might prevent your attendance at multiple games throughout the season. Talk to your children and see if one of them feels more strongly about your attendance. It's likely that your kids have different preferences. Of course, if you tend to be available for one child's games more than the other's, then attend the child's games you least attend. Your kids are counting!

# To Summarize...

- Balance is an ongoing search.

- Saying no to commitments and events will help you say yes to your child.

- Be your own advocate, and don't keep yourself from balance with excuses.

- Make time and space for your family, even when it's not easy. And don't lose focus on you!

# Chapter 16

## Care: Being There and When You Can't Be There

There are many ways to care for your child well, and it's easy to get caught up in other people's views. Sometimes we don't feel like we have choices, and even if we do, deciding on child care can be intimidating. In this chapter, you will read about the benefits and challenges of a few options.

Your child doesn't have to be trilingual or calculus immersed to have a robust and loving child care experience. In fact, in one 2002 study, researcher Marcon found there were no significant differences in academic achievement between children who attended an academic-focused preschool and children who attended a more progressive, play-based approach.

Don't forget that you can always change your mind (and this applies to many of your parenting decisions). Once you recognize that you can *always* make a change, you can focus on finding the most consistent and loving environment for your child. If you decide to go back to work and enroll your child in a day care and you don't like the way it's working, you can always change the situation. Your options might include finding one-on-one care, changing to a more flexible work schedule, choosing another day care provider, finding a share-care situation, or temporarily leaving the workplace. Whatever it is, take a deep breath and start with one informed decision to lead the way.

# Full-Time Parent

Without question, full-time mother was the most enjoyable, fulfilling, satisfying job I have ever held. That said, it was also the hardest, most emotionally grueling, and least financially compensated. The choice to stay home is not an easy one—and not always a practical one. If you can afford it financially and in terms of your career stage, if you're interested, and if it works for your family, go for it. There's nothing like it, and you'll never have the opportunity again. Though you might feel daunted by the prospect of aging out of your career or starting over in your professional field, you will never have this time again with your child. If you are willing and able to try, embrace the challenge and the luxury wholeheartedly. And you can always change your mind.

However, if the idea does not excite you, if you cannot afford it, if you can't envision leaving your job, or if you just know it will not work for you, working full or part time is an equally valid choice. It is not only okay but arguably preferable to do what you do best and model that for your child.

When you are at home with your child, you will have both great moments and

## Writing Your Own Job Description

If you're a full-time parent, try to devise a job description that captures what you really want out of your time with your child. Think about the day-to-day and think about the overarching goals. This will help you to refocus your efforts and curb your frustration when needed.

**Perspiration**

some of the lowest moments of your life. You might doubt your decisions, find yourself frustrated, and even become lonely or bored. At some point in the day, think about, and even begin making notes about, the times of the day that are the most positive and the times that feel the hardest. As you find patterns in each, you will be able to expand the positive moments and work to diminish the negative ones.

Some days, it will be easy to enjoy your time with your child. Your child's growth and discoveries will seem magical, and you will deeply appreciate the fact that you won't ever have the chance again to watch it all unfold firsthand. On the other hand, some days will be very difficult. There will be meltdowns, miscommunications, messes, discipline snafus, and a seemingly endless cycle of things to wash.

When you are down in the dumps, and you will be, know that it is okay. It will get better, and you can work to figure out when and how to find your own reset button. Even if it breaks your routine, might you put on a children's show and give yourself a half-hour bath or tea break? Would it lift your spirits to move lunchtime and go for a walk with your child? Will it help you to schedule a park date with a good friend where you know your child might be engaged and you might have a much-needed adult conversation? Try to recognize and honor your own feelings.

Remember that you're working to raise a strong, self-reliant, and responsible adult. So when your son lies to you and denies that he cut a hole in his carpet with the scissors and screams that your chosen consequence is unfair, know that he is learning and you're doing the hard part of your job. You'll reap the rewards when he comes around and admits next time he knows he's done something wrong. Then you can be proud he's made a good decision and owned responsibility. When you become a full-time caregiver, you may well witness the full cycle of these behavior patterns multiple times a day. Every job has challenges. This one is no different.

## Day Care

Choosing a day care provider can be challenging. The best place to start is by getting references from friends and neighborhood families you respect. There may be online networks or books published in your geographic area that can help you learn more about the different more established care facilities.

Consider picking up a copy at your local library. If you are willing, ask people in the supermarket, at the park, or in front of a local school. People are frequently willing to share ideas and explain the pros and cons of their own day care choices.

Once you have a list, be sure to visit the facility. If you can, visit with your spouse, partner, coparent, grandparent, or friend. It's good to get two perspectives on the place and to have someone with whom to discuss the options. Prepare a list of questions.

**Inspiration**

## Aspects of Day Cares

Here are a few questions to consider when you are looking at day care establishments:

- What is the routine?

- What is the philosophy on discipline?

- Is there an academic component? If so, does it feel age appropriate? Does it feel too rigorous?

- How does the staff meet each child's own physical, emotional, social, and cognitive developmental stage?

- What structure is in place to continually meet each child where the child is and to further the child's development?

- What is the emergency plan?

- Does the facility provide meals, or are you expected to pack snacks and a lunch?

- What is mealtime like?

- What does parent communication look like?

- Are electronics (television, videos, computer) used during the day?

- How are breaks and staff rotations handled?

Once you have decided on a facility or two, ask to visit with your child to observe a typical day. If the facility does not allow visits, ask for an explanation or remove the facility from your list. When you visit, try to sit on the perimeter of the action to observe without interfering with the children's play. Be there for your child, but try to let your child be there without hovering so you can get a good feel for the care your child might receive during the day. Once you make the decision, trust in it and let it happen. Also trust your instincts if you change your mind. Remember, you can always change your mind.

You might consider keeping your child home until preschool. Consider for that experience whether or not you are looking for a play-based program or a skills-based instructional program? This is an important question to ask yourself, and the answer will likely change as your child grows or your family situation changes. Use all resources to which you have access (including **Chapter 17,** which discusses education) to understand the research and choose a day care situation that most supports your family's educational and care philosophy.

# Family Help

You might be lucky enough to have family members who are willing and able to help you with child care. Many in this position understand the incredible fortune of this setup and also the delicate communication needed for it to work. If you have a grandparent, an in-law, an aunt, or an uncle who is willing to watch your child, be sure that this prospective caretaker feels physically up to the challenge. There might not be a need for your loved one to run sprints or to sit "crisscross-applesauce" for an hour, but whoever cares for your child should be capable of the basic activities needed to keep the child safe in the space or neighborhood in which the care will take place. If there is a need for physical accommodations, such as a different chair, a confined space to avoid stairs, or a special stroller, try to provide any helpful equipment.

You might consider opening a conversation about care expectations by asking your relative what you can do to make the job easier. Would it help to prepack all snacks and extra emergency noshes? If the care will happen at the relative's house, would it make it easier if you pack a small container with art and toy materials that might be opened before and then cleaned after each day? Emphasize how appreciative you are to have help by offering a coffee or a treat or an invitation to stay for dinner after you return home. Depending

# Care Looks Different at Different Stages of Life

## Zero through Five Years Old

Care for a very young child requires a great deal of attention and time. Care at this stage should include safety, an environment that provides opportunities for physical, social, and cognitive development, and dependability and flexibility in case of illness.

## Six through Twelve Years Old

By this age, children are in school, so care is usually reserved for before and after school. Care at this stage should definitely include a strong social element, comfort, and structure. Children need to know someone is there for them to help them with homework or a difficult day, or to celebrate a success.

## Thirteen through Eighteen Years Old

Adolescents need care but not constant supervision. In fact, they need to experience independence. Parents should offer opportunities for teens to be left alone at home and to venture out into the community. Care at this stage requires listening, understanding, and a great deal of patience. The need for independence at this stage is not a substitute for quality time together.

on the nature of your relationship with the family member, ask if there are ways you can help. If a particular toy or activity really pushes buttons, make sure that toy or activity is not an option while your relative is with your child.

Finally, take a deep breath and recognize that it is very likely that the rules will be different with a grandma or an uncle from what they are with you, and that is fine. You may offer the rules you and your partner have for food and electronics, but you might have to be flexible with relatives. Be reassured that kids are very good at compartmentalizing situations. They understand very early that it is possible to behave differently at home, in school, at a friend's house, or with grandparents. Your regular family rules will not be ruined by an occasional predinner ice cream date or an extra thirty minutes of a television show. If your child will be with your relative for a significant number of hours each week, you might have to come to an agreement about the most important rules. However, if your child or children will not be in this situation for the majority of the week, then count your blessings and celebrate the fact that you are lucky enough to have loving and free (or affordable) care for your children.

## Nanny

A nanny is often a comforting option to new parents because there is a sense that you can maintain your own parenting (via someone else), and your child has one-on-one attention. Also, if your family grows, you have someone there who understands your family dynamic and can help adjust through the transition. There are also share-care options (discussed shortly), in which case your child might still receive more attention than in a group setting, but the attention is not one on one.

### Trust Your Gut

If your instinct is telling you that you need a nanny cam with a live feed to your office computer, keep looking or consider an alternative care situation for your child. A nanny should be a trusted person.

Inspiration

Finding a nanny can be an exciting adventure, one that will hopefully lead to a lifelong friendship and bond. It can also be nerve wracking and scary. It is natural to feel anxious about letting another

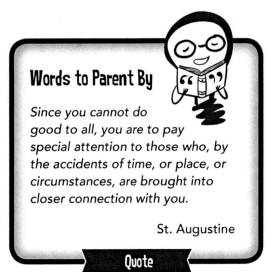

parenting figure into your child's life, one who might already have more parenting experience or who might have opinions that are different from yours. You are, after all, choosing one of the most important things in your life—a person who will take care of your child! Try to relax and enjoy it as much as you can. As with any of the decisions in this chapter, you can usually trust your gut and you can always change your mind.

The best way to start looking for a nanny is, again, references. Ask friends, family, and neighbors. Many neighborhoods now have parent listserves. Get on these and post that you're looking for someone. You'll likely see postings for a nanny who's leaving a current job. Most parents wouldn't post such advertisements for someone they didn't trust and believe in, so take those recommendations seriously. Perhaps you have friends with school-aged children. If that's the case, ask them to ask around. Finding someone through a personal reference will make you more comfortable. You can also post on other digital boards (like Craigslist). If you find someone through a more anonymous source like this, be sure to get a background check and be thorough with references.

Once you find a prospect, invite the nanny over to spend time with you and your child together. You will want your time together to feel natural and comfortable. Does the nanny play with your child? Talk to your child? Seem genuinely interested in your child? Ask questions: What do you love about being a nanny? What interests you in this job in particular? What routines do you stick to? What is your discipline style? You will also want to go over important aspects of the job (the large and the small stuff). Review nutrition requirements you have, sleep schedules, routines (nap, bed, mealtime, snack, outside/inside activities, for example), appropriate behavior and expectations in the home, social opportunities (like playdates), and any additional needs you may have (laundry, errand running, or tidying up the house, for example). Be very clear about your expectations for electronic media use (television, mobile phone, computer) during care hours.

Be sure to do a reference check. And when you do, ask questions—don't be shy. Is this person reliable? Punctual? Kind? Sensible? Mindful of parent requests? Safe? Clean? Willing to do anything else you might need? And if the nanny in question is not willing to provide references or simply doesn't have any, that is a major red flag.

Share care is often more affordable than having a private nanny, and it provides a great opportunity for social interactions. A share-care setup involves sharing a nanny with another family (or possibly multiple families) and can be structured in different ways. It might be that the nanny watches your child a few days a week and a neighbor's children other days. You might also arrange it so that the nanny is responsible for both your and others' children at the same times, possibly alternating houses. This option might be especially nice for an only child or a child whose siblings attend school during the day.

When deciding whether to pursue a share-care setup, you will have an added layer of reflection in addition to your process of evaluating the prospective nanny. A share-care system can easily strengthen a relationship with another family, yet it can also destroy the bond. As circumstances change, one family may want more or less of the nanny's time and attention. Changing school or work schedules may create conflict between families. The nanny's care style might be more in harmony with one family's philosophy than with the other's. If you decide to create a share-care, put as much time into creating an agreement between families as you put into the nanny's contract. How will you communicate schedule change requests? How will you decide additional family needs? How will you both communicate with the nanny about issues that might affect all the children? How will the pay structure be determined? Will you feel comfortable communicating with the other family (or families) about potentially delicate and emotional child-rearing issues? There is a stronger possibility of a share-care arrangement being a positive experience if you enter into it with a clear plan.

## Co-Op

Co-ops are a happy compromise for parents who have some time available and also want a highly socialized environment for their children. Many co-ops operate similarly to day care centers or preschools in which all adults are licensed professionals. Often you sign up for a certain number of hours of

## Co-Opportunity to Go Out

My sister and her husband started a babysitting co-op for the weekends. They alternated watching friends' kids and having their kids watched for sleepovers with a few other families. The co-op is still going strong, twelve years and five additional children later. It has created a community and helped with child care on a very reliable basis.

**Pure Genius!**

care and commit to a smaller number of co-op hours. This can allow you to have periodic coverage and participate in the caregiving at other times.

Usually the only major difference with this arrangement is that some of the caregivers will be parents of the participating children. Another difference that accompanies the co-op structure is the possibility of more transitions as different adults join and leave the group. This does not have to be disruptive, especially if the professional staff creates co-op schedules that work with the natural flow of the program. There can also be inconsistencies in a program created by parent participation, some of which can be absolutely wonderful. In one example, each participating parent brings a unique set of skills and assets.

The son of a friend of ours attended a co-op in which another child's parent was an accomplished woodworker. She led the children in building a kid-designed play area using basic tools and wood, and every time she appeared, the kids would cheer. While not all participating parents may have earned cheers for co-op appearances, all were able to offer special contributions to the program while also encouraging their own children to play with peers.

One inconsistency that can be a drawback at a co-op is that the very different parenting styles can result in awkward interactions with other parents. For instance, in our friend's situation, one parent insisted on playing a vigorous game of chase each time he arrived, disrupting any current activity. In another instance, a parent often came from work in a traditional setting, and she wore clothes that could not get messy. She often spent her co-op time standing in the kitchen area working to prepare snacks or put away clean dishes. In these instances, the professional day care educators can be invaluable in coaching each parent to appropriate and optimal participation.

# Character in Action

### Zero through Five Years Old: Can't Spoil a Good Thing

Your mother has offered to watch your infant daughter, but she and your wife do not agree on screen time limits. When your mother has watched your daughter in the past, you've come home to them watching television together, and your wife is adamant about her daughter not viewing television until the age of three because that's what the experts suggest. Take a moment to thank your wife for being so diligent to know what the experts suggest and for making sure your daughter is well cared for. Take another moment to thank your mother (with your wife) for the offer.

The biggest question to ask yourself is to what extent your mother will listen to you and your wife and how comfortable you are talking candidly with your mother about these kinds of issues. If you are comfortable, sit down and go over all the rules and routines you have in place right now that you want her to observe. Also mention that other things may come up, and make sure she understands how grateful you are and that you would be most comfortable with check-ins. This would be the ideal. You have to know that when your mother is in charge, even if she wants to follow all your rules, she will have her own opinions and likely bend the rules. She is Grandma, after all.

Now, if the above suggestion doesn't work for you and you don't have that kind of open relationship or your wife is adamant, then you should likely find a different regular-care situation so as not to introduce constant strain in your relationships with your wife and with your mother. That said, definitely make sure your mother has ample opportunities to be with your daughter recreationally, if not for a regular-care situation.

### Six through Twelve Years Old: Incident Report

Your six-year-old son comes home from day care and says that another child stuck a pencil in his ear. You were not notified by the day care, and he seems fine. If he is fine, great! These things do happen. Go ahead and mention it to the teacher at drop-off the next day to check in and make sure the situation was handled. If the teacher didn't know about it, you might ask about supervision and how something like this could be handled next time. Don't get too worked up that the teacher didn't see it (if that's the case). Things happen, and this is a great opportunity for your child to learn about self-advocating. Role-play with your child about how to let a teacher know about something that makes him uncomfortable (and you can even ask the teacher for some good phrases to use with the other child and the teacher). If you have concerns after talking with the teacher, then feel free to bring it up to an administrator, but do try working with the teacher first.

### Thirteen through Eighteen Years Old: Homeward Bound

You have a babysitter after school every day for your kids, and your fourteen-year-old son asks if he can be in charge. The very fact that your son has asked for this is a sign he is ready. That doesn't mean he has all the know-how. Has he watched your younger children in the past? How is he with them? How is he when you leave him on his own?

You'll definitely want to give him some practice leading up to being in charge every day after school. Make sure that he not only knows what to do in an emergency but that he also knows what is expected on a daily basis (homework for his younger siblings and him, dinner preparations, cleaning up after themselves, and anything else that you would expect).

This is a responsibility, and he needs to continuously earn it. You definitely need to think through the logistics and the safety of the situation as well. How will they get home? What will they do if he forgets his key? How can they contact you if they need to? Has he taken any babysitting classes? Is he first-aid and CPR certified? These are classes he can sign up for to help him prepare himself.

Don't forget that parents still need to care for their kids even when they're older. So even as you offer independence and you're not as present as you used to be, stay connected through conversations and helping your child prepare for these independent experiences.

# To Summarize...

- There are many options when considering the choice to work or stay home with your child.

- No choice is right or wrong in general, so consider the options and decide what's best for you.

- Make an informed decision about care with confidence.

- Know you can change your mind if the care situation is not working for you, your child, or your family.

# Chapter 17

## Education: Supporting Your Kids in School in a Productive Way

### In This Chapter...

- Why educate?
- What to consider with your choices in education
- Positive and appropriate communication with your child's school and teachers
- What to expect in the various stages of education

All parents want their children to get the very most out of their school experience. However, many are unsure of the best way to interact with schools when questions and concerns arise. This chapter contains some practical suggestions and outlines typical stages and benchmarks your child will experience throughout the learning process.

Though productive communication can make the difference between a good school year and a difficult one, parents must keep the big picture firmly in mind. Some researchers have calculated that Americans spend about

5 percent of our lives in school, which means that we are doing most of our learning outside of school! It is very unlikely that one year will make or break a lifelong process of education.

# Why Educate?

It's crucial to make sure that your child's early education (and hopefully entire education) is challenging in a healthy and motivating way and supportive both emotionally and socially. This requires you to work at education. It may begin with finding a school that's a good match, but it also requires your involvement throughout your child's education. The more positive the education experience is from the start, the better the base will be for all future learning and development. The early years lay a foundation because young children are naturally curious and have an instinct to learn and grow. They rise to the academic and social challenges. Think of the time and energy you invest in the early-childhood education experience as an investment in all future education. Your child will link all future concepts to the knowledge developed during these years. It's not an investment in facts or knowledge but an investment in the how and why of learning. An early love of learning can help your child face challenges in less structured or less supportive environments.

Your involvement in your child's education, both in and out of the classroom, will be a tremendous support. By involvement, I mean visiting the school to meet teachers and attend special events, checking in with your child, being cognizant of the curriculum, being aware of engagement and challenges for your child, reading together, taking your child to parks, museums, libraries, and other places that provide exposure to culture and different experiences, and talking with your child about the importance of education in general. You might consider moving to a different district or investing in a private or religious school to find the appropriate challenge and support for your child. If you are not interested in those major commitments or are unable to move, pay for tuition, or make other education-based changes in your life, don't worry.

In all likelihood, there have been changes in education since you went through the school system. Moreover, your vivid memories of school may (ahem) be less than accurate and are certainly based on your perspective as a child. From changes in school standards to new social supports to specific district-adopted curricula, you might be surprised at how many variations there are in our educational system. As your child reaches school age, research your school's philosophy, mandated or unique programs, assessment and homework policies, and more. By gathering this information in varied ways, you will be a more informed educational participant.

First, visit your school's or district's Internet sites. There you will find information about school initiatives, specific program elements, and school leaders. Many schools have links to parent organizations and after-school programs, both of which can provide you with a strong sense of community involvement. Additionally, you can get a sense of whether there are opportunities to participate in the educational system that might match your interests and availability. Second, talk to parents in your neighborhood or at a local park. Ask questions such as, "What do you think are the two strongest aspects of School X?" or "If you were able to change one thing about the school or program, what would it be?" As you talk to more people in the community, you should get a sense of the school's strengths or its weaknesses. Look for red flags in your research. Some of those might include:

- Disgruntled parents

- Lack of easily accessible information

- Conflicting messages from administration and parents

## Words to Parent By

*Live as if you were to die tomorrow. Learn as if you were to live forever.*

Mahatma Gandhi

**Quote**

Finally, visit the school. Call the office and make an appointment to visit. Visit a class, meet the school principal, speak with the teachers. You will probably get a strong sense of the overall school environment by walking in the halls or observing a recess. However, you will likely gather more specific details by asking direct questions. Create a list of topics that are important to you and spend some time deciding what you will ask about each topic and who is best positioned to provide that information.

While the sources mentioned above—websites, informal conversation, and school visits—are by no means exhaustive, these sources can provide a rich portrait of a school. School evaluations on public rating sites can be skewed toward complaints or overly focused on test scores, so use that data cautiously. Most importantly, never stop gathering information. Even after you have entered a school system, know that your child and your school are both dynamic and changing systems!

# Choosing a "Good" School

Ideally, your neighborhood school is a good fit for your child and your family. You may be fortunate enough to have a choice of schools, and choices in education can happen at every level. Choosing a school can feel like a monumentally important decision. It can feel like deciding to get married or have children. Just remember that you can change your mind. Parents can fall victim to the belief that if they screw this up, their child will pay throughout life. Why is it that we think the preschool our child attends will influence college acceptance or earning potential?

Take a deep breath and relieve yourself of this worry! I was recently chatting with some mothers I know casually while we waited for our children's music class to end. We were talking about the pressure we feel, homework loads for our older children, and other topics of the sort. We each shared our own school experiences and realized that one had attended a prestigious preparatory school on the East Coast as well as an Ivy League college, one had attended public schools on the West Coast through college, and one (me) had attended a progressive school, a preparatory school, and a public college. We were a diverse group of women with a diverse set of educational experiences, and one of us was working, one was picking up a few contracts here and there, and one was home with her children. Three women with three completely different backgrounds—we all enrolled our children in different schools—all found ourselves enrolling our children in the same neighborhood music class. We all shared at least some common values. The notion that our different educational backgrounds should have led us to wildly different futures was patently untrue.

There may not be such a thing as an ideal school, but finding one that is a match for your family, philosophically and logistically, as well as your child's learning strengths will likely support a wonderful educational experience.

Keep in mind that a school that suits one child may not meet the needs of another (i.e., a sibling) and that a school that satisfies one parent's ideals may not be optimal for a particular child. In keeping with the ideas earlier in this chapter, educate yourself about the choices you have. Schools can be public or independent, parochial or nonsectarian, and can fall anywhere on the spectrum of traditional to progressive philosophy. Most independent schools identify with one or a few philosophies, such as Waldorf, Montessori, or Reggio-Emilia.

Plan a meeting with your coparent to think about the broader goals you may have for each phase of your child's education. What do you want out of the

## Visiting a School

Some things you might be interested in asking during a school visit are:

- Does the school group students by ability, or does it strive to create mixed-ability groups? Are there special pullout opportunities either for support or for enrichment? If so, how are those opportunities distributed?

- What is the school's media policy? What percentage of the day are kids in front of screens? What is the nature of screen time?

- How are students evaluated in the classroom? Is it always in written form, or are there opportunities for oral assessment, visual assessment, and more? What kinds of evaluations are given weekly (for instance, spelling tests), monthly, or less frequently?

- What do report cards look like? What formal methods of communication does the school have for documenting learning?

- What are the school's policies around parent communication with teachers?

- What kinds of professional development do the teachers engage in, and how much time do they spend on this in a given school year?

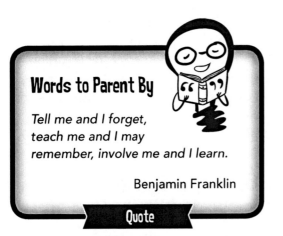

**Words to Parent By**

*Tell me and I forget,
teach me and I may
remember, involve me and I learn.*

Benjamin Franklin

Quote

early-childhood experience? What are you hoping for in elementary, middle, and high school years? What does your child's personality tell you about the kind of school setting that might work best? You may or may not come to perfect consensus around each goal, but you will open a thoughtful discussion about the educational values you each hold dear. This will be invaluable when thinking through choices at every level.

Remember, each type of school has its own philosophy, and some are hybrids of more than one type. Here are brief descriptions of some of the common types you will likely find in your search. There is no one right choice, and you will want to follow the guiding principles above in selecting yours.

## Independent

These schools are independently funded and have their own missions. They are deemed autonomous from religious and government practice. They often charge tuition, although many offer financial assistance. Many are affiliated with professional accreditation and certification organizations.

### Waldorf

Waldorf is a specific philosophy that originated in the early twentieth century. It encourages self-sufficiency throughout three different phases of child development: early childhood, middle childhood, and adolescence. Instruction is infused through the arts and the child's experience. Most Waldorf schools function as independent schools.

### Montessori

Montessori education promotes guided independent instruction that is often self-initiated for students. It is based on children's innate desire to learn. Montessori classrooms house specific materials that allow students to explore their world through physical and intellectual exercises. The teacher is seen as a guide.

## Progressive versus Traditional

All schools are on a progressive-to-traditional spectrum. Progressive education finds its roots in the early twentieth century and is based on the work of several philosophers, including John Dewey. Progressive education is often student centered and visions the teacher as a facilitator of building knowledge. Traditional education is typically more didactic and teacher centered, where the teacher is seen as the de facto leader. While all schools are on a progressive-to-traditional spectrum, many schools have classrooms that would also fall at different places along the spectrum.

## Parochial or Religious

Some religious schools are more devout than others and include theological classes. Many families that don't associate strongly or at all with a faith still choose these schools because the academics and culture are value driven.

## Public

Public schools are schools that are available to all students in a specified district. These are "free" schools, but often what makes one different from another is the financial and community support parents can offer.

### Charter

A charter school operates in a public system and has its own unique mission. While these schools are funded by the district, they often choose to raise their own funds for certain programs and staff. Students apply to attend charter schools, unlike other public schools.

### Magnet

Magnet schools are public schools with specialized academic programs in a certain field (for example, science or math). Students usually apply to magnet programs.

## Homeschool

Parents can choose to educate their children at home. Each state issues requirements and guidelines that help parents keep their children on track. When choosing homeschooling, parents should consider offering opportunities for social development in many different settings.

# Stages of Education

There are four general stages in education for young childhood through early adolescence: early childhood or preschool, elementary, middle, and high. The exact ages in the ranges vary depending on school or district, but typically preschool covers ages two through four, elementary school covers ages five through eleven, middle school covers twelve through thirteen, and high school covers fourteen to eighteen.

## Early Education

Early-childhood education truly begins at birth, but in terms of formal schooling, it can start anywhere from eighteen months to five years old. Preschools range from day-care-type facilities to intensively academic programs. While it's important to make sure you are stimulating your child's brain, it's also important to make sure the school you choose fosters creativity and age-appropriate development. There is no need for academic rigor in preschool. In fact, research does not show that it helps in future academic achievement at all.

### *When to Start*

It's important for your child to have social experiences, and those can happen in and out of school. If you are home with your child and offering plenty of social experiences (parent-and-me classes or playdates at the park, for example), then there is no need to rush the school experience. For children who are in a day care or other care situation, school might be a good financial choice and will offer plenty of social experiences. Children don't *need* to start school until kindergarten, and if a child's first school experience is kindergarten, it most certainly does not decrease their chances of getting into college!

### *What to Expect*

Preschool is a big step for kids. It's a superimposed routine on top of the home routine and involves many more players. As with any stage of

# Education Looks Different at Different Stages of Life

## Zero through Five Years Old

Education in these early years is about physical, social, and cognitive development. The focus should be on exploration and play, learning how to socialize, and enjoyment of reading and mathematical thinking. The best educational environment parents can offer to a young child is safety, comfort, consistency, and intellectual and physical stimulation.

## Six through Twelve Years Old

The elementary years are the time for building the foundation of academics, including reading, writing, and basic math concepts. Education should focus on academics but also include a strong social-emotional element. Children are often referred to as sponges because they are naturally curious and often excited by new information. For this reason, education should provide a challenge. As kids move through to middle school, they are ready to begin to think more analytically while continuing to see the fun in learning.

## Thirteen through Eighteen Years Old

During adolescence, teens are ready for deep critical reasoning. Education at this stage should continue to challenge as well as develop maturity, responsibility, and independence. At this stage, it's important to consider higher education and alternative professional opportunities to help support the transition to adulthood.

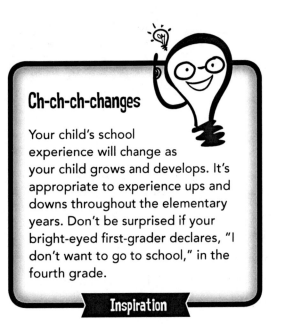

### Ch-ch-ch-changes

Your child's school experience will change as your child grows and develops. It's appropriate to experience ups and downs throughout the elementary years. Don't be surprised if your bright-eyed first-grader declares, "I don't want to go to school," in the fourth grade.

**Inspiration**

education, offer time for transition and be prepared to need some time to transition yourself as well. Your child may struggle with acclimating to the new place, people, and activities. You might have to plan to be there for the first few days, then definitely cut the cord. The teachers should be making you feel like it's okay to leave your child, and if the transition is a bumpy one, ask for informal reports. Assuming you receive mostly positive feedback, your child is probably fine and making a scene just for your benefit. Your child may start and love school but go into a post-honeymoon phase during drop-off or pickup times.

My oldest son's first day of preschool was prophetic. I had visited the school, we had visited the school, we talked about school, we purchased his lunch box. Everything was in order, and we went in for his first day. Oh, how I had prepared him. "Mommy will take you, and then you will be there without Mommy…" We walked in, bravely holding hands. I took his jacket and went just outside the door of the classroom (where I had dutifully taped family photos earlier) to hang it on his hook. He turned as if to search the crowds for me and asked, "Mommy?" I rushed back in quickly, "I'm right here—don't worry," to which he replied, "I thought I was supposed to be by myself today." Well, I couldn't have been prouder, but how the tears did flow—out of my own eyes.

### Elementary Education

The elementary years are bliss. Kids in kindergarten through fifth grade are playful and open to new ideas. They are beginning to think more about others and how the world beyond their immediate sphere works. They are still idealistic and enjoy time with friends and family without too much concern for social pressure. These years are perfect to casually explore the fine arts, musical arts, and a variety of sports.

### *What to Expect: Navigating the Bigger Playground*

You can expect your elementary-aged child to have a generally accepting and excited view of school. Your child is likely open to new ideas and learns organically—and is not usually too stifled by failure. Naturally, your child may run into academic or social issues from time to time, but if you sense that your child is not thriving, talk to the teachers and administration. Find out specifically what's at the heart of the matter. Not all problems require a class or school change. Remember that most issues that arise are normal, so stay calm and approach school staff with the big picture in mind.

While a big part of the elementary years are full of fun, discovery, and the sincere desire to learn, some kids start to develop physically and emotionally as they near adolescence. This can be particularly hard for children who are developing faster—or slower—than the majority of their classmates. Be cognizant of these disparities, and talk to your child about them. There's no way to always fit in, but try to encourage and support self-confidence in your child and promote healthy habits and expectations.

In preschool, children share a playground (either at school or in a local neighborhood) with others primarily their age. They have a sheltered play experience. Elementary school opens up the playground, the lunchroom, the classroom, and many other aspects of school. Kids are expected to take responsibility for their actions in a much bigger way. Where discipline issues such as pushing would hopefully be dealt with in preschool, it is often punishable in the elementary years. Conflict resolution is a huge part of the elementary development.

### *Introduction to Homework*

It's probably safe to say that this is no one's favorite topic. Many students (and parents!) have become increasingly overwhelmed with the amount of homework that is assigned in schools. And, believe it or not, many teachers even cringe at the word. What is your part in homework, and how do you know when to get involved and when to step back? There *are* things you can do to lessen any homework-related stress and/or anxiety that your child may be experiencing.

## No Cheating

Don't do your child's homework! I know this sounds silly, but it happens all the time. I hear the excuses: "She understands it; it's just that she's so tired and simply doesn't have the time." Or "He's confused and his teacher didn't go over this concept in class." No excuse is a good excuse.

**Perspiration**

As an educator, I am not a fan of homework. In my perfect world, the school day would extend by an hour or so, all classes would include practice time, and kids could go home to be kids after the school day. We don't live in this world, and we must find a way to coexist with homework (with the few exceptions of schools that have no homework). Try to see the positive effects of homework: opportunity to practice concepts and skills and to build responsibility as well as opportunity to go deeper in a subject and to allow students to share work with family. Accept homework as a reality and support your child the best way you can. Help your child contend with homework by providing a work space that suits your child's needs. Find a time in the day that works well with your family schedule and during which your child is able to focus. Maybe your child is a morning person and might do better waking up early to get homework done rather than right after school.

Allow for some successful failures—leaving it at home, missing a few points, or forgetting to do it. These experiences all build resilience and responsibility. And if you allow these failures to happen in elementary school and don't intervene, the lesson will be learned and hopefully these things will happen less when the stakes are higher.

## Middle School Education

Middle school students are able to think critically about literature and are still game for fun! Oftentimes, middle schoolers get a bad rap because they can be moody or withdrawn. They are extremely self-conscious. They want to stand out as individuals and yet fit in perfectly. This section will explore the wonder years (as they were adequately termed by the 1988 television series) and the benefits and challenges associated with middle school grades.

### *What to Expect: Navigating Cliques and Homework*

Middle school students live dichotomous lives, conflicted between wanting to play like children and wanting to be serious and grown up. They understand, with minimal depth, about the emerging social groups and the forming of intimate relationships. They are beginning to study more seriously. After all, the math level for a student in seventh grade predicts the freshman math track level in college. They have enjoyed the free nature of elementary school and still want to play. But they also want to hunker down and learn more about school subjects, sex, pop culture, and growing up.

The physical and emotional changes at this stage can be overwhelming at times for your child—and for you. You will likely have a reaction to your child's changing body and mind. Remember that these changes are normal and can, and often will, make your child feel awkward. This awkward feeling can affect mood and behavior.

Be supportive. If your child develops a few zits (and who doesn't?), don't immediately assume it's a problem. I am guilty of projecting my own issues with acne on my children. It's tempting to *fix* problems, but acne is normal and may not be a problem for your child. If your child has a bad case of acne, by all means treat it. But the takeaway is that a zit here and there won't hurt, is normal, and isn't a reason to cover your face and hide for a week.

Offer space when you can. Your middle schooler will likely be moody at times: It's hard to manage all the expectations of school, social pressures, and family life when you're twelve or thirteen and constantly thinking about your appearance and fitting in—not to mention sex. Your middle schooler still needs you, just less so when it comes to school. Experiment with a hands-off approach: hands off homework, hands off playdates, and hands off some decisions (like whether or not to run for student council). Allow for independence and encourage it. It's hard to let go, but your tween will be better learning and practicing some of this independence now.

Homework typically piles up in the middle school years. It's great for children this age to take on more responsibility for their learning. Most kids can handle it. If your child is struggling, try to pinpoint the issue: If homework is taking too long, determine what is taking so much time. Is your child processing the actual work slowly or is your child distracted? Is your child doing homework at an ideal time in the day? If homework is too hard, consider your options with your child's advisor or counselor. Before complaining about the amounts, know what the problems are.

Don't forget to practice hands off! Check with your child: "Have you done your homework?" If the answer is yes, smile. If the answer is no, ask if there's anything you can do to help make sure it gets done. Do not pull it out of the backpack. Do not read through it. Just support your child in doing it. The stakes are a little higher now. If your child doesn't do the work, does it wrong, or forgets it, the consequences will be bigger. That's okay. A few missed assignments won't lead to a desolate life. Use these moments, when you know about them, to talk about the natural consequences (grades, participation in sports, etc.). Don't dwell unless this is a consistent problem.

## High School Education

Teens want to be treated like adults, and they can and should be—some of the time. Their bodies are ready to lead adult lives, but their minds are still developing. Teens can demonstrate extremely mature and immature behavior in one fell swoop. It's an exciting time: trial and error, sex, drugs, and alcohol. Even if teens aren't involved in the weekend party scene or aren't dating, they are exposed to a more adult world and need the independence to experience it. This section will discuss ways to help them refine their filters so they can do so in the safest way possible. It's not easy to give teens space when so many aspects of their lives are so scary, but parents need to trust in our decisions and our parenting. You made your own mistakes, and your child needs to make them too.

### *What to Expect: Transforming to Adults and Applying for College*

We're big fans of musicals in my house. I used to dance with my babies as I'd rock them to sleep, listening to tunes from all different sorts of shows, including *Kiss Me Kate* and *The Music Man*. I recall tearing up when I would hold any of my three as infants and sing to them to "Sunrise Sunset" from *Fiddler on the Roof*. For those of you who don't know this song, I suggest listening to it right away. It's a wonderful ballad about children as they grow into their own people, and it captures the dismay, heartache, and pride a parent feels.

Your adolescent is close to becoming an adult. It's hard to believe your baby's almost all grown up, but right now, your teen needs you—albeit in a different way from ever before. Continue to set limits, enforce rules, and teach right from wrong. But the conversations get even more intense, even if they are less frequent. Take the time to dig deep. After all, you have only a few more years of daily banter with this amazing person.

Adolescents are expected to manage their own lives, and they are leading busy ones. You can count on them remembering activities that are important to them (dances, games, or hanging out with friends) and forgetting some that are important to you (family time, piano practice, or homework). And if they don't forget, they simply might not prioritize in the same way you would. It's hard to find the balance, but you need to let them go and manage most of their lives. You are an advisor to them, and your opinion should be made clear. Allow them to make decisions and see through the consequences, good and bad. Be there to talk through the consequences and learning moments.

A college education is a hope many of us have for our children. While I recognize not all of us have this hope, and college is not right for all people, I think that generally speaking, it's a good thing to expect your child to go to college. Set the expectation early, but don't pressure the application process before it's time. Be aware and prepare. Do not assume you know what to do based on your own experience. Testing, applications, and visits have changed dramatically. Set your child up for success. Ask for advice from college counselors and friends who have been through the process. Get advice, talk about your options, and explore. Most important, let your child lead the process. If that strategy isn't working, push a little. If your child simply isn't ready, consider waiting. Time off from school after high school doesn't mean your child will never go to college. It also doesn't mean time off. It means taking time to explore and learn in a new way.

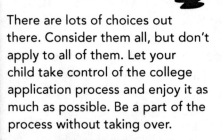

## Controlling the College Choice

There are lots of choices out there. Consider them all, but don't apply to all of them. Let your child take control of the college application process and enjoy it as much as possible. Be a part of the process without taking over.

**Inspiration**

# Communicating with the School and Teachers

Parents have all been to school and hold a host of educational memories—both good and bad. As a result, it's easy to feel as if you "know" what is best in an educational setting. You might be the most knowledgeable about your own child's feelings or development, but keep in mind that professional educators have a wealth of experience and understanding about how to help children learn in a school environment.

Keep in mind the professionals in your child's school probably have more education and experience with teaching than you do. And, on top of that, they also are less biased than you about your child's education. They have a stake in the game. (Trust me, they are not there for the money.) Assume good intentions. Sure, in any profession, you find a few disgruntled types, but for the most part, teachers, administrators, and counselors are there because they love what they do and they want the best for your children. (Yes, I am biased in this arena.) They don't always know the right means to the end, but they try, and they care about the success and well-being of the children in their schools.

Many schools, especially in the early years, host parent-teacher conferences. These are a wonderful opportunity to start and carry on a running dialogue about your child. Some schools will offer prompts to steer the conversation. With or without these prompts, be prepared with any questions you might have. If the school does not host conferences, feel free to ask for one. It's never a bad idea to make contact. Usually with older children, you can contact a counselor or advisor who might help coordinate the multiple teachers involved in your child's education. If your child's teacher or school community does not feel approachable, find someone you are comfortable with, and inquire about what you can do to set something up.

Being as prepared as possible for these kinds of interactions helps pave the way for more effective communication

## Your Place

Remember this is your child's experience, not yours. Try not to make it about you. Check in with the teacher to better understand the expectations for parents, and don't just rely on something you heard another parent say.

**Perspiration**

between parents and schools. Given how important a quality education is for our kids, support in this area can serve to make your child's school experience even richer. In the event you need to discuss something specific (your child's progress, a cheating infraction, or a social issue), it's ideal if you've laid the groundwork for communications as outlined just above. However, it's never too late.

Whenever approaching teachers, administrators, or counselors, be aware that you are just one out of many parents they serve. Be appreciative of their time and of their experience. Listen to what they have to say, no matter how heated the topic. Share your concerns calmly and consider their suggestions. If you need to continue the conversation, don't be afraid to ask. They will be more likely to want to continue to support you if they know you are listening and you are reasonable. It will also make sharing these suggestions with your child easier if you are all on the same page.

# Character in Action

## Zero through Five Years Old: Drop-Off Drama

Your thirty-month-old son just started preschool. He seemed okay to try it out in the beginning, but it's been only a few days and now he is very difficult at drop-off. He kicks and screams as you are forced to pull him out of the car. His teachers report that he is fine once you go, and he seems engaged in his play and with other kids, although sometimes he gets weepy at nap time.

If he is getting good reports from the teachers, he is probably displaying a strong separation anxiety. Do your best to establish a routine and make drop-offs as pleasant as you can. Create a routine in the classroom, in collaboration with the teacher, as to how you should leave your child. Some schools have a drop-off through a carpool line, which might be perfect for your child because he can simply leave the car quickly with a teacher escort. If you prefer (or the school requires it) to walk in, then establish that practice. Either way, prepare your child for how you will say goodbye. Go over it every night before bed, and maintain it—as much as you can—each day. Spy on your son every once in a while so you are reminded that he is happy and in good hands. If possible, try having a different parent or caretaker drop him off to see if the transition is easier. He may be playing on your emotions, or it may simply be easier to do with someone else.

### Six through Twelve Years Old: "C" Failure for What It Is

Your eleven-year-old daughter has been doing well in school, generally. She seems to be managing her work on her own. She says she studied hard for her latest test and was really disappointed that she got a C. She's moping around like she failed and still commenting on the grade days later. Your immediate reaction is to contact the teacher and ask about a retest because your daughter is disappointed in herself. Consider the big picture: A C grade *does not mean failure*! This is a C—neither good nor bad, but an indication that your daughter knows 75 percent of the material tested. If your child is truly disappointed in her grade and wants a retest, then go ahead and let her explore that option. Do not contact your daughter's teacher.

### Thirteen through Eighteen Years Old: College Choices

Your eighteen-year-old daughter is applying to colleges, and her list of schools is drastically different from yours. Talk with your daughter about the differences in her list and yours. Listen to your child's reasons for her choices. Here's where you need to trust your daughter but also your daughter's college counselor. If you're in a school where you feel the support is strong, let the staff help you both in the process. If you don't feel well supported, seek outside help. There are nonprofit organizations and private counselors who can help navigate the college admissions process. If your daughter's list seems appropriate after listening to her reasons and her counselor's insights, then encourage her to follow her heart and let her take the lead. The only reasons to reassess the list might be financial considerations, her counselor's input, or your strong feelings about one or two you really think would also be a good fit.

# To Summarize...

- Be clear on your purposes for educating your child.

- Consider your choices and aim for a good fit for your child and family rather than worry about public opinion.

- Communicate with your child's school community with a respectful tone and an open mind. Understand conflicts and problem-solve; don't make things worse with your anxiety and reactions.

- Be aware that as your child changes, your child's experience with school will inevitably change as well.

# Chapter 18

## Health: Inside and Out

### In This Chapter...

- Ideas for keeping your balance through a balanced body
- Why is bedtime so important?
- How to manage stress
- How to encourage your children's healthy choices

**W**hile it seems logical that you need a healthy body to function, carving out time and energy to take care of your health, along with that of your child, can be daunting with a busy schedule. It's easy to let work, household, family, and financial burdens fill every second of the day, forcing our attention away from a few key factors that can make all the difference. In this chapter, learn about how to preserve your own health in order to protect and secure the health of your child.

It is much easier to provide a safe, comfortable, and nurturing home when you feel confident and satisfied. While it may not be realistic to get _____ (fill in the blank—maybe it's a hike, lunch with a friend, a special coffee drink) each day, you can and should make time for those important parts of life. Check in with yourself throughout the day and try to note when you feel energetic, rested, calm, happy, or focused. These might be times in which you are doing a good job nurturing your own health!

Your health and happiness are paramount to your child's health and happiness. Let's explore different ways to focus on both your own health and raising healthy kids inside and out. I will present research-based recommendations for sleep, nutrition, fitness, and stress. It's also very important to talk to your child about healthy choices with regard to sex, drugs, and alcohol. It's never too early to broach these topics, so long as you approach them in an age-appropriate way and are talking with, not at, your child. Keeping the long-term view in mind, I will offer ideas to help you foster your child's own ability to make healthy decisions.

# Rip Van Winkle May Have Been onto Something

Sleeping for years may be a bit much, but our society appears to have wandered too far to the other side of the spectrum! We seem to be a nation of sleep-deprived people—from children to adults. Common sense and experience remind us that too little sleep makes us irritable, moody, unable to focus, and without energy. It seems obvious that lack of sleep affects our memory, our problem-solving abilities, and our ability to form sound judgments. Research has exposed even more serious consequences linked to sleep deprivation. Too little sleep is associated with increased weight gain and a greater risk of diabetes. It is also correlated with higher chances of heart trouble, depression, and substance abuse. Attention disorders, poor reaction times, and lack of resilience in the face of everyday challenges can all be attributed to too little sleep.

While many experts provide sleep guidelines or ranges, almost all note that sleep is different for all individuals. Moreover, sleep can be different for the same individual throughout the week or the year, or depending on activities. However, even noting individual differences in sleep needs, health experts— from the Mayo Clinic to the National Sleep Foundation—offer some sound guidelines for the majority of people. There is a small possibility you may fall on one or the other side of the range, but in all likelihood, you are among the majority of the population and need the following range of sleep:

- Infants and toddlers, 12 to 15 hours

- Preschool children, 11 to 13 hours

- Elementary-school-aged children, 10 to 11 hours

- Adolescents, 8.5 to 10 hours

- Adults, 7 to 9 hours

Are you shocked? Has bedtime been creeping backward, later and later each night, until your fourth grader is going to bed at ten o'clock? Are you calculating your own sleep and your child's and realizing that you are very close to, or perhaps on the wrong side of, these margins? Start working to change your sleep habits today.

While it might look easy to decide to change your family's sleep patterns, habits can be hard to change. Give your family some time to adjust, and keep in mind that you will all be better rested, more energetic and focused, and a lot more pleasant to be around once you have found a healthy sleep pattern. As you are establishing your new sleep schedules, use all resources at your disposal to help those schedules be successful. Keep all media out of bedrooms—TV and computer in a common area, cell phones charging in the kitchen, and all digital devices stowed outside the bedroom. Turn all bright screens off at least thirty minutes (if not more) before bed to allow the body to release its own natural sleep hormone, melatonin. Avoid vigorous exercise, caffeine, alcohol, or heavy meals close to bedtime. Create a "winding down" routine for yourself, and work with each family

## Make a Family Sleep Plan

Put as much thought into your family's sleeping hours as you do their waking hours. Start with the times each family member needs to be up in the morning and work backward to find a good bedtime. If the schedule varies throughout the week, experts recommend choosing the earliest start time as the consistent one to help the body be in the habit of going to bed at the earlier time. Adjust the family activities to be sure that a late TV program, loud conversation, or wakeful music does not interfere with any family member's sleep schedule.

**Perspiration**

member to help create his or her own winding down routine. This might include a warm bath or shower, some calm music, and preparation for the next day (packing purse or backpack, setting out clothes). Adequate sleep is an essential factor for both immediate and lifelong health!

# Nutrition: Free Range, Organic, Locally Sourced—Is It Edible?

Food is marketed with a bewildering array of adjectives. I remember being shocked by the difference in price between organic and conventional produce when our local grocery store began carrying organic food. Now, however, the majority of stores seem to carry a range of products, and the price difference, while still noticeable, seems to be less dramatic.

I found a fantastic resource in the people who work in the store. The produce department has information about where certain foods were grown and how far they have traveled. The fish and meat departments often give me a heads up about upcoming sales or price reductions. People in each department are able to give me advice about different products. Try to find a store where you can ask questions of the employees and even form a relationship with some.

Even if you cannot afford, don't care to spend on, or don't have access to organic, the benefits of eating fresh fruits and vegetables versus prepared and processed foods are huge. You should feel good about yourself just for preparing meals yourself with fresh ingredients, even if you didn't get them at a high-end specialty grocery store.

Children of any age can be a part of creating your family's healthy food plan. We often shop for the week on Sunday. On Saturday, we talk about what kinds of foods we want for the week. All three kids make their own lunches (with some parent cooperation, depending on the food and the child), and they each have

### Food Fun

Enjoy eating with your family. If you've got food issues, face them up front and get help. Know that your child will learn eating habits from you. Make smart decisions and look for resources if you don't know what those look like. Consider talking to your pediatrician. There are also countless food blogs, magazines, and cookbooks out there to refer to.

**Inspiration**

different ideas about what they might want to eat every week. If we do not have time to take everyone to the grocery store, we note each family member's food ideas and add those to the grocery list. If you are just beginning this process, it is worth having some discussions about eating food that is relatively unprocessed and fresh. Share with your child (and let your child share too!) about the importance of eating a variety of foods, colors, textures, and tastes. Also, as your child ages, it's important to revisit this and support consistent good habits.

Help build your family members' independence and personal habits by allowing some reasonable latitude with meals. Though it is not realistic to allow full choice at every meal, let them test out a fruit-only lunch or an all-white dinner. Then talk to them about what they like about it and what they do not. You might be surprised at how even one meal might leave your child wanting a different experience—more savory or sweet, or less soft and more crunchy. Ask your child about it: Did it leave a feeling of hunger, energy, lethargy? Your child may or may not be able to explain a particular snack or meal's effects, but you will be connecting food's impact on the way we feel. Eventually, your child will understand that our food affects our energy, our mood, our ability to make decisions... everything!

As with all cognitive filters, your goal is to help your child develop, talk about, and practice healthy eating choices independently. At a school lunch, your child will be left to decide: "Am I full? Should I stop eating?" At a party: "No one's watching; I could take twelve cupcakes." Talk about self-monitoring and model good behavior. Dessert, sweet treats—these are not the enemy. Include them in your repertoire. Teach enjoyment of food. As with so much in life, moderation is key with sweets (salts, fats, and the like too). My family enjoys dessert almost every single night at dinner. I used to have my own dessert late after the children's bedtime, sheltering my kids from the demons I loved so much. But when my kids were older and started enjoying them with me, I lost so much weight because I was doling out much more reasonable portions.

# Find Your Fitness Groove

Yoga? Pilates? Zumba? Running? Weight lifting? I have to confess that I have tried all five and more in the quest to find an exercise plan that I love. I find plenty of excuses to do almost anything else—really, anything!—rather than buckle down to my exercise regimen. At the same time, I notice the dramatic difference in how I feel and think when I do exercise regularly.

Thirty minutes of sustained activity most days is enough to help most people thrive. One of the biggest barriers to exercise might be the daunting task of carving out time in the day. Use some of the research around habits and change to find a plan to address your fitness goals. Are you looking to get back into exercise after a hiatus? Are you hoping to change your pattern of exercise to break out of a rut? After you have checked with your health care provider and know what the safe limits are for you, begin with some planning.

As you find your fitness groove, determine what your intentions are and give yourself a timeline. For most people, setting goals is one step toward changing. Then reinforce your goals and model a healthy attitude toward change by sharing your goals with your family. Let your child and your support team cheer you on as you begin your plan. The plan should be manageable, realistic, and flexible. If you know that you have never been able to get up at five in your entire life, steer clear of setting your new morning exercise time at five! If thirty minutes each day is not possible right now, start with fifteen or twenty.

It is highly possible that the shifts you feel from starting a new exercise plan will positively affect the rest of your life and may help create new time in your schedule. Exercise promotes better sleep, more efficient work, better mood, and higher energy. As you start taking small steps to find a plan that works for you, you may find enough time to exercise thirty or more minutes most days of the week. Even if you can't squeeze in dedicated exercise time, modeling increased activity can be just as important. Consider walking or biking to your child's school or taking the stairs instead of an elevator or escalator. Going to the movies and watching television are fun when you need some downtime, but taking kids to the park or on a hike are also great alternatives for family time.

# Health Looks Different at Different Stages of Life

## Zero through Five Years Old

Very young children need sleep, a sensible diet, constant supervision, and time for free, unstructured play. Health is pretty clearly outlined by pediatric standards, and parents can document benchmarks that are readily accessible on the American Academy of Pediatrics website or several parenting books. (See the **Appendix.**) Parents can refer specific questions and concerns to their family doctors.

## Six through Twelve Years Old

In these years, children are more able to care for themselves on a daily basis. Parents can encourage them to take responsibility for physical hygiene, nutritious eating habits, and fitness, though they will likely need support and reminders. As children approach puberty, it's important they understand the changes in their bodies and know where to go with questions.

## Thirteen through Eighteen Years Old

Teens should be caring for themselves independently (hygiene, eating, and fitness) in addition to taking responsibility for asking for help with any physical or emotional needs. Health at this stage might include sexual health. It's important for teens to have an array of people and places to go with questions and concerns. Parents will want to keep in constant communication with their teens and make it clear that health is a priority.

## How to Keep the Saber-Toothed Tiger at Bay (Managing Stress)

Stress has been a part of life forever. In prehistoric times, humans might have experienced the stress of finding a next meal or avoiding becoming the next meal of the local saber-toothed tiger. This would have been a natural, temporary form of stress: I am hungry, so I will find food. Or I don't want to be eaten for dinner, so I will run away quickly. However, in modern times, we experience stress on a much more consistent basis. We might have work deadlines, complicated schedules to navigate, or numerous transitions each day. Rather than feeling stress every so often, we feel it for sustained periods, even days. Our heart rate increases, our brains release stress hormones such as adrenaline or cortisol, and our bodies experience a host of reactions that directly affect our health.

Too much stress can affect our eating habits, mood, and ability to function well. Luckily, sleep and exercise are two of the most effective ways of decreasing a feeling of stress. Even something as simple as walking for twenty to thirty minutes each day (no need to train for a marathon!) can significantly reduce stress and anxiety. Just as you are paying attention to the times you feel well rested, happy, and energetic, you can also take note of times you feel particularly stressed and frazzled. What are your stress buttons? Punctuality? Preparation? Traffic? Your boss? The first step toward taming the stress beast is recognizing what your stressors are. Once you know what stresses you out, you can work to either avoid or diminish those hot buttons in your life.

Stress can affect kids too, and sometimes it can manifest in different ways. Be aware of your child's mood and behavior, and look for signs of stress. Symptoms can include a change in diet, a change in weight, stomachaches, headaches, sweating, moodiness, disengagement, or hyperengagement. Try to reduce stress in your child's life through reducing time commitments, easing off on performance pressure, and carving out time for play or sleep. The best method to reduce stress is to be proactive and look for areas of weakness in your schedule or habits. If your child is tired after school, don't plan much for then (even if "all" the other kids are going to the park). Our schedule used to be very regimented to keep activities right after school so we could get home at a decent hour for dinner and get to bed on time. We noticed with our daughter that as her homework load increased along with her activity level, she seemed distracted and less enthusiastic about her schoolwork and even her extracurriculars. She is a night owl and enjoys free time after school. It took some reconceptualizing of the whole family schedule, but now we try to schedule her piano and dance lessons later in the day so she can come home to chill, have a snack, and be on her own. Sometimes that time is playing with her guinea pig, and sometimes it's napping. And sometimes, on a rare occasion, it's even getting right to homework. We've asked her to advocate for herself as well. We explained

## Conquer the Stress Monster

When you have time during the day or possibly at the end of a week, jot down what happened to cause you to feel stressed. Create a T-chart with the title "If…" on the left and "Then…" on the right. Write one of the situations in which you find yourself stressed under the "If…" column. On the right, brainstorm some possible solutions. For instance, if the morning routine leaves you stressed and anxious each day, how can you make it more streamlined? Make lunches (better yet, have your kids make their own lunches) the night before? Set the alarm for ten minutes earlier? Write a list each night to prepare for the following day? Assign each family member a new task for the morning to decrease your own list? List as many possible ideas as you can and test them out!

| If… | Then… |
|---|---|
| Mornings feel rushed | Wake up earlier |
| | Prep lunches at night |
| | Have kids make their own breakfast and lunch |
| | Have kids choose clothing at night |
| | Keep shoes and backpacks by the door |
| | Maintain a chore list to check each morning |

that we cannot always know when she's feeling overwhelmed by her homework or her schedule—so now, with some reminders and practice, she is considerably better at identifying when things get to be too much for her and will ask if she can wait to do her homework or take a break. It took a while to get to the place where she was comfortable saying, "I need..." But just knowing what you need in life is a huge step toward getting it.

Teach your child how to destress too (or at least compartmentalize). If your child shares a challenging moment or issue on the way home from school, take the opportunity to think about what would help, and follow your instincts. If the weather is nice, take a walk together before homework or after dinner. You don't even have to talk about the problem at hand, and this doesn't have to be a daily routine, but just get out there and walk around. Encourage your child to take some time off before homework or getting ready for bed. See if your child might be interested in writing in a journal or drawing. Sometimes it's nice to address the stress in the moment, and sometimes the destressing can be completely unrelated just to give your child's mind and body a break. Help find out what destressing looks like for your child by encouraging new things. And don't feel guilty if destressing is more like indulging. It can look like going to bed early, eating a bowl of ice cream, or spending an hour in front of the television. We all need to find ways to treat ourselves.

# Puberty and Sexuality

Kids all develop at their own pace, and it's an exciting and scary process all at the same time. Your little girl goes from being that sweet-cheeked, sassy, bobbed-hair climber to a clever, graceful, flirtatious young woman in what feels like no time at all. And your loving, running, thoughtful boy turns into a broad-shouldered, confident young man. And in between, there is a lot of transition—much of which is awkward.

Talk to your child about what's to come. Celebrate the changes when you can, and prepare for the awkward moments as best you can. Buy books for your child that describe the changes that will take place. Read some of the books together, and leave some for private reading so that your child can return to a trusted resource if it's ever needed. When you know your child's school is going to talk about sex education, extend the conversation at home, even if it's just a check-in. Children realize they are losing their innocence as they grow, and they can associate the change with shame. They are curious about what's out there and feel they need to hide the curiosity. Explain that while much of the development and curiosity your child has may be private, it's not shameful. There's a big difference. Make it clear you love your child through all these changes.

Kids, for the most part, are having sex in their teens. There's no denying it. According to the Centers for Disease Control and Prevention, most teens start having sex around age seventeen. The longer kids wait, the more likely they will experience healthy and safe sexual experiences. Sex in the late teens is definitely more advantageous than in the early teens, so the longer the wait, the better your child's chances at emotional security. But hoping your child will wait and act responsibly won't do the trick. You have to involve yourself and educate early and often. It won't always be an easy conversation, and it will most likely be awkward. Just hunker down and do it. The more you talk, the easier the conversation will flow.

Your child will be calling the shots in this realm whether you like it or not, so be sure to talk early and often about sexual feelings, relationships, questions, and concerns. It's better to be prepared and support the relationship than to play ignorant and hope it all turns out okay. Educate your child about the true facts—inclusive of what happens physically and what happens emotionally. It's important to talk about possible outcomes. Pregnancy and sexually transmitted diseases are obvious topics, but sex changes relationships and self-identity as well. Be as open and honest as you can. This doesn't mean you have to share

## Oral What?

When my friend heard rumors from other parents about sexual acts, including oral sex, happening with kids in her sixth grader's class, she approached her daughter and began a dialogue. Her daughter had not heard the rumors, didn't understand, and was horrified by the description. At first, my friend worried she shouldn't have brought it up. But as she talked with her daughter, she realized that she wanted her daughter to hear this information from her instead of her peers, who may well have conveyed inaccurate information. She ended the conversation by inviting her daughter to come to her with any questions and suggesting other trusted adults she could talk to.

**Pure Genius!**

intimate details about your own experience, but you can share your emotions and your hopes for your child.

Give your child the tools to make healthy and responsible choices. Talk about birth control and taking responsibility. Sex is a very serious act, but it can and should also be something beautiful. The best thing you can do for your child's sexual identity and experiences is preparation and education. Prepare your child for sex and for saying no. Talk about your hopes, beliefs, and value system. If abstinence is something you believe in strongly, help your child understand that and talk about the challenges involved. Support your child through this decision.

Be a support and offer other supports for when you can't be there or your child doesn't want to go to you. Identify a few family members and friends your child can contact with questions. Make it clear to your child that you trust these people and you are okay for them to have confidential conversations. Talk with these people and share the same with them so they know that if and when they are approached, they may use their best judgment to help your child. Your child's physician may also be a great resource. Allow and encourage private time during routine physicals for any questions your child may want to ask without you in the room, and let your child know that this information will not be shared with you. Most states have minor consent laws that allow teenagers to seek medical care for family planning and sexually transmitted diseases without parental consent or knowledge, whether from your own private physician or family planning clinics. Give your child this information (and perhaps information about a clinic near you) in case it is too uncomfortable to seek advice from the pediatrician. You can read more about building a support system in **Chapter 21.**

# Character in Action

## Zero through Five Years Old: Insomniac

Your five-year-old is an insomniac and cannot get to sleep. You know she needs ten to twelve hours, and she gets eight to nine most evenings. You might establish a bedtime routine, keep the lighting low, read a quiet story together (maybe even the same one every night), bathe her, play soft music, play white noise, or get the room as quiet as possible, use a weighted eye pillow, or even offer a back massage. (Hopefully she will repay you for that one when she's older.) Experiment with these ideas and see what works. If she simply is wired to be up late, make sure she's calm and not up playing. Let her know not to be anxious and that sleep will come. Encourage her to find something quiet and calm to pass the time: listening to recordings of stories or music, reading, or maybe even snuggling with a sibling or pet. Allow her to nap during the afternoons if she needs it. Most kids don't need sleep aids. Feel free to consult with your pediatrician, but don't jump to medical intervention just for convenience. If she's productive and able to get through the day, just work as best you can with her schedule.

### Six through Twelve Years Old: Brooding Boy

Your seventh-grade son arrives home from school with a smile on his face as he bids his friends farewell and then enters a brooding slump the moment he walks in the house. He barely says "Hi," and when you ask how his day was, he replies with something along the lines of "Fine." You dig deeper but it gets you nowhere. Stop digging, and give him space. I know that seeing him like this makes you want to hug him and bring back that sweet little boy with the big smile on his face as he regales the tails of second grade. But what your son needs now is space, and his affect is signaling to you that he's not interested. He should snap out of it after a snack, when homework is complete, after some time alone, after a practice or activity, or certainly by dinnertime. If he remains in this mood constantly, consider talking with your pediatrician and getting a referral to a therapist. But if his moods go from low to high on a regular basis, take comfort in knowing that your son is developing and his hormones are active.

### Thirteen through Eighteen Years Old: I have a Friend...

Your fifteen-year-old daughter confides in you that her best friend had sex. Your head is spinning, and you're desperate to get this right. What do you do? First of all, it's very likely that your daughter is coming to you with this because she is confused and overwhelmed and because she is the one who is in this hypothetical situation (or could be soon). Express gratitude that she came to you and trusts you, and let her know that she has not misplaced her trust. Cover your privacy ground and let her know that you will not share this with her friend and that she can ask you any questions she has (and that her friend can come to you as well). Talk with her about the concerns you might have about your daughter, or her friend, having sex at her age. The longer she waits, the more likely she will find an emotionally healthy relationship and have positive experiences with sex. Also, be sure to let her know that no matter when she begins to have sex, she can always say no the next time. It should always be her choice when she does have sex, and she should make smart and safe decisions regarding birth control and sexually transmitted diseases. Remind her that no matter how awkward this conversation feels, she can continually come to you for more information, even if she's embarrassed by her decisions. If she does decide to have sex, she will need your support more than ever. She will also likely need reminders that you still love her and that she has not lost her place in the family.

# To Summarize...

- Sleep is more important than you realize. Make time for it!

- Fitness and nutrition are crucial to a balanced life.

- Keep stress at bay for yourself and your child.

- Support your child through fun, natural, and awkward stages of physical development.

# Chapter 19

## Play: It's All It's Cracked Up to Be

### In This Chapter...

- The evolution of play from infant to adolescent
- Collaboration at its best—and most fun!
- Making room for play in your busy schedule
- What to do with "I'm bored"

**P**lay evolves as your child grows. With today's hectic schedules for kids and parents alike, it's often easy to overlook the need for improvised, freely chosen, unstructured playtime for kids of all ages. Research shows that kids develop important social, emotional, and cognitive skills when they have opportunities to "just play." This chapter will outline why it is important and strategies for you to create time and space for play for your child.

Benefits of play include the chance to develop creativity, try on leadership roles, solve problems, release energy, and engage in physical activity—just to name a few! Understanding the importance of play will help parents in making choices about where their children attend school, selecting

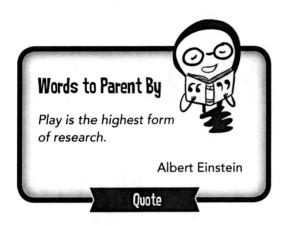

**Words to Parent By**

*Play is the highest form of research.*

Albert Einstein

Quote

extracurricular activities, and planning family time.

Downtime is part of play. It contributes to the development of both creative thinking and resiliency. The American Academy of Pediatrics suggests that free play helps with brain development. It is worth revisiting the definition of play: any improvised, freely chosen, unstructured activity. Soccer practice and violin lessons and watercolor class may all be very fun, but they are not usually play. If your child participates in a very student-directed, full-of-choice, and open-ended extracurricular option, it might be wonderful. Those types of extracurricular offerings are rare, though, so I offer a few important guidelines to help your adolescent maintain a healthy balance and minimize possible areas of conflict.

My husband and I work from home most days, and we are grateful because it offers great flexibility and time with our children. That said, summers can present a challenge with our kids home too. One day in August, as the lazy days rolled along, my husband had a brilliant idea. He gave my oldest twenty dollars and told him to take his siblings out in the neighborhood and not to come back until two thirty. He offered them a list of suggested destinations— library, park, ice cream shop—let them take what snacks they could carry, and ushered them out the door. The kids returned home with stories beyond stories of their tales in the hood. It was clear our eldest practiced his leadership and our younger ones had to practice their collaboration skills (because my husband also warned that he'd better not get a call from a storekeeper that his kids were messing around). All that, and they got to run around and play.

Play can be any freely chosen, self-directed activity. It is something fun and satisfying without having a defined or extrinsically rewarded goal. From the toddler years on, humans can become so focused during play that they enter a state, coined by researcher Mihály Csíkszentmihályi, called flow. When you are in a state of flow, you are so immersed in your activity that you lose track of time and become disconnected from the ordinary world all around. There is exciting research about the amazing cognitive, emotional, and physiological benefits of flow. Moreover, it is just plain fun. From toddler age on, it is important to carve out enough play time in the schedule to allow flow.

Parents need play too! Play is not only fun, but it has also been linked to a boosted immune response, improved sense of well-being, decreased stress hormones, and more. For some adults, play might be a trail run. For others, it might include creating a beaded necklace. Whatever you choose to do that allows you an escape from ordinary life—a good book, yoga, painting—you are entering a state of flow. We all know how it feels when life gets "too busy" to squeeze in our favorite activity. You might be feeling it right now. If so, please put this book down and go play! We are more patient, energized, able to focus, and perceptive when we have given ourselves even a small gift of play. Beyond the many benefits to yourself, you are modeling the importance of play to your child or children. You are sending an implicit but very clear message that finding something you love to do is important.

I was up against a deadline at work, and my kids could clearly see that I was stressed. They said supportive things like, "Don't worry Mom, it'll all be okay." I would smile and continue to work, typing on my laptop, making yet another call after bedtime. It occurred to me that my stress was so great, it was seeping into my family life—and it simply wasn't worth it. How could I encourage my own children to let loose when I wouldn't do it when I so clearly needed to? I made a huge effort to put my work aside the next day so that I wasn't working into the late hours. We had a brief family game night after dinner. I worked while my kids did their homework, and then we all went to bed on time. It was a great night, and I woke up refreshed the next morning and more able to face my deadline. It didn't take much time or energy to play a game with my family, and it made all the difference to focus on enjoyment rather than my smartphone.

## There's More to Play Than Tummy Time

As it turns out, that tiny bundle who just joined your family has some needs beyond the obvious ones of being fed, diapered, and put to bed. Infants form an understanding of the world through interaction and play with primary caregivers and family. While they find the entire world fascinating, they

## It's a Date

Make a pact with yourself to accept the next invitation you receive from your child for some good old fashioned play. Whatever it is, make the time then and there, or set a date and time to do it. For young children this might mean a puppet show or playing school or tea party. For older children it might look like a board game, cooking, hiking, or simply kicking back and watching television.

**Perspiration**

learn the most through short bursts of play with one-on-one contact. Given the dramatic development that occurs in the first twelve months of life, play for a one-month-old looks very different from play in a twelve-month-old. However, there are two important facets of play that parents can emphasize: physical exploration and language development.

Physical exploration is a behavior essential to human development. As they are learning to move their own bodies (hey, who just stuck their finger in my mouth?), infants learn through their own physical sensations and from the reactions of caregivers. They begin by grabbing, pulling, and wiggling—and they slowly construct an idea of how to use their hands, arms, and feet. They practice rolling and crawling and eventually walking. The best way to foster this development through play is to create a safe environment in which your infant can explore and then get down on the ground and discover with your infant.

Infants need and enjoy some variation in surface, color, and pattern, but there is no need to redecorate. Begin by thinking through safety concerns. Can nearby objects be swallowed? Are they sharp? Unstable? Might my infant fall? Add some interesting things to the space—a blanket, a ball, a big plastic spoon—and then allow your infant to explore. Mobiles, fans, or leaves are excellent visual stimuli for precrawlers. While you and your infant are on the floor exploring, you can engage in the second facet of play: language development.

Language is essential to robust verbal development. Shower your infant with different words, intonations, nonsense sounds, and pitches. Let your baby know what you are doing. Describe visual, auditory, and tactile things in the environment. Sing songs—no matter how self-conscious you might feel about your singing prowess. Early childhood songs with finger plays and child-centered themes are great, but singing your favorite pop song can be just as good! Many infants will begin babbling (early verbal play!) near six months and will start responding to your verbal cues. This early language play will set the stage for a lifetime of both verbal development and play.

# Mobile Me

Life is play for a toddler. Now, with mobility and a beginning grasp of communication, toddlers are capable scientists. Almost every object or statement is worth an exploration: What will happen if I throw this over there? What will the peas do if I put them in my milk? What noise will the water make if I splash it? Why? Toddler play builds on the exploration play of infants. Now able to stand, toddlers expand gross motor skills through climbing, throwing, running, hanging, and more. Set your child up for safe tumbles to encourage balance and coordination by monitoring the new navigation skills on stairs or furniture or during park play.

Toddler play requires a flexible schedule and a space for mess. As anyone who has ever played with a toddler knows, a toddler's idea of schedule is not always compatible with an adult agenda. Remember that toddlers experience a deep and powerful new understanding of the world through play and can be reluctant to move to a new activity. While allowing for flexibility in your schedule, you can also begin teaching your toddler about time. If you need to be somewhere or want bath to end at a certain time, use a kitchen timer. Let your child know that you will set it for three minutes and that the alarm will signal cleanup time. Then involve your toddler in the cleaning. (Feel free to refer to the section on chores in **Chapter 14** to learn more about having kids help with cleaning up.) Avoid asking "if" your child would like to clean. Rather, ask "what" your child would like to put away first. Let your child decide how to stack items and, if possible, where to stow them. Kneel on the floor with your child and model the power of cleaning as a team. When you keep toys low and accessible, you help foster both play and good cleaning habits.

Encouraging mess is another aspect of robust toddler play. Educators and researchers now know that messy play is linked to a willingness to take risks and make mistakes later in life. Mess fosters inquiry and spatial development,

## Cleaning Up after Play

Keeping your toddler's toys organized in a simple manner will help your toddler keep on top of cleanup after play more easily.

**Inspiration**

creates an understanding of consequences, and is just plain fun. Find a space inside or out for your toddler to explore water, dirt, and sand. Make play dough at home and encourage practice rolling and shaping dough. Cover a floor with a protective barrier and allow finger painting, vegetable stamping, or newsprint art. Blocks and commercial toys can be fun, but a bucket of water and a turkey baster can provide an equally rich play scape.

Toddlers often engage with peers and siblings in parallel play. The children might be side by side playing with separate objects but seem to rarely interact. As it turns out, each child is acutely aware of the other "player" nearby. They listen to each other, observe the other's play, and notice the exploration going on even as they continue in their own play. Though they seem to not be playing together, a brain scan would reveal incredible neural activity as they both play and also notice how a peer plays.

Toddlers become so engrossed in play that they can now enter a state of flow. The activity may have no particular goal or script, but it remains completely gripping for a period of time. If they are lucky, they will be able to find this state for the rest of their lives. I hope I never forget the image of my toddler daughter I saw one afternoon. While I was busily doing laundry, getting dinner ready, and doing goodness knows what else, I walked quickly by her room and paused for a moment. She was sitting with her stuffed animals all around her, reading a book. She knew the book so well she even recited it with intonation. I was especially impressed when she would stop to see if any of her stuffies could identify pictures: "Can you show me where his toes are?"

## Create and Compromise

Around the age of four or five, many children become more excited about playing with peers. They begin to develop an awareness of friends and might decide they have a "best" friend or two. It is very natural for them to experiment with friends at this point, which makes play a wonderful opportunity to develop essential social skills. Whether they are conquering the world, taking a doll to the doctor, or inventing a new ball game, kids are practicing conflict resolution, cooperation, leadership, and compassion. Cognitively, they are bolstering their planning skills, creativity, language acquisition, and more. If your child is lucky enough to spend part of the day at a child care or preschool facility, some solo time at the end of the day might be a relief. If your child is home with one caregiver, it might be a thrill to go to a busy park.

If you and your child decide to schedule a playdate, set yourselves up for success. Keep the time short. A one-hour playdate might be enough for a five-year-old, a two-and-a-half hour one should be ample for nine-year-olds. Invite only one friend. Juggling more than one friend at a time is an art that children do not develop until later in life. While supervising safety from afar, let them be. Allow them to negotiate ideas around what to do, even if they struggle for a few minutes, and give them the gift of letting them figure out how they want to play. You will be sending the message loudly and clearly that you value their autonomy and have confidence that they can direct their own play. I learned this accidentally one day when we hosted a playdate for our older son. I had begun the playdate by driving my son, my younger daughter, and my son's friend to our home. I had set up snacks and planned to introduce a board game and some sidewalk chalk. My daughter had other plans, and tired of waiting for me, my son and his friend ventured off to his room. By the time I made it upstairs to check on them, they were engaged in imaginary play that resembled some form of playing house. They occupied themselves for the duration of the afternoon and protested the end of the playdate when his friend's mother arrived.

## Put Your Child in the Driver's Seat

While some children expand their social world and are excited to have more playdates around the age of five, many are not. Be reassured that there is an incredibly wide range of healthy socialization. Allow your child to drive the playdate schedule (as much as your schedule will allow it, of course) and remember that solo play can be just as rich as coplay.

**Pure Genius!**

Kids use their rich vocabulary and developing imaginations to play fantasy games, imitate behavior they have observed in their world, and create elaborate fictional worlds. Dress-up becomes an essential facet of play for most children aged four to about ten (a range that can vary considerably, depending on your child). Keep hats, scarves, and any old adult clothing accessible for spontaneous dramatic play. If you do not have dress-up clothes handy, brown paper bags are stellar substitutes. They can easily become hats, vests, hula skirts – you name it. A week rarely goes by in our home without some sort of theatrical production put on by our youngest. A director in the making, our son has pulled together many stagings, including *Anything Goes*, *The Wizard of Oz*, and *Grease*. He becomes engrossed with these productions, working on them for weeks. He will put aside clothes he feels will work for his characters, write out scripts (with his adorable inventive spelling), and approach friends and family about playing roles. The actual productions, while not quite ready for Broadway, show a clear vision and a true immersion. He is lost in his art, and it's beautiful.

As you did with your toddler, allow time for your child to create both flow and mess. Let your child initiate play and allow time to improvise and get lost in the activity. Provide opportunities to make a mess in the kitchen, the bathroom, the yard, or anywhere—and involve your child in the cleanup when the playtime is over.

## It's Not a Playdate; We're "Hanging Out"

Play for a tween can turn from resembling child play to mimicking teen play in an instant. They might beg to watch a movie with a friend, and then fifteen minutes later, they begin building a fort. With the barrage of media cues urging children to mature increasingly earlier, I urge you to emphasize child play in your home. Keep the dress-up collection, the building materials, and the art supplies handy to allow developmentally appropriate exploration to continue. If possible, have a movie camera available for your tween to use. Child-directed filming facilitates imaginative dress up and adds an element of maturity to the drama.

Tweens can become conflicted about how to play as they straddle the worlds of elementary school and middle school, so some careful adult involvement can be helpful. Some tweens remain happy to spend an afternoon playing board games or Legos, but some are more excited to explore the larger community. Invite increasing autonomy by allowing your child to construct a fun scavenger hunt. For instance, have your tween and a friend "design a

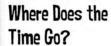

## Where Does the Time Go?

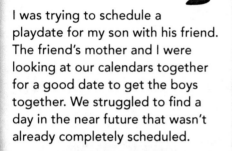

I was trying to schedule a playdate for my son with his friend. The friend's mother and I were looking at our calendars together for a good date to get the boys together. We struggled to find a day in the near future that wasn't already completely scheduled.

**Uninspired**

day." Let them choose a location (feel free to point out cool science museums, art centers, or music events, but be okay if they choose a local mall) and collaborate to write or draw clues about what they have seen. At the end of the visit, they can test you and see how many clues you can answer. If they worked solo, they can quiz each other! And, if they prefer to be on their own, celebrate the fact that they do and are able to express it. Let them be, checking on them occasionally.

Your tween might want to explore more detail-oriented hobbies or art projects. Ideally, your tween will initiate some ideas to pursue with a friend or with you, but feel free to offer suggestions if a nudge is needed. Note that for many children, the enthusiasm with which you suggest an activity is often inversely proportional to their willingness to try it, so try to keep your tone neutral! Magazines, the library, and the Internet are all stellar and available sources of hobby, craft, and activity ideas. Delegate the research—visit the library or help your tween use a search engine—and allow your child to plan as many aspects of the project as possible.

Some tweens are capable of navigating a group playdate, but the one-friend-at-a-time model remains optimal. With younger kids, playing with one friend allows a more manageable environment in which to develop communication skills. With tweens, playing with one friend can decrease social anxiety and exclusion issues. It allows them to safely practice moving between the world of children and the new world of adolescence.

## Don't Ask; Just Play

Play for an adolescent begins to resemble play for adults. Dramatic play continues for teens who pursue theater, but it transitions to a more cerebral exploration of self for most teens. In fact, a pivotal aspect of teen play is imagining possible adult selves. Teens might lose themselves in a book,

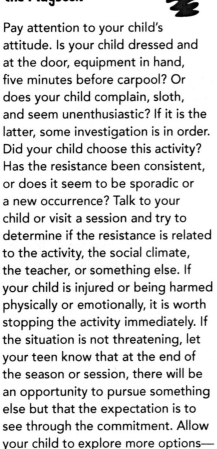

## Rewriting the Playbook

Pay attention to your child's attitude. Is your child dressed and at the door, equipment in hand, five minutes before carpool? Or does your child complain, sloth, and seem unenthusiastic? If it is the latter, some investigation is in order. Did your child choose this activity? Has the resistance been consistent, or does it seem to be sporadic or a new occurrence? Talk to your child or visit a session and try to determine if the resistance is related to the activity, the social climate, the teacher, or something else. If your child is injured or being harmed physically or emotionally, it is worth stopping the activity immediately. If the situation is not threatening, let your teen know that at the end of the season or session, there will be an opportunity to pursue something else but that the expectation is to see through the commitment. Allow your child to explore more options—possibly including your child in one of your chosen activities.

**Pure Genius!**

daydream for extended periods, or beg for more online fantasy game time. Daydreaming does not have to be sedentary. It might take place on a hike or in a pool. Adolescents begin to project what they might be like and, equally importantly, what they might not be like in future years. Along with sleep, healthy food, and exercise, unscheduled downtime is an essential component to healthy development. Ignore the misguided idea that teens—or anyone, for that matter—should be busily engaged at every moment. The time adolescents spend "spacing out" enriches self-analysis and future planning.

The intense need for downtime is balanced by the need to connect. Adolescents, like all humans, have an incredibly wide band of "normal" social needs. Allow your adolescent to take an expanding role in planning social time with friends. (For more ideas on socializing, read **Chapter 24**.) Take advantage of interesting cultural centers in your area and then let your teen and friends set some reasonable parameters for participation. If they want to be dropped off, find a way to let them have some freedom while still staying safe. Let your teen invite friends over to family meals and events, and you will honor the need to connect with peers while also staying connected to the family. Let your teen play in the kitchen by picking a night every so often to plan and cook dinner. Pick a theme such as *Top Chef* or backward night; let your teen try to make sushi or pasta sauce from scratch. Cooking is a wonderfully creative, open-ended, and useful way to play!

Many adolescents are involved in extracurricular activities. There has been an unfortunate trend toward increasing those extracurricular activities. There are more offerings, and many athletic activities now offer year-round and camp-intensive opportunities. Some families have added activities in hopes of helping their child to stand out in the college admissions process. Working parents now have options to enroll their children in focused undertakings rather than in a less-guided care environment. For these and other reasons, adolescents are now bombarded by scheduled activities.

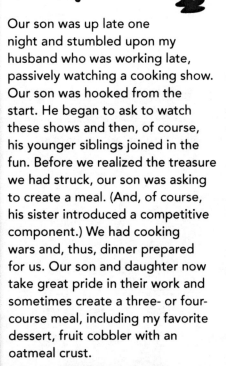

## Sous Chef in the Making

Our son was up late one night and stumbled upon my husband who was working late, passively watching a cooking show. Our son was hooked from the start. He began to ask to watch these shows and then, of course, his younger siblings joined in the fun. Before we realized the treasure we had struck, our son was asking to create a meal. (And, of course, his sister introduced a competitive component.) We had cooking wars and, thus, dinner prepared for us. Our son and daughter now take great pride in their work and sometimes create a three- or four-course meal, including my favorite dessert, fruit cobbler with an oatmeal crust.

**Pure Genius!**

If your adolescent enjoys an activity or two, be aware that more is not better. The dramatic rise in overuse injuries is one of many pieces of evidence that focusing too heavily in one arena can lead to burnout and even physical damage. Be sensitive to the dramatic physiological changes adolescents can experience, and listen carefully for reports of continued soreness or joint trouble. In addition, keep in mind that most sports experts encourage youth athletes to play different sports in order to develop and challenge the entire body.

Parents are often tempted to insist their child continue with an activity—especially if the child seems "really good" at it. Consider the conflict you invite when you insist that your adolescent participate. It may be that you and your coparent believe the activity is so central to your family that it is a battle worth fighting. In many cases, however, letting go of your idea about what your child "should" be doing results in a happier and healthier home. Substitute a forced activity with some freely chosen adolescent play time, and it will be a win-win.

# Play Looks Different at Different Stages of Life

## Zero through Five Years Old

The main work of a very young child is play. Even in infancy, children discover through unstructured play. They make use of their senses and learn about their bodies and the world through play. Play looks simple in the early ages, such as lying tummy down or grabbing feet, and then evolves to include playing with objects and then other people.

## Six through Twelve Years Old

Play is as important at this stage of life as it was in the early years, but it often disappears due to the increasingly busy schedule of elementary-aged children. Play in the elementary years can include hanging out at the playground, enjoying a board game, or writing and directing a production with some friends. Resist the urge to turn the television on at the first sign of boredom. (While television is often a fun and appropriate way to unwind, it's different from play.)

## Thirteen through Eighteen Years Old

We don't always think of play when we think of teens, but teens need to play. They have an increasing list of responsibilities and activities and need to let loose and rediscover their creativity and pure joy. At this stage of life, play can include texting or talking on the phone, hanging out with friends, going on a date, or listening to music.

# Character in Action

### Zero through Five Years Old: The Reality of Sharing

You and your toddler are playing in the park. In a very developmentally appropriate moment, your toddler decides to take something from another child. Embarrassed, you demand that your toddler give the item back while at the same time the other parent insists the other child share the coveted item. Your child is upset, by both your reaction and the idea of returning the item. ("I want it!") The other child is upset by the idea of sharing. ("It's mine, and I am using it!")

Sharing is an idea most children do not develop until they are about seven years old. It is not an appropriate expectation for a toddler and, frankly, not easy for adults at times! Work on restoring the item to its owner. Let your toddler know that you won't let the same thing happen in the reverse situation, so it is not okay to grab a friend's toy. Offer a realistic and firm choice, "Would you like to hand it back, or would you like me to?" If necessary, gently take the object and hand it back to the child. Depending on your child and the situation, the reaction you get will vary. Your child might be unfazed and return to independent play. It is more likely you will have to redirect your child's attention to something else. If there is another similar object (many child care facilities will avoid this situation by having multiples of the same object), offer it to your child. You might offer a snack, a move to a different spot, or simply a hug. It's fine to say something like, "I know you are disappointed that you can't have that right now. I bet we can find something else to do." Your calm and clear message will help your toddler get back to the business of play. If things really go south, be sure to model the behavior you'd want: "Here, I'll give back the toy. Sorry for taking it. We'll work on sharing."

### Six through Twelve Years Old: I'm Bored

Your eleven-year-old is hanging out with his classmate. They know the computer is off limits, so they poke around the board games for a while. They wander into the kitchen and announce they are bored. At this point, you have a few options. You're in the kitchen—a natural place to offer a snack. They can fix it themselves, which would provide an activity and a place for them to chat. You could stick around if you feel welcome or leave them to it. If you get the sense they need more structure, suggest an activity that has routine or rules: Take a walk to the park with a basketball, suggest a specific board game you know your son likes, or maybe work on an art or creative project like a science or magic kit. It's good for children to be bored. And while it's fine if you suggest a few activities, it's best to let them make the final decision. Necessity is the mother of invention, and boredom is the father of creativity.

### Thirteen through Eighteen Years Old: Finding the Flow

Your fifteen-year-old son sleeps in on Saturdays until noon and spends two hours on video games or watching television. He used to get up raring to go to the park to shoot hoops or hop on his bike and tour the neighborhood. You even enjoyed Saturday morning at the farmer's market once a month with him. You've suggested that he get up and going or that he join you, but he continues with his new routine. As long as he is engaged in other areas, such as getting his school work done and interacting with friends, let him have his Saturday mornings. Adolescents have a very distinct biological clock, and it's not set to the standard business hours we live by. He needs his sleep, and he's carving out time for himself to just chill. If you're concerned that he's withdrawing from more than just Saturday mornings, it might be worth investigating more with your pediatrician and his teachers or school counselor. Most likely, he's doing exactly what he needs to nurture himself.

# To Summarize...

- Play is an important aspect of emotional, cognitive, and social development.

- Play changes throughout development.

- It's crucial to make room for play in your busy schedule.

- Boredom is the father of creativity.

# Chapter 20

## Transitions: Adapting to Changes

### In This Chapter...

- Welcoming siblings into the family
- How to think of divorce and marriage as changes for the family
- How to maintain connections throughout a move
- Dealing with illness and loss

Families experience transition on many levels on a very regular basis. This chapter will address large-scale transitions, such as divorce, loss, and new additions. The strategies suggested to approach these changes are also applicable to smaller ones, such as fostering an animal, changing school or work routines, and traveling. This chapter will help you approach transition as a parent and will outline some strategies to help your child navigate change.

# New Additions

Just remember you'll make it through the transition of bringing baby home. Sometimes these transitions are dreamy and easy at first, and sometimes the challenges are present at day one. If this is your first, you'll want to read up on the experience—but probably not too much, or you might get nervous. You want to be excited about bringing baby home. I won't lie: Labor isn't fun, but it's worth it. And, as my mother says, "Most people go back for seconds." If you're adopting or fostering a child, you've probably had to jump through many hoops. Often the process can take years, and it is exhausting and financially draining. Try to keep the joy in it if you can. Once you're holding baby, you'll know it was all worthwhile.

If this is your second or third (or, goodness, your fourth), you can count on an inevitable adjustment period. Just as with your first, when you and your partner, spouse, dog, cat, or friends got ready, you will need to prepare everyone in the house again. Talk about the baby. Do not tell others without telling your children first. They will undoubtedly find out, and then you'll have lost control of how you deliver this critical news.

Once the baby is home, work through the feelings. Let your older child be sad and miss your attention. Talk about your older child's feelings. Don't be alarmed or overreact if your older child should utter

---

## Credible

My youngest was a week old. My daughter loved *her* baby, but she couldn't stand to see me loving him. She would vacillate between loving him so much it made me proud and being very angry with me. I knew this was normal, but it still hurt. One day after school, she announced that her friend had a "credible doll" from the Disney store. I didn't know what the heck she was talking about, but I packed all three kids in the car and immediately took her to buy a credible doll (a character from the movie *The Incredibles*). Purchasing a guilt gift wasn't my proudest moment, but rather than argue about need versus want, I decided to splurge and make her feel special for a moment in a very difficult period. Incidentally, it was the first time I ventured out with all three in tow on my own and will remain in my memory as a moment of triumph.

**Perspiration**

something like, "I hate the baby; let's send it back." This is normal, along with probably most everything else that your child will utter.

Let someone take care of the baby so you can spend some extended, baby-free time with your older child. But also make sure you begin to foster the sibling relationship. You want your older child and baby to have time (preferably supervised) together. They will develop a relationship, sure enough. The best method for fostering it is modeling it: Do you have a nice relationship with your own siblings, cousins, friends?

# Marriage

Marriage, like parenting, is a collaborative and long-term commitment. Don't forget that it's malleable. While you and your spouse will always be who you are and have many constant traits, you will also grow and evolve as you move through different experiences. In terms of your parenting, you will grow as individuals, but in a marriage, you also have to grow as a parenting unit.

Many parents start off married, but others marry when their children are already part of the family unit. Some parents move on to second or third marriages while parenting. It's important to include your child in any of these transitions. Don't shield your child from what's happening. Marriage is a good thing. You are modeling commitment and bringing love into your home.

You can include your child in the ceremony, but even more importantly, ensure your child has a strong role in the relationship. It's crucial when you commit to another person that you spend time and energy on the relationship. So definitely make time with your spouse and enjoy one another. But don't let it cloud your time with your child. Include your child as much as possible so that you can truly create a new family unit. Try to make special time to be with your child individually as well. And, if you are in touch with an ex, make an effort to do things as a combined family unit. Each family is unique, and we live in a time where communities, more than not, are open to different families. Be open and honest with your kids and your community about the relationship. You don't have to share all your laundry—clean or dirty—for people to know how you love.

I have had the honor of being at several second weddings of people with children. I am impressed and moved by the capacity of love in these situations. I know one couple that married recently. He had two children and she had none. They were open with the school community, sharing the relevant details and including my family in some of the celebrations. This helped us get to know the family better and support the children through the joyous part of the transition. It also encouraged us to be more understanding of the challenges the family was facing. The ceremony itself was lovely, and the couple included the two children at the altar, exchanging vows and a symbolic bracelet with them in addition to vows and rings with one another. I was touched by the inclusion and outright spotlight on the kids, honoring their part through this change.

These situations can often be difficult on the former spouse. A friend of mine is extremely supportive of the new relationship between her ex-husband and his new wife. It's not been an easy transition for any of them, but in the end, she loves him and wants him to be happy, and she wants her children to know a stable home environment. It can often be difficult to share this kind of personal information with the community, so when you learn of changes going on in yours, be open and supportive. Don't jump to conclusions. And if you're going through it, you might worry about what people think. Sometimes you cannot help it. Try to leave that part behind as much as possible and throw yourself into making the transition one you can be proud of and raise your children proudly through.

## Divorce and Separation

If you are separated from your spouse or partner or your marriage ended in divorce, do your best to maintain a friendly relationship with your ex. This may be a challenge, and you can only try your hardest. Attempt to show your child that you were in a loving relationship and that you still care for one another and, most importantly, for your child. It will make all your decisions that much easier. There is no perfect way to end a marriage, but positivity toward your ex will benefit your child and make your life more manageable.

It takes as much energy from you as it does from your ex to keep the family moving forward. In other words, to make this change work for the children, you need to put in more: more time for the kids, more effort to get along with your ex, and more time on the actual transition (whether that's a move for you or your former spouse, a reduction in expenses, etc.). Negativity and speaking

## Lean on Community

Lean on your community—neighbors, school folks, and family—to help you support your kids. The more you include others in your life, the more they will come to know and love you for the family you are and the less likely they will be to judge you.

**Perspiration**

poorly of one another will not get you anywhere and will only stand to hurt your child's relationship with your ex and you.

I remember talking to my husband about divorce before we got married. I asked him if he was nervous we wouldn't make it because his parents had ended their marriage. He responded with such confidence that, in fact, his parents' model taught him about the importance of family. Even through their difficulties and divorce, his parents, he told me, never changed in their affection for him. He can't recall dramatic arguments or either of his parents trying to win his loyalty. In fact, his mother moved just a block away—a fact he says proudly—so that he could get to either home easily. Both parents attended sporting and school events without a trace of anger. He recalls all of this with great admiration and love to this day.

I have a dear friend who separated from her husband. No matter her feelings about the subject, she never said a word in anger in front of her children. That's not to say they didn't see the pain or unease this transition left. The whole family was under strain, but she didn't feel the need to share the burden of her angst with her children and wanted to protect the family that would always exist even after the marriage dissolved. I always admired her acceptance of the situation and her effort to maintain what she could for her children and the man she loved—but no longer was in love with.

## Moving

My mother and I were driving a car chock-full of my dearest possessions. (Everything else was with my husband in the U-Haul on its way to our new home.) We hadn't gone forty miles before my son had an explosion in his diaper. I pulled over, stooped over my son, and used a makeshift diaper-changing station on the roadside because the car was too full. I had no clothes to change him into, just a fresh diaper... Everything was packed too tight. I just started to laugh—better that than tears! My whole life was about to change, and I had to focus on getting my son clean and in a new set of clothes. We were moving three hundred miles to a new home, a new city, a new job, and the unknown!

Moving is rarely fun, even if you're excited about the prospects. It takes much coordination, time, and effort. It's often a time laden with stress, unease, and fear. Even in the best, most convenient situations (maybe your employer is paying all costs), a move with a family is made even more complicated. Depending on the age of your child, you might be considering local public versus private schools, specific extracurricular activities nearby, or competitive

---

**Inspiration**

## Ideas for Leaving One Home and Introducing a New Home

- Talk about what you'll miss, and make plans to return for visits.

- Make an effort to help your child maintain special friendships (via Skype, email, snail mail, text, phone, etc.).

- Make an effort to return with your child to see family, friends, or favorite restaurants.

- Host a party or arrange playdates and dinners with friends and family that you will miss.

- Create mementos for your child, such as a box of special items from your home, CDs, or an album of photos and letters from friends.

- Share photos of the new country, city, or home.

- Visit the new country, city, or home.

- Provide resources that might be of interest to your child (including brochures of local teams, museums, or activities).

- Talk about the benefits and reasons for moving.

leagues in the area. On top of employment, a suitable home, and all the other criteria you may have for yourself, there are many considerations for your child.

Don't spring a move on your child. Find a moment when you can really talk it through and answer questions. Provide as much information as you can to help your child paint a clear picture of what to expect. Also, if at all possible, make arrangements to maintain memories of your old home.

Share your reasons for your move. If the decision is made, it's made. Do not propose it as an option unless you truly want your child's input in the decision. Make it clear this is a necessity for the family. Be supportive and understanding of fears and concerns, but do not give in to them. Change is hard on everyone, and kids are generally resilient and the first to adapt.

## Illness and Loss

It can be very scary when a child or parent is seriously ill. I have a friend who suffers from cancer. She was nervous at first to share that fact with her two sons. The truth is, the number of doctor visits alone gave her away. It's nearly impossible to hide this kind of condition. Not to mention her hair loss, regular medications, exhaustion, and mood changes. It's good to share openly with your child about illness, whether it's you or another loved one who is sick. It's not wise to scare your child with all the details, but it's good to answer questions openly.

Everyone experiences loss in their own unique way, and there is no right way to grieve or deal with it. When your family faces a loss, it can tear you apart or it can bring you closer together. All too often, marriages fall apart after a loss. And there is no greater loss than the loss of a child.

My family experienced the terrible loss of a child six months along in the pregnancy. At the time, I thought there was no greater pain. I still cry when I think of it. My husband stood by me and demonstrated patience beyond belief. In addition to the loss, I was also postpartum, so my moods were all over the place—not to mention I didn't enjoy how I looked. On top of that, people who saw me would ask how far along I was or, worse, congratulate me on the birth and ask about the baby. Each day there was a new surprise heartbreak. The poor mother I saw one day at my older child's preschool pickup was not expecting tears when she asked me what we had named the baby.

## Sharing Is Caring (Even When It's Hard)

My friend kept her illness quiet at first, until she was able to come to grips with it and until she, her husband, and the doctors had a plan. She desperately wanted to share with her children, but she wanted to wait until she could also present a solution to them so they had a plan to count on. When she had that plan of action, she talked her kids through the whole situation. They could see she was scared and sad, and this helped them know they could be scared and sad too. But they also knew that they could trust her and that she would keep them in the loop.

**Pure Genius!**

With time, I learned that I would always grieve that son of ours but that I had much to live for as well. It was a struggle for my little ones to understand at the time how very sad I was. They were also a great reminder to me of why I had to get out of bed each morning. I am often honest to a fault with my children, but I've learned that it's truly been best for us to share openly. When they asked, I answered. This included detailed questions about how the baby died. It wasn't easy, but often, especially with young children, a brief answer is enough. This open sharing kept us all on the same wavelength and able to share in our emotions. My children learned what I needed from them, and I came to understand it was time to move on, as they were ready and waiting for me.

The loss of a child is certainly difficult, to say the very least, and the loss of a dearly loved family member or friend also affects families. And these losses, unfortunately, are inevitable. I encourage you to be open with your child about death and to allow your child to share in your grieving. It will help your child understand what is happening and why you are so sad or taking time out to be with family or friends.

I recall taking our children to my husband's grandmother's funeral. It was a very difficult time for our extended family and our own nuclear family. His grandmother was (and still is) a widely adored mother, wife, and friend, and a highly regarded woman in her community. To say she was loved and missed would be a large understatement. My mother-in-law was surprised I kept our children by my side during the viewing, the funeral, and the burial. She suggested we consider keeping our distance. But as we all left the cemetery that day, she and I both agreed it was good to have them with us.

Not only did it offer my children closure, but it also helped my mother-in-law to have their hands to hold.

It's often hard to think about taking care of your family after a big loss. Take your time and read about your specific situation. Books are a great resource that allow you to be alone to process your feelings. I also recommend support groups if you prefer to be surrounded by people.

# Finances

The ups and downs of our earnings and expenditures can have a large impact on our lives. While financial security doesn't always equal happiness, the comfort of money can create a sense of security that should not be taken for granted. And the strain of a lack of money can create a lack of stability.

Larger income is usually associated with a good life. Don't forget to keep your kids grounded if they are enjoying a privileged life. Often people get an inflated sense of self with the accumulation of more material goods. Privileged people fall victim to wanting more as much as anyone else. See **Chapter 11** for a discussion on moderation for more on this topic.

A reduction in income is often a very difficult transition for a family. Often in these situations, there are a lot of unknowns: When will my spouse or I get a new job? How long can we go without the income? What will we do if we cannot recuperate? Where can we move if we have to? How do we communicate this? Do we have to communicate this? Talk with your kids. You don't have to (and you shouldn't) share all the nitty-gritty details with your child. A toddler won't likely need many details, if any at all, but an older child will sense what is happening. Your child will be more comfortable with an appropriate amount of information rather than just sensing uncertainty. While you should be realistic and present practical options, don't scare your child. You can share that you're unsure about the future and that the unexpected can make you nervous. But assure your child that you will make it through as a family. It's okay not to have the answer so long as you show your commitment to the family.

Parents in this situation are usually quite stressed. While you can share the situation and let your child know you are nervous, I suggest you put on a brave front and try not to get too emotional. If your child catches you crying or in the middle of a deep discussion, don't hide, but try to keep a positive attitude.

# Transition Looks Different at Different Stages of Life

## Zero through Five Years Old

The lives of infants, toddlers, and young children are constantly in flux. At these stages, children are changing every day, growing bigger, and increasing their skills repertoire. Change is actually quite natural at this stage of life and can be supported with strong routines, encouragement, and a positive attitude. Transitions in the early years can include a parent going back to work, trying a new diet, or starting school.

## Six through Twelve Years Old

The elementary years are also full of transition. Each year of school brings new challenges, excitement, and skills. Parents should continue to support change with routine, encouragement, and a positive attitude. At this stage, kids are also more aware of the world around them and can understand change more and can sometimes be a part of decisions. Transitions in this stage of life can include the onset of puberty, a new best friend, or taking on the responsibility of a new pet.

## Thirteen through Eighteen Years Old

During adolescence, change can be a challenge. While teens make more independent decisions than they used to and are able to better navigate the larger world around them, they are also anxious about impending adulthood. When possible, empower your teen to be a part of the change and choice. Transition at this stage can include dating, getting a job, or learning to drive.

My husband and I were once in a financial pickle. I had been home with our children for ten years and we needed more income. There were so many unknowns as we figured out what to do: What was the minimum or maximum level of debt we could take on? Should we sell our home? Where would we go if we did sell our home? Should I go back to work? Should my husband try to find another job? (He was already working two.)

We decided to sell our house so we could have some time to make some more long-term decisions. We stayed in a friend's one-bedroom apartment while the house was on the market. (A house with five, mostly young, residents doesn't market very well.) Our house, our one big investment, didn't sell. We didn't expect that. We were in contract twice, and both times it fell through due to financing… We felt doomed. What now?

Everyone has choices. Even in that awful situation, my sister reminded me, we had a choice. We could allow foreclosure. We could declare bankruptcy. I could go back to work. We could rent out our home. So we went to plan B, and I looked for work. Luckily, I found something. The transition marked an extended period of financial uncertainty as well as the fortitude needed to help my children adjust to their working mom's new schedule. That, along with moving back into the house, took a lot of effort and a positive attitude.

It took a long time to get back on our feet, but how proud we are of ourselves and our family that we did. The two tricks to making it through were keeping perspective—we really did have a lot despite what we were giving up—and getting through it together.

# Character in Action

## Zero through Five Years Old: Welcome Home

You've just purchased a new home—much larger than your last. You overhear your four-year-old son pronounce to a friend during a playdate, "See my new house? Now we're rich!" Your instinct might be to step in and say something right then. Likely, at four, this will be a passing comment. Assuming the playdate continues in a positive fashion, let it go in the moment. Be sure to come back to this comment later on when you can talk with your son. This is a tricky situation because he (and you) should be proud of your new home. Often people associate money with shame. It's good to

### Words to Parent By

*If you don't like something, change it. If you can't change it, change your attitude.*

Maya Angelou

Quote

be successful and own a home you're proud of. You can use this moment to teach your son about being proud and honest. Talk about the comfort and joy of having enough money. Bring in aspects of gratitude, hard work, and splurging. Highlight aspects of pride and effort. Then talk about modesty and privacy. Money is nothing to be ashamed of, but it isn't an appropriate conversation topic for children on a regular basis.

### Six through Twelve Years Old: Visions of Reconciliation

Your marriage is on shaky ground, and your wife has moved out. She's telling you that it's over and telling your eleven-year-old daughter that while you're in two separate homes, nothing will really change. Your daughter is counting on the fact that you're going to get back together with your wife. Speak to your wife (if possible) and see if you can find some common ground. Try to talk to your daughter together. If that just isn't going to happen, *you* need to be honest with your daughter and let her know the reality of the situation. If you're hoping that the marriage is not quite over, it's certainly okay to share that so long as you also provide the fact that it may in fact be over. Share your feelings with concrete words. While it's okay to show your feelings in front of your daughter, make sure that you experience some fun and happy times together as well. Don't let this event shadow your entire lives together, but let it be part of it.

### Thirteen through Eighteen Years Old: Moving On down the Field

Your sixteen-year-old daughter seemed set on earning an athletic scholarship at a local college. She is a strong soccer player and has played since she was seven years old. She's been competing on travel teams since fifth grade. Once she got to high school, she continued with her travel team and started up on her varsity high school team. She announces she wants to quit the travel team because she wants more time for homework and friends. Is it time to push her to work through a difficult time, or do you let her take the lead on this?

At sixteen, your daughter has a pretty strong grasp of what's involved in staying competitive and is evolving into her adult self. Soccer has been a part of her identity. It's important to talk through the decision in great detail. For example, she should understand that she might be passing up the athletic scholarship and college play time should she stop the travel team. However, most colleges have robust intramural sports that allow high school athletes to continue to play but with a more flexible level of commitment. That shift might be okay with her, and if it is, it has to be okay with you. Be sure to dig deep into her reasons. Is she not getting her homework done, or is she up very late finishing it? What is it that she wants to do with her friends? Is there another activity she is interested in? It would also be a great idea to talk with the coach and your daughter together to find out if anything has happened or if her play has changed. If the options are reasonable, by all means support her decision. There are some practical points to consider. What financial alternatives does your family have for paying for college? Is a four-year college something that you all really want for her? Is it something she is counting on? Is it a realistic hope?

Depending on your financial situation, there are several options for college, including scholarships and financial aid. After all, there is no guarantee, even if she sticks with the travel team, that she would qualify for an athletic scholarship.

# To Summarize...

- Divorce doesn't have to mean splitting everything down the line.

- Marriage with kids is about more than just the bride and groom.

- Stick together no matter where life takes your family.

- Be open and honest about the changes in your life.

# Part 4

## Fostering Community

Part of living in this world is sharing it with others. We need to teach our children how to live within our own nuclear families, as well as within our extended families. Beyond that, children need to learn to partake in the world and contribute to their communities, both immediate and beyond. Raising a self-reliant, motivated, and healthy child is futile if that child is left to live in a vacuum of selfishness. We must learn to create and enjoy our communities and give back to them with an expectation to improve them.

In this section, we will consider elements of collaboration among parents, children, and the communities we live in. We will establish the positive aspects of competition and how to rein in the negative. We'll talk about how children progress through different stages of relating—and not relating—with others, and how that translates within the community and, specifically, with peers. These socialization skills will help you and your child positively contribute to your neighborhood and to society.

# Chapter 21

## Collaboration: Parenting with a Partner and/or Community

### In This Chapter...

- How to find and form your village
- Can't we all get along—or at least try?
- How to communicate with your partner and village
- Who's doing this parenting well anyhow?

Parenting is hard enough. Make it easier on yourself by building healthy support systems. One of the benefits of raising a family in this century is the ability to connect easily, but one of the difficulties of raising a family nowadays is that connections are often quick and superficial. This chapter will offer insights about how collaborating can help you raise your child and how your child's collaborative skills can help build strong, productive relationships.

I cannot tell you how many times I've shared a parenting challenge with a peer, only to have the other parent respond with a blank look that makes me feel abnormal just for *admitting* I have the challenge. Let me share one of these moments with you:

Me: "We're really struggling with the homework this year. I can't argue with the content, but it's taking my son more than the recommended twenty minutes a night. I am also working with him on it more than I think I should, but I don't think he can do it on his own."

Peer: "Huh—my son does it by himself, and I don't usually even see the homework. He does really well so I haven't really noticed the content."

In that situation, I felt both embarrassed that my son couldn't keep up and shamed for sharing an issue that the other parent clearly didn't experience. Whether or not the other child was having problems with homework, his parent was so focused on defending her son's image that she missed the fact that I was seeking advice and support. Building and maintaining a network of support is a wonderfully positive parenting perk. Recognizing who is not part of that network is equally important. In that particular moment, I just ended the conversation quickly. Moving forward, I sought out other people I felt more comfortable talking with.

## Trust in Your Partner

If you are parenting with a partner, enjoy this partnership and cherish it. That's not to say you need to agree with each other about everything, but respect each other's opinions, listen, and present a united front. Support each other through your decisions. Help each other talk out issues large and small. When you approach important decision points, discuss how you will handle them before critical choices must be made. Is it a year when sleepovers might begin? Will middle school dances or high school curfews soon become an issue? Exploring these parenting decisions before the moments arrive allows you and your partner to collaborate with less pressure. In addition, it fosters a climate of cooperation in which other decisions—bedtime, media rules, food choices—can be discussed with relative ease.

If you are parenting with a spouse or lifetime partner, be sure to nourish your own relationship and hold each other in high regard. There is a reason you have chosen to spend your life with this person, so be sure your spouse or partner knows this to be true on a daily basis. It's important to carve out

# Collaboration Looks Different at Different Stages of Life

## Zero through Five Years Old

Collaboration for a very young child is usually imposed by the adults or older children in the young child's life. Collaboration at this stage of life can include taking turns using a seesaw at the playground, sharing food with a parent, or winning *or* losing a game of Chutes and Ladders equally well.

## Six through Twelve Years Old

At this stage in life, kids are generally open to collaboration and have the social and cognitive skills to listen empathetically, articulate opinion, and understand perspective. While these skills are accessible, they often need to be prompted and supported. In the elementary years, collaboration can include creating a science fair project with a classmate, inventing a new game with friends, or agreeing on a movie to watch with siblings.

## Thirteen through Eighteen Years Old

Teens are developmentally able to collaborate. At this stage, parents can encourage collaboration by listening to issues that arise rather than offering solutions to them. In most cases, teens are ready to problem-solve independently. In adolescence, collaboration can include participating in a school or community play or band, volunteering with a food bank, or working on a research project with a group.

## Guess How Much I Love You!

Ever read the book with the same title as this sidebar? It's about a parent and baby rabbit competing to love each other more. It's a fantastic and fun game to play with your child. Have you expressed your love for your spouse or partner today? Make sure you do. Better yet, show it with a kind word, a foot massage, a special meal, or ... !

**Perspiration**

time for the two of you to be together and to carve out time when your spouse or partner can be alone. Your loved one deserves respect, so go ahead and show it! And expect it for yourself as well. After all, your child will grow and leave, and you two will remain.

Trust your partner. Try to avoid becoming one of those "it needs to be done my way" parents. Children thrive with many role models and influences. Let your spouse or partner be as important as you are. Beginning with infant care, share the responsibilities of child rearing. Even if you truly believe your swaddling technique is the best, let your partner take part as well. It's okay if you cut off the crusts, but when you're not there, perhaps the crusts stay on. Your child can avoid the crust. In fact, your child might like to eat it!

Trust your spouse or partner to make the right decisions for the moment. You can second-guess, but stay calm if you are second-guessed. You may disagree, but how important is this issue? Do you need to discuss it before making a decision? Is it okay to let this one slide? If it seems important enough to discuss, wait until you have time to reflect and can discuss the choice without your child overhearing. Sometimes it's hard, in the moment, to determine how important the issue is—and then in retrospect, you realize you should have just let it slide (or wished you hadn't). This comes with practice. So if you're unsure, then talk it through. Make your lists (pros and cons) and really determine how important it is to you.

Money, time, and energy can all be limiting, but make an effort to get away with your partner When you recharge your relationship, you make sure each of you knows you are cared for. This might include date night, a Sunday morning bike ride, or (heaven, yes) a weekend in a hotel room! You might also consider a late-night dessert while children are asleep, a weekly show ritual, or an early-morning coffee date. You need to recharge your relationship and make sure each of you knows you are cared for. It's no easy feat to carve out that time, but you can lean on your friends and family if you and your partner are in dire need of time together. You don't have to pay a sitter to go out. Swap evenings with a friend, or look into co-ops where you can alternate watching a group of kids. Not only will you enjoy nights out, but the kids will become part of a tight network too.

# Create a Village

It's important to find a community in which you feel supported, challenged, and comfortable. Surround yourself with families that you respect, admire, and enjoy. Don't waste your time with families that make you feel insufficient or lacking. There is a difference between being impressed and inspired and being intimidated and made to feel nervous. For example, there are parents around whom I feel supported and challenged: "Oh, your daughter plays piano and plays on the basketball team. How do you fit in the practices for both throughout the week?" And then there are the parents who make me nervous and insufficient: "Aha, your child is a chess master, pianist, star basketball player, and speaks French fluently. When did Johnny begin to learn French?"

It's okay to find a support system in which you may question another parent's choices, but it's not healthy when you are simply at a loss. There are families out there that can maintain a crazy pace and whose children seem to thrive. They either put on a good show, will burn out soon enough, or are simply unique. Know that these families are rare and that you are in charge of how you live.

You can begin to build your network through parent-and-me classes or through casual park encounters and can continue to build it through your child's college years. It's good to have multiple people to go to, as you will have a variety of needs and questions as your child goes through different phases in life. Through your involvement in your child's activities, for instance as a co-op parent or through play and volunteer situations, you will notice other parents whose responses resonate with your own or who express interesting ideas. You can foster those bonds by offering to meet at the park or initiating a playdate.

For those of you not parenting with a partner, this village will be a huge part of your parenting. Hillary Clinton was dead on when she said, "It takes a village." Not only will you need people to lean on, learn from, and talk with, but your child can benefit from the people around you. Your child will be influenced by everyone around, and at least you can choose some of those people. Within your village, identify people your child can go to. For example, if you are a single mother, let your son know (many times and throughout the years as he changes) that he can go to Frank or Tim anytime he feels he cannot go to you. Even if you aren't a single parent, it's good to have a go-to person or people on hand. Your child may end up in a sticky situation and feel uncomfortable going to you. Understand that it is natural for children to be more or less comfortable discussing things with different people and focus on creating a network of trusted people to whom they might turn.

Once you forge these friendships and as your village grows, be bold and let people know where they stand in your circle. Let them know that you might need a little help or that you or your child might go to them for advice. Ask whether they feel comfortable being a touch point for your child. Let them know you are there for them too. Talk about how you might handle situations as they arise. As with a spouse or partner, you may not see eye to eye on everything. That's okay as long as you feel your friends are reasonable and caring adults. Create your village actively, and then trust in this village and let its members care for you and your child.

Remember to enjoy your village. Schedule time away with your trusted friends. Weekends away, lunch out on the town, dinner after the baseball practice. Wherever you can find the time, make the time. When you are out of the hustle and bustle of your life, you will be able to make deeper connections. Some sleep-away camps, temples, and churches offer retreats or family weekends. These can be a wonderful way to get away with friends and to make new ones with similar interests and values. If you have an only child, vacationing with other families can provide a sense of community.

## Communicate, Communicate, Communicate

Whether it's with your spouse, partner, child's teacher, child's coach, your friends, or other parents at the playground, be sure to talk. It's crucial to maintain and attend to the bonds you have with other parents, even when you are too busy (especially when you are too busy). Don't be afraid to share what's going on and to ask questions. That said, use a filter. Do you know your child's baseball coach well enough to share concerns about your child's learning style? Is it appropriate? Maybe, maybe not. Be sure to think that through before opening up about a potentially delicate topic.

## Where to Start

Develop an organic network of parents that you can depend on. You will want some at the same stage as you, some with older children, and some with younger ones. Share openly and provide a safe place for members of your network to share with you. Here are some ways to start (or continue) building that network:

- Join a parent-and-me class and really put in the effort to get to know the other parents in it.

- Research a moms or dads group to try to find peers around your age with similarly aged children in your area so that you can get together conveniently.

- Hang out with your child at the park and socialize. Sometimes casual conversation can lead to deeper ties.

**Perspiration**

If you have a coparent at home, talk, talk, talk. Talk—even celebrate—when you're sure of a decision you made, and talk when you think you made a bad choice. (Remember, the theme of this book is learning from our mistakes.) If you talk about the goings on of your day-to-day parenting experiences and choices, you will better understand each other and your child. You will also find that parenting decisions emerge more naturally as you create a habit of communication.

Listen too! It's as important to hear your spouse or partner as it is to weigh in and make your thoughts known. You might reconsider a point or find agreement that you can fully trust. If you are not coparenting, listen to trusted friends and parents in your community. It's okay not to know the answer. It's also okay to mess up. If you talk about it, you can find reason and hope through conversation.

One of the limitations of today's parenting is the pressure to put on a show. There is a lot of pressure to raise your child to be fantastic at everything, to have a passion, to do well in school, to be polite, to get into a good college—and the list goes on. Some of the holiday cards that arrive in

## Role Playing

Role playing can be very helpful to practice your communication skills. Lean on friends and family in your village to help you work on your style. Practice makes perfect, and if you're unsure in a situation or need help reinforcing your point, repetition can be helpful. Ask for honest feedback and practice suggestions.

**Inspiration**

the winter months are a bit over the top, "Charlie made the travel lacrosse team, continues with piano, enjoys soccer in the off season, designed his own video game that is for sale on Amazon, and is excited to be in third grade." Please, let your child live a little and find other topics of conversation.

If you are not coparenting, be sure to put yourself out there and have conversations about decisions you are making. Allow people to weigh in on what's going on. Don't make it an exercise of judgment but rather an exercise in reflection. You know what's best for your child, but that doesn't mean you always make the best decisions. Of course, you should have confidence in your decisions, but you should also be aware that you can learn from others and help inform your decision making in the future.

## Strive to Compromise

You would prefer your kindergartner to be home or at the playground every day after school, and your spouse or partner cares immensely that your child try a team sport. Remember to give and take. Maybe try a recreational league for soccer or basketball, for example, that meets once a week and is low pressure and focused on fun. If your spouse or partner becomes one of "those" parents on the sidelines (coaching, screaming, etc.), then it's time to speak up. Perhaps your partner is so involved in supporting your children that she or he is not aware of the behavior being demonstrated. Otherwise, let your spouse or partner explore this opportunity with your child. If a musical instrument is a nonnegotiable to you, speak up and be willing to step back on another issue.

Give and take is not all about extracurriculars. This concept applies to discipline, education—you name it! One of you might feel strongly about your child going out on a weeknight, staying out past curfew, being with a peer of the opposite sex behind closed doors, or owning a particular electronic device. Here's where listening comes into play. Your spouse or partner might have a good argument that differs from your own. It's okay to stand by your opinion.

Generally, it is better to err on the side of the more conservative opinion when you really cannot come to an agreement. So when your spouse wants a fourth baby and you just don't see that happening, it's better to stick with three than to have a resentful parent on your hands.

Now, if your wife wants your child to spend two weeks away at sleep-away camp—and your kid is game, but you aren't—consider it. This is where being conservative isn't always a better bet. It's okay to say no, but give your child's ideas serious thought. If you can't give permission now, can you agree to consider the idea the next year, after you take some time researching a possible middle ground? Whether you completely agree in the end or not, it's important to back one another up when talking with your child. You can continue the active debate in private, but try to maintain a united front when with your child. It is also okay to calmly discuss your different opinions in front of your child as long as you keep it balanced and emotionally neutral. Children benefit from seeing adults model a discussion in which they disagree and come to a compromise.

It's also okay not to care about every decision. And it's okay to admit it. You can also feel comfortable about minimizing the importance of some parenting choices; going with your gut is usually the safest bet in these situations. When can your toddler start chewing gum? I chose too early for my oldest, and of course he

### Dinnertime

I have fond memories of lively dinner conversation growing up. Dinner was a time to be together and share. We learned a new tradition of reporting news and offering gratitude each night at the dinner table from our friends. Now our conversations are in depth and build off one another's experiences. If sharing gratitude or reporting news does not work for your family, something as simple as adding a few candles to the dinner table can create a calm and welcoming space for family time. You'll be surprised how quickly a different family dynamic can emerge. Ask families in your network how they handle dinner or any other common situation and learn from their ideas.

**Pure Genius!**

swallowed the first piece. Not such a big deal (unless you're one of those who really believes it sticks to your esophagus for seven years). My husband thought we should have waited longer. The decision wasn't a major one, and my husband moved on. With the next child, we waited a little longer. This is where perspective comes in handy. (See **Chapter 8** for more on perspective.) Talk with your kids about your decision making as well. Let them know what's a big deal, what isn't (to you), and what influences your decision.

## Mentors are Parents' Best Friends

You've probably had a role model or mentor in some professional or personal capacity during your life. Well, it turns out that parents need mentors too. Identify people in your community who can be role models for you. You might like how one family on the block seems to have the most responsible kids (whom you hire as babysitters, perhaps). Seek them out! Observe how the parents interact with their kids; ask questions about how they deal with situations. Flatter them. People love to talk about themselves and are usually eager to share ideas when they can.

There may be a parent at work who talks about being at soccer games each week, and that may inspire you to attend your child's sporting events. Perhaps your child's friend from school spends time with family during walks to school or a family game night. Whatever it is that inspires you, let it lead you. Don't be afraid to try what works for others! Take your own walks to school, make time for a family game night, or make plans to attend a sporting event together.

## Character in Action

### Zero through Five Years Old: Preschool Pariah

You get a call from your preschooler's teacher, and he's been biting! Oy. Yes, you are now *that* parent with the biter—the parent who is always apologizing to other parents in the park after school. Your knee-jerk reaction is to apologize profusely and ask for suggestions from the teacher and then to punish your child when he gets home (though you cannot think of an authentic punishment at the moment). One friend in your trusted group suggests biting your son back. Another trusted friend suggests you work through a reward system.

Please don't bite your son! When in doubt, remember to model what you envision in your own child. Two wrongs don't make a right, and so on and so forth. Talk with your preschooler and make it clear that biting is wrong and can hurt. Reassure him that you can see that he is (or was) frustrated. Also be reassured yourself that biting is a very common reaction, especially for preverbal children or those just learning how to use their words to express feelings. A logical consequence is lack of interaction with people he bites. So if he bites you, explain that you want to be alone and that while you really enjoy playing with Legos with him or reading, right now you are going to separate yourself. You'll look forward to playing again when he's ready to be with people and to use words or get help when he is frustrated.

This sends a very strong message. Hopefully the school can back you up and separate him from other students by delivering a message similar to yours. Don't worry. He'll grow out of it. (Remember, Hannibal Lecter is a fictional character!) You've shared this issue with friends, and now they're going to want to know what you've done. You're nervous they will judge you. You're probably right, but if they are true friends and you've created a strong village, they will respect you for doing what you think is right. Chances are, they have experienced a similar situation. It's your prerogative to keep your disciplinary decisions to yourself. But don't feel like you have to be embarrassed by your decisions either. The point of creating a strong support system is to help you better understand yourself and your parenting, not to hold you accountable. Your child will do that plenty.

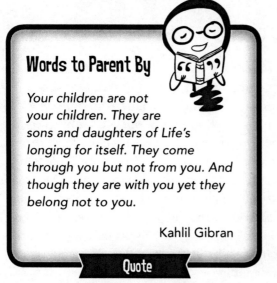

### Words to Parent By

*Your children are not your children. They are sons and daughters of Life's longing for itself. They come through you but not from you. And though they are with you yet they belong not to you.*

Kahlil Gibran

Quote

## Six through Twelve Years Old: Middle School Musician

Your spouse is very invested in music education and believes strongly that your children should each play one instrument and as part of an orchestra. You have two children, and the older one, a middle schooler, is now committed to five days a week of practice and rehearsal. She would like to try to join the school basketball team. Your spouse is against the idea of joining the team because it will take away from homework time, which is already tight. What do you do?

Listen. Remember to listen and honor your spouse's opinion. And listen to your daughter. If she has a good point and you believe the basketball will be a good fit and opportunity, share that with your spouse. It's okay to have different opinions. Point out that your daughter has a strong commitment to music and try to suggest some workable solutions, like which practices or rehearsals you could cut out during the basketball season. If you and your spouse can find agreement, talk with the music teacher(s) and work together with your child to find the right fit.

So that didn't work, and your spouse won't bend? Have your spouse read this book. The right answer is to find balance. It's okay to have a nonnegotiable (like a musical instrument), but it's not okay to shut out other child-initiated requests. Keep in mind, denying your child an opportunity to explore may backfire. A key to maintaining intrinsic motivation to learn and grow is autonomy, and children's opportunities for choice should expand as they develop. Is it possible to continue the instrument for a year without participating in the orchestra? One year of autonomy may lead your child back to enthusiastic participation or might lead to a whole new set of activities in which your child is truly invested. Lean on your community to help you through this kind of decision. Your spouse may benefit from hearing other opinions.

### Thirteen through Eighteen Years Old: College or No College—That Is the Question!

Your eighteen-year-old, who's always done well in school and is likely able to get into a number of colleges and universities, has expressed that she is not ready for college. She is burned out and wants to take a year or two to do something other than school. It's a good argument, but you know in your heart of hearts she needs a college education to get anywhere in life, and this really isn't an argument you are willing to have. You wish she'd just let you send her off to college and get through it and then she can do whatever she likes. After all, you're willing to let her choose the school and her course work. Your partner agrees and wishes she would just go to college. However, he points out that your daughter is making a brave decision here and would like to follow it through for a year to see what happens. After all, he points out, she is eighteen and is legally an adult.

Well, the answer in this situation is not clear (as in so many parenting decisions). However, what is absolutely necessary is the need to listen. Hear each other and your daughter out. Then talk through the long- and short-term consequences. Try to support her through the decision making. Even if she goes with her gut and doesn't listen to you in the end, you've shown her that you respect her, you love her, and you can live with her decision. You don't have to cut her off just because she makes a decision you don't believe in, and you don't have to support her financially either. Offer her suggestions on how to make it on her own without a college education, be there for her when she finds her decision wasn't the easy way out, and celebrate with her when she finds moments of joy and appreciation for her choice. You might want to begin with a compromise and let her know that you will support her for a year if she also agrees to apply to colleges in the fall of this year just in case she realizes that she will want to attend college later.

You might talk with friends in the community who did not attend college, friends who took time off between high school and college, and friends who found alternative paths. If you also involve your daughter in those conversations, they will not only help her but will also help you. You need support in this situation, and you need to find out if your gut is telling you something because it's familiar or because there's more to it than that. Lean on your spouse and your community in this decision, and remember that there are many possible paths in life. Some circles are more accepting than others, and consider how you'll feel about sharing this information. There is no need for you to feel compromised during this decision-making process. Be honest with your peers about your feelings and ask them for compassion and understanding, acknowledging that some might frown on the decision not to go to college.

# To Summarize…

- Lean on your partner, spouse, and village.
- Be willing to compromise.
- Communication is key.
- Find a role model.

# Chapter 22

## Competition: It's How You Play the Game

### In This Chapter...

- What limits make sense with youth sports leagues?
- How to focus on learning and not grades
- What's your status quo, and does it matter?
- How do economics play into parenting?

ompetition is everywhere. Schools and sports teams are ranked. Students are graded and compared with peers on standardized test reports. Restaurants, books, shows... Our culture is rife with ranking. While a little healthy rivalry can be productive, too much can be emotionally, intellectually, and physically stifling. In this chapter, you will read about how competition influences parenting and how to help your child nurture an intrinsic desire to strive without losing sight of the big picture.

Some children appear to be born with the desire to compete. Some react to conflict by completely shutting down. Regardless of your child's personality, you can start exploring healthy competition by finding and developing your child's intrinsic motivations to work hard and succeed.

# Youth Sports

Athletics are a complicated arena in the United States. While Americans have an ambivalent relationship with lifelong health, we have a very strong love affair with sports. Making the right choices when it comes to sports can lead to fabulous outcomes and opportunities for children. However, today's children are joining organized sports teams at very young ages, and this can lead to a host of unanticipated consequences. Despite the statistics revealing relatively few athletic scholarships, rampant overuse injuries, and troubling adverse consequences from playing certain sports, we continue to support a robust youth athletics system. Youth sports have grown into a very profitable enterprise in recent years, and it is not always clear which sport, team, or club will serve your child best. Knowing the right questions to ask and how to find the right fit will help set the stage for healthy and happy experiences.

The first and often unasked question is, who chose this sport? Did you choose it for your child? Did your child ask to play? Did a friend invite your child to participate? Is your child playing just because an older sibling plays? It is easy to get caught up in a family or community pattern without asking the individual child. For some children, this approach is fine, as they enjoy being with friends and learning something new. In fact, sports teams often provide an early social opportunity for children.

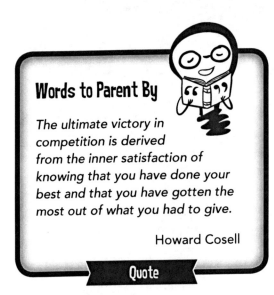

## Words to Parent By

*The ultimate victory in competition is derived from the inner satisfaction of knowing that you have done your best and that you have gotten the most out of what you had to give.*

Howard Cosell

**Quote**

For other children, team participation quickly becomes a forced activity or burden and may lead to them opting out of sports completely. If your child meets you with serious resistance when it is time to put on the cleats or get out the jersey, talk about what is going on. Better yet, have that discussion before the season begins. Does your child really want to try this sport? Do you and your child understand

## Did You Say Team Sport?

Here are a few physical alternatives for you and your child to consider:

 Swimming

 Fencing

 Ice skating

 Tennis

 Gymnastics

Each of these can have a competitive component but can also be enjoyed recreationally.

**Perspiration**

the commitments expected by this team and this league? Do the team and league philosophy support your family's ideas of positive sportsmanship, skill development, and healthy competition? Depending on the age of your child, you can work through some or all of these questions together.

Conversations can often be quite simple with younger children: Do you want to play? Are you ready to go to practice and games every week? But as your child becomes more and more heavily invested in a sport, it's important to weigh in more. Sports can become a serious financial commitment with all the equipment and league fees, combined with possible travel. Also, obligations for one child can take away time from the family and impact a sibling's ability to commit to a team.

There are options, and it's up to you to find the right one for your child. If your child or you are not ready for intensity, stick to rec leagues. It's harder to find them at the middle school level, but they exist. Don't feel the pressure to get your child in young and working toward a college scholarship. Whether or not you choose a competitive or rec team, make sure you are comfortable with the coach and the relevant policies. You can't likely change the latter, but you and your child can learn them and decide whether or not you can live with them. And if you're ready for the highly competitive team, go for it. And be okay to step back if it isn't working for your child or your family.

If you are having trouble getting your child involved in a physical activity, try to think outside the box. Your child doesn't have to join a team. There are all kinds of classes out there. There are free options too: Take a hike, walk to school, or ride your bike to the grocery store with your child—or form a neighborhood club.

# Competition Looks Different at Different Stages of Life

## Zero through Five Years Old

For very young children, competition should be internally focused around developing language skills, building gross and fine motor skills, and developing compassion. Parents can offer small moments of competition at these young ages with a fun and accepting attitude. At this stage, competition can include getting better at climbing a structure, racing home from the park, or playing a game of Candyland.

## Six through Twelve Years Old

All elementary-aged children can be encouraged to compete in a friendly manner with low stakes and even with increasing stakes if the intrinsic motivation is there. Parents can encourage competition by offering a variety of sports and activities that align with a child's interests. In these years, competition can include playing a game of four square with friends, participating in a competitive swimming league, or working hard for a good grade.

## Thirteen through Eighteen Years Old

As teens approach adulthood, they have the increasing desire to perform and succeed. Competition is part of that. Parents can nurture a healthy competitive attitude by offering plenty of opportunities for winning and losing, success and failure. Be patient and allow for feelings of disappointment. Celebrate success with a gracious attitude. In adolescence, competition can include beating a personal running record, applying to a high-reach college, or trying out for an elite volleyball team.

# Grades

Why do we have grades? Grades are a very efficient way of providing learners with credentials and feedback. A student has earned this grade in this subject, and may move on to the next level. While there is often educational debate around grades, it seems unlikely that they will disappear in the near future. Luckily, many educators are aware of the many downsides to grades and have made thoughtful adjustments to policies. Some schools have eliminated or modified student-ranking policies. More teachers allow revision and emphasize process instead of focusing on one final product. Fewer teachers pass back tests in order of score or shame students by posting grades publicly.

Despite the thoughtful and spirited debate about grades among educators, grade competition is still evident in parking lot conversations, dinner table discussions, and elsewhere. First, know your school's attitude toward grades. At Back-to-School Night, ask questions of the teachers and the administration. How are homework and classwork assessed? Does effort or participation play a role in the grade? What are the rules for late work and/ or revision? Are students allowed to discuss grades with other students? Do teachers ever announce grades? If you have concerns about the grading system, ask the teacher if you can schedule a meeting. Be understanding about teachers' demanding schedules. They often teach all day, have recess and lunch duty, and supervise carpool lines. They use their few spare minutes to check in with colleagues, set up activities for future lessons, and meet with students who need help—all in a nine-hour day. Many also have their own children and might need to rush to drive a carpool or pick a child up at after-school care. When you contact your child's teacher, provide a few windows in which to meet in person or by phone. In addition, you might want to send some of your general questions—not criticisms—to the teacher through email to allow the teacher a chance to think through some answers before you meet.

No matter what the policy is at your child's school, you can control the conversation around grades in your house and your carpool. It seems simple but can be hard to do—yet you can avoid asking about grades. Ask if your child learned anything surprising today. Ask if your child helped or enjoyed a friend. See the scenario below for a list of questions that can give you a great insight into your child's day without asking the dreaded, "So, what did you get on that test?" If your child is quick to compare with peers, be as quick to point out that the grade is a reflection of one assignment and has no connection to other students. Furthermore, the grade is a small snapshot of this assignment from one moment in time and can be thought of as a step toward a new goal on the next assignment. Use this conversation to ask your child about schoolwork: What is your child proud of? What does your child want to improve on? Perhaps most importantly, ask this same set of questions after big assignments, no matter the grade. Hopefully your child can find something to be proud of and something to improve upon for every assignment. In this way, you reinforce the importance of process over any one product and are helping foster lifelong learning.

Competition is natural and very human. Don't be surprised or upset if your child is comparing grades and getting competitive. Try to encourage your child to learn rather than achieve grades, but also be proud your child wants to do well. And, inevitably, your child will not always have the better grade. This is also a good learning moment. Remind your child that, again, grades are one snapshot and not the whole picture. That said, it's okay to be bummed out. More importantly, learn from the errors and try to improve.

## Status and Peer Pressure

Peer pressure is not just for adolescents. Parents can fall victim to peer pressure just as easily. Everyone else has a stroller worth $1,000, so why shouldn't you? This dates me, but when my oldest was born, the expensive, fancy strollers that everyone had to have (and, yes, I did too), cost $85. I remember my aunt being shocked by the price tag. Of course, she just used an umbrella stroller that she bought at the five and dime. The newest model may be truly awesome. Who doesn't want a cup holder and shock absorbers? But is it the right choice for you, your child, and your family? We can easily get caught up but need to resist.

Think about how you feel about your own place in the world. Are you happy and confident? Are you competitive about your status and concerned about how people see you? It's not bad to want status, but what does it really

**Projection**

When you notice your child is consistently looking for more status, it's probably an indication that you're not content with your own status.

**Uninspired**

mean? Is it the be-all and end-all? No. When I speak to parent communities, the overwhelming majority of parents want their children to be happy, confident, and self-sufficient (not necessarily rich or famous) and to have healthy relationships. Status is not required.

Okay, so status is not required. Then why do so many people strive for it? It's human to be competitive and seek out something better. Teach your child to seek status for fulfillment and to truly feel better, not for the sake of appearance. Teach this by living it. If you've been longing to join the board at the local hospital, then go for it. But do it for the right reasons. Are you joining to help advance research and support people who are in medical need? Or are you joining because you know that people running in your circles are on boards of large organizations? So you're the CEO or the partner in your firm. You belong to the golf club. You went to an Ivy League college. Bully for you. That's terrific! Is that what defines you as a person? It might be. It certainly has an influence on who you are. Are those the things that you want to define your child? If so, which parts? Chances are, if you're driven to be the upper of the upper crust, your child will learn that status is very important.

Be careful to avoid comparing yourself with other adults. This may seem obvious, but small comments about other parents, the neighbors, or acquaintances can inspire your child to compare and can lead to petty behavior.

Part of you might *want* your child to be popular. That's likely because you don't want your child to face difficult social situations or exclusion. So rather than focus on the status, focus on the long-term benefit you want for your child: to know acceptance and belonging. You can't eliminate exclusion, but you can "accentuate the positive"!

Your child will have to deal with status in social circles, in extracurricular activities, within the family, and later on in jobs. Teach your child to

## Watch What You Say

Be mindful of your own comments about your status or judging yourself in a cavalier way. Comments such as "I'm not as good as Sally's mother" or "I know you wish you had him for a father" will suggest to your child that you are constantly comparing yourself and that you care too much about what others think, including your child.

As with many parenting techniques, modeling can be more powerful than any discussion or activity. First, be careful to avoid comparing yourself with other adults. This may seem obvious, but small comments about other parents, the neighbors, or acquaintances can inspire your child to compare and can lead to petty behavior.

**Perspiration**

understand what status means: What is a label, and how does it define someone? Talk about the positives and drawbacks about labels. We label our children so early on: She's shy, he's sensitive, she's an alpha girl, he's a bully, she's popular, he's a class clown—and the list goes on. These labels will undoubtedly offer some sort of status to your child. It's up to you to make sure they don't define your child.

Once your child achieves some sort of status, it's okay to celebrate that, but be clear on what it is you're celebrating. If your daughter is elected class president, celebrate her hard work on her campaign and the possibilities with her new power. Don't let it consume her and let her begin to think she is more important than her peers. You might comment, "That's terrific honey! I am so proud of the work you put into the campaign. Now you get to enjoy the privilege of being a leader. What are you most excited about?" Let the conversation flow from there, and use your judgment, keeping in mind this should not become her singular label.

Depending on your child, social competition can be a consistent challenge or a cyclical one. For some children, there is a surge in social competition right before and around kindergarten that may die down until middle and high school. For other children, it is a more persistent feature of peer relationships. You can help your child steer clear of unhealthy social competition by developing empathy (see **Chapter 3** for a discussion on empathy) and modeling.

# Economic

There is no denying that money is important in this world. That said, our bank accounts do not define us or our children. Do your very best not to compete financially with your peers. Your child does not need an Xbox just because Susie Q has one. It's hard enough to stay afloat in this world balancing your work, family, and bank account. Don't make more work by constantly comparing yourself with other families, and don't let your child waste time doing that either. It won't get you anywhere. No one is suggesting that money doesn't matter and that more wouldn't be nice for pretty much every family out there. But refer to **Chapter 5** for a discussion on gratitude before comparing yourself with other families in terms of money.

Your child will learn to appreciate finances based on your modeling. If you are driven by money, then your child will likely be as well. Be careful about how you talk about it and the importance you place on it. Are you talking about money a lot? If so, your child will pick up on its importance to you. Do you hear your child talking about money or how much friends have? Bring the conversation back to values, and take the opportunity to make it a teachable moment.

Many people equate money with success and happiness. Of course, we know money can't buy us love, as the Beatles sing true, but then it does seem to make life easier. There will always be someone richer than you, so learn to enjoy what you have. If more is what you want, then likely you'll never be satisfied, because you can always want more. Talk with your children about need versus want. Talk about how money offers different perspective in life. My family had its own personal mortgage crisis in 2008 along with the rest of America. In the end, after lots of havoc and maneuvering, it was a great way to gain perspective. We were (and I know this is Pollyannaish) rich with love, with experience, with friends, and with fun. It helped us with the conversation around money because our kids heard much of what was going on around them. They too grew appreciative of what they had. We made cutbacks that they could feel, so we asked them to help us with some of the decision making around those.

Family discussions about economic competition are prime opportunities to discuss charity. When you have achieved a comfort level in your home that you can sustain, you can consider giving money to organizations or charities that you want to support. Allow your child to be part of the decision. Perhaps you can offer a small allowance for your child to donate. Remember that charity begins at home, so supporting a local library, pet rescue, or school can be quite meaningful to your child.

# Character in Action

### Zero through Five Years Old: Soccer Slight

Your five-year-old daughter has played soccer on a rec team for one year. You hear on the sidelines that next year, several of the teammates are going to move to a travel team, but no one asked if your daughter was interested. What do you do? This is not a statement about your daughter's worth as a human being. It's likely not even a statement about her ability to play soccer. This is symptomatic of parents who are über competitive and are pushing for a different experience for their children or of kids who are really driven and have asked to be a part of something more challenging. If your child was really raring for this experience, you would likely have pursued these tryouts. That said, if you talk to your daughter and she wants to try follow suit, you can call around and probably get her a few tryouts. (Nothing is set in stone, ever.) If your daughter is not interested after you discuss the option, or if you cannot afford it, or if you simply cannot make more practices work with your schedule, then find a rec team she can join—or consider taking a break from soccer.

### Six through Twelve Years Old: Testing Trauma

Your eleven-year-old son took a standardized test at school, and when you see the score, it suggests he is not competitive academically with your community. He's in the thirtieth percentile in verbal skills, twenty-fifth percentile in

## Charitable Giving

There's no time like the present to begin a charity practice at home. Begin to put aside money with your child and choose a place to donate it. No matter the amount, it's most important to see how the money is used. If and when possible, give of your time as well. This will demonstrate your true understanding of charity.

**Perspiration**

reading, and thirty-fifth percentile in math. Your friend calls you when the test scores sent home to parents reveal her son is a genius. What do you do? Ask yourself why she is calling you. Is she excited and trying to share something with a friend? Is she trying to get information from you? Is she gloating? If she is a true friend and is sincerely excited, celebrate with her. Now you can choose to share your concerns about your child or not. If she really is a true friend, then go ahead and share your concerns and ask her opinion. (Refer to **Chapter 21** to read about how to trust in your village.)

If you are not ready to share, keep the conversation short, don't say anything snide, and excuse yourself. Then think about the importance of these scores. Do they reflect what you and teachers have seen in your son? If so, does he need added academic support? Is he a strong "C" student and excelling socially?

Remember, you're the parent, and you lay down the expectations. But don't simply demand your son be an "A" student. If he has the potential and is truly not working hard enough, push a little. If he's happy and doing well enough, let him do well enough and support him in his development as a good person.

## Thirteen through Eighteen Years Old: College Crisis

Your eighteen-year-old daughter is a senior in high school, and her two close friends have received acceptances to their first- and second-choice colleges. She got in to your local college and confides she is disappointed she will not have the chance to leave home and doesn't have the choice to make. She comments that she's simply not as smart or impressive as her friends.

There are probably a few truths to this story: One, it's a numbers game, and not everyone gets in where they want to go even if they fill out one hundred applications to their top one hundred schools. Two, maybe her application wasn't as good as her friends' in terms of academics, extracurriculars, or essays. Three, did she apply to reachable schools? These are all things you've hopefully explored before the process, but even afterward, it's not too late.

You and she may be surprised by the new and exciting experience she can still have at a local college. If you can afford it or acquire funding, perhaps she can still live on campus. Maybe she can plan to spend a year there and reapply to other schools when she has a better idea of what she wants to study. She can always transfer. The important thing to stress is that she isn't "not as good" just because she didn't get what her friends got. Everyone's got to face the challenges of life, and right now, this is hers. The more she compares herself with others, the more beaten she will feel. This is a grand opportunity to seize the moment and make the best of it.

# To Summarize...

- Play sports for the love of it and not the scholarship.

- Grades are just one way to rank.

- Status matters only in how it matters to you.

- Economics are a fact of life—so accept yours and live!

# Chapter 23

## Relating: Your Relationship with Your Child

### In This Chapter...

- Making time and making the most of the time together
- Setting limits
- The importance of listening
- Understanding your own limits

Relationships change as kids grow, and it's important for children to know how to forge and maintain them. In this chapter, read about how your relationship with your child will change and how to preserve it as well as how to support your child's emerging relationships through the ages.

"I think Mary's not my friend anymore." "I don't like it when kids tease me." "I wonder what it's like to kiss a girl." "I'm afraid I'm failing chemistry." These are things you might hear your child utter when all else is calm and you take a moment to be together. Often as kids wind down, they decompress and share more than they were willing or able to right after school or amidst a busy family meal. My husband and I try to make time in the evening to listen in case our children open up on the events of the day.

Our kids can manipulate us at bedtime, a routine we've finessed to perfection. We used to bathe them, read to them, and put them to bed. It couldn't have been easier. So why do we now allow them to stall at bedtime? Because I know that some day we won't have cuddle sessions any longer. Sometimes my husband and I will work late, after bedtime stories have been read. The kids will then pop in and ask, "Can I have a snuggle?" My husband and I would often sigh or reluctantly go snuggle with our children in bed. It occurred to us as our children grew older that we had to remind them about bedtime stories and hugs. So, yes, they may be stalling at bedtime, and we may be tired and ready for Mommy and Daddy time, but they also won't be inviting us into their beds to cuddle forever. Seize the moment.

Your relationship with your child changes as the years go by. As infants and young babies, children are completely dependent on their parents. The sweet cooing that is their language represents how they feel for you. The crying is a loss of your attention or immediate need such as food or sleep.

As they move through toddlerhood, they declare independence but still need you significantly. Declarations of "Hungry!" or "I do it myself!" imply they have choice over what they want or need, but you still need to help them achieve it in most situations. Essentially, they can walk, talk, and manipulate you.

During the elementary years, children may enter a blissful stage during which they will share openly with their parents. You might hear "Mommy, I feel so excited when you come home" or even "None of the kids want to play with me at recess." The emotions are there and gone, and children in this age group are excited to share and curious about what you think. They are still very focused on themselves, and you are their main representative.

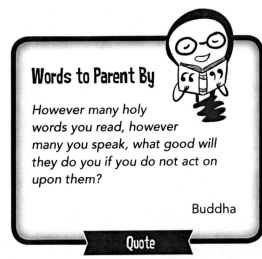

## Words to Parent By

*However many holy words you read, however many you speak, what good will they do you if you do not act on upon them?*

Buddha

**Quote**

Up until the tween years, many children aim to please their parents and share the family's values. As they become prepubescent and eventually go through puberty, they explore an entirely different form of independence— one that can fall anywhere on the spectrum from gentle separation to flat-out rebellion! This change can seem magical one day and impossible the next. This is when peers begin to have a bigger influence on your child's thoughts, convictions, and opinions. Young teens want to please their peers and fit in (or at least not stand out too much). You might hear a mix of comments like "No way!" and "You just don't understand!" You will get fewer glimpses into the goings-on at recess or the friendships forming and disintegrating.

Once children enter their teens, they are in various phases of developing new and more selfless versions of themselves. They are often rediscovering their independent toddler selves, still wanting to fit in but also wanting to express their own identities. You might hear more about inner thoughts or happenings at school, such as "I'm really scared I won't get into college," "I thought she liked me, but I guess she was using me," or "I can't believe so many kids are cheating." Teens find themselves hoping to please their parents once again—though they seldom admit it. Through all the stages, your relationship with your child should be as open and honest as possible.

## Family Dinner—Yes, It Makes a Difference

Research shows that sitting down for a family meal twenty minutes a day, five days a week can make a huge difference in your child's life. The time spent together at regular family meals acts as a protective factor for children and as a safety net in times of future hardship. It makes perfect sense that a child who feels loved, valued, heard, and enjoyed would be more stable and confident. Family meals offer you time to share your own convictions and expectations and to explore options with your child. And if that's not enough to convince you that, on average, children who partake in regular meals with family see higher achievement and fewer behavior problems than their peers who do not. It's not as hard as it may seem, but it does take effort and consistency.

The earlier you can start this routine, the easier it will be to keep it in your schedule. That said, it's never too late. Don't be afraid to simply carve out the time and make it very clear to the entire family how important it is. This is family time, and it's to be observed. If your child has a late baseball practice, then consider changing mealtime to earlier or later. This can be tricky, but it's well worth it. When my oldest had Hebrew school until six thirty across town, the younger two and I had a large, healthy snack and played board games until he got home. The board games became a part of our Wednesday ritual. I know it sounds serene and lovely—two kids and a mom cozied up in the living room playing Sorry! into the dark hours and sipping cocoa. It wasn't always as idealistic as that—there was still homework to be done and dishes to be cleaned—but the memories are. By the time my husband arrived with our oldest, we were able help them transition to home time, tend to any emotional middle school dramas, and sit down to share a meal together.

Go easy on yourself and be okay with what it takes to make this dinner happen. If you don't have the time, energy, or know-how to cook a family meal, then by all means order out, let someone help you, or eat frozen dinners. Of course, it's important to keep your and your child's diet healthy, but don't worry if not every meal is 100 percent organic and made from scratch. There are healthy options—and, yes, it's great to aim for them—but the time with your family and teaching healthy eating habits is more important than the ingredients.

### Dinner Duo

Friends of ours do a dinner swap with another family. Our friends cook dinner for eight people instead of their family of four. They give four of the servings to another family of four. They do this two times a week and then receive dinner from the other family two nights a week. This reduces the preparation time and effort of dinner and allows for a home-cooked meal four nights a week.

**Pure Genius!**

Though I mention the importance of dinner, note that you can adapt the importance of family meals to your own situation and schedule. While dinner is a nice option, there are breakfast and lunch too. Weekends also count—if your weeknights are nuts. Look for a good time that works. Maybe you are morning people and pancakes and bacon are just your thing (with fresh fruit and a vegetable scramble, of course). Sunday brunch is a popular time for families to gather as well.

You might be surprised by the conversation that takes place at a family meal. When my oldest began middle school, he was quite anxious about remembering his locker code. I remember sarcastically suggesting he carry all his books around with him, when my daughter chimed in that he should have an extra copy of the code in his pencil case and maybe keep one in his pocket. What a simple and perfect solution—which he accepted. A family meal is also a great time to start a practice of sharing news and gratitude with one another. I will often share struggles I am having and am always pleased by the suggestions my children have on how I can troubleshoot. (Read more about gratitude in **Chapter 5**.)

# Discipline

Discipline sounds so negative, but in fact, it can include positive reinforcement and routines that can help set you up for smooth(er) sailing. Kids of all ages feel better when there is structure in place. They may not always demonstrate their appreciation for rules and the like, but they do need and want it. And guess what? So do you. When they're babies it's important that kids have a nap, eating, and bedtime routine. As they grow, it's just as important that they continue to have routines. It's not to say you can't change your schedule at the last minute (because, honestly, who could live that way?), but once a routine is established, a child has a better sense of the world and how to maneuver within it.

In addition to routines, children need limits for behavior. When they test those limits, it's your job to let them know. If you opt to be your child's friend, or the good cop, your child will develop tendencies to push you farther. You could be damaging the relationships between you and your child, you and your partner if you have one, and your child and your partner. It's important when parenting with a partner that you back one another up. It doesn't mean you always have to agree, but when it comes to discipline, it's important to honor your partner's place

## The Punishment Should Fit the Crime

Logical consequences are always best when possible. For example, if your child cannot sit nicely in a restaurant, leave. Be sure to let your child know why you are leaving and repeat yourself a few times. Before you go out again, remind your child of what happened last time and ask if your child is ready to go back.

**Inspiration**

## Take a Breath

When you do feel frustrated, consider taking a deep breath or counting to ten. While it may sound cliché, these simple actions do work. And if they're not right for you, find what is right that takes you away from the situation and helps you clear your head. No one has the right response to every situation every time it comes up. But if you know yourself well, you can often prevent yourself from responding when you're not ready. Be comfortable letting your child know that you need a parent time-out to reflect before reacting. You will be offering your child two powerful gifts. First, you are taking time to think through your response carefully. Second, you are modeling a healthy process for removing yourself from the fray.

**Perspiration**

and save discussions and questioning for a private conversation.

My husband and son used to lock heads over things that didn't seem worth it to me. (Bedtime would come, my son would stall, and my husband would get more frustrated than I thought was necessary.) When this would happen, I would sternly suggest to my son that he try to read the cues from his father and ask him if he could think of why his father seemed frustrated. My son needed this coaching because he was naturally pushing limits and not realizing that it was going farther than a fun joke. I noticed this as a pattern after a while and decided to talk to my husband about it. I suggested that, yes, it is annoying when kids don't follow the bedtime routine perfectly and that, yes, I could see it was irritating him and that he was annoyed with our son's behavior. All that said, I suggested to my husband that perhaps it wasn't really worth getting upset over. First of all, it was a predictable mess, so one option was to let me handle bedtime for a few nights in a row. Second, we talked about the possibility of my husband being a little more flexible in the moment. I was worried that this would come off as critical and annoying to my husband, which is likely why I let it go on longer than necessary. On the contrary, he was so grateful that I had pointed out the simplicity of it and that he didn't have to be frustrated at what should be a fun and sweet time with our children.

In the end, nothing works quite as well as "sorry." For you *and* your child. If you misbehave and lose your cool, be sure to acknowledge it and apologize. You don't have to be sorry for being angry, and you can even be clear about why you did misbehave: "I was so angry at what you did, and I didn't react well. I'm sorry." It's important to teach your child to apologize to anyone your child has wronged—and that includes you. My mother-in-law taught me something very important about saying you're sorry when I was visiting with my oldest, who was a toddler at the time. When your child apologizes, it's really not enough to say, "Sorry." It's more important to understand what you're sorry for. See more about forgiveness in **Chapter 4**. What does that do for the situation? I ask my own children, "What are you sorry for?" Once they have answered, I ask them, "How will you show me you're sorry?" They often respond that they'll "never _____ (fill in the blank) again." It's important for them to know that mistakes and bad judgment happen and that they may, in fact, do _____ again. In this case, I remind them that they should definitely aim for that, but the important thing is that they learn from the mistake.

## Talking and Listening with Your Child

My husband and I were in the Ballroom Dance Club in college. An instructor once taught me never to do a trick (turn, dip, etc.) more than three times in a row because the audience would get bored. If you ever find yourself repeating something to your child regularly and your child still doesn't appear to listen, chances are your tactics aren't working. Take the time to sit down and truly talk with your child about the issue at hand. Have you ever found yourself rushing your children and uttering, "Hurry up," "Let's go," or "Time to go"? If you find yourself repeating these phrases with your child still idling by the closet looking for a jacket, then your words are not really helping. Have a conversation—when you have the time—about the need to get

### Demonstrate You Are Listening When Your Child Is Talking

- Put down the phone, mail, food, whatever it is that you're paying attention to.

- Physically turn your body toward your child.

- Make eye contact.

- Try your best not to interrupt.

- Hear in addition to listening.

- Respond thoughtfully and when you really have something to say.

Perspiration

# Relating Looks Different at Different Stages of Life

## Zero through Five Years Old

Relationships for very young children are primarily with parents, caregivers, and other adults and children in the immediate family or community. Parents can support relating at this stage by talking and listening. Be patient and don't dismiss your child's ideas. Your young child may demonstrate a special connection with another peer, but don't expect a BFF bond to develop at this stage.

## Six through Twelve Years Old

As elementary-aged children move through the grades, they learn to navigate all kinds of relationships. Parents can encourage relating at this stage by continuing to keep the lines of communication open and asking for opinions. At this stage, relationships include those with classmates or teammates, friends inside and outside of school, teachers, counselors, and coaches.

## Thirteen through Eighteen Years Old

Adolescents are generally able to maintain relationships and forge new ones with a variety of people in different roles. It's key to continue to communicate with your teen and protect your relationship, even if it means sacrificing here and there. For example, you may lose an argument with your teen, but think of it as your child legitimately winning it. At this age, relationships outside the family are likely to become more intimate. Teen relationships to nurture include friends, teachers, advisors, coaches, and girlfriends and boyfriends.

going, and find out what will help get your kids moving faster or whether they simply need more time to get ready.

And then, when your child is talking, listen! It's so easy to get caught up in our own emotions or goals, but it's even more important in those times to listen to your child. Ask specific questions (not the rhetorical "What were you thinking?") and provide space to generate an answer. There may be a perfectly good reason why your five-year-old is leaving wet towels on the carpet after a bath and, as hard as it may be to understand, why your seventeen-year-old is staying out after curfew. Even if the reason isn't good enough for you to change the rule, it's important to listen so you can help your child understand how to change the behavior. Be clear. It's not a democracy; you're in charge. But be a benevolent dictator.

That means you should make every attempt to listen to your child, even if the timing isn't convenient. Stop whatever is preventing you from engaging. The child who feels heard will talk more. You will learn so much from your conversation with your child, and when you listen, you will open up your relationship for future conversations. Talk as much as your child will listen, but then listen again. Be patient when the discussion gets heated or troubling to you. Remember that your child will be more likely to come to you again if you can be trusted, if you can be helpful, and if you show you care more about your child than you do about the situation and possible outcomes.

## When You Need More Help

Sometimes you need answers you can't find in books. I talk about the importance of community and creating a village in **Chapter 21**, and that's a great place to start. Talk with friends, other parents you know, and your own family members about your relationship with your child. Don't go talking to everyone when you have a problem with your kid, but find someone you can go to. If it feels like more than you can handle and the advice you're getting isn't working, don't give up.

It's important to understand when you need professional advice, and a great place to start is with your child's pediatrician. It's important for you to be honest with yourself and with the doctor. If you aren't comfortable opening up, it's time to find a doctor you can do that with—possibly your own physician.

# Character in Action

### Zero through Five Years Old: Who's Fit Is It Anyway?

You took off work early to be there with your child and even remembered a snack. Yet your two-year-old son is having his third fit of the day, and it's all because you packed regular Cheerios instead of Honey Nut Cheerios. He threw the cup on the floor and pitched a fit in the middle of the playground. It's all you can do not to yell back something unfit for the park.

Take a deep breath and wait a moment before reacting. Try to block out the external factors. (Okay, so maybe people are watching and judging, but no matter what you do, you cannot help that.) Focus on what needs to be done. Try to reason with your child, which likely won't be easy if he's truly pitching a fit. Stay calm, physically remove him from the park, and take him home (or to your next destination). If it's nap time or mealtime, offer that. If not, it's okay to give him a little space. Perhaps you both need a time-out to gather your nerves. Make sure he's safe; it's okay to just let him cry or scream while you figure things out. Be sure to keep him safe, and let him know that you understand he's upset and that you love him. He needs to know this, and he also needs to know that you cannot be with him when he is like this.

Sometimes, in great frustration, it is nearly impossible to reason, and you need to wait it out. You may not have a lot of choices. Maybe you are stuck in traffic or cannot go home at the moment. Do your best to give your son room to let him have his fit or to get him something to comfort him. And if you have the time and physical space, allow yourself to regroup.

### Six through Twelve Years Old: Finger Graffiti

Your eight-year-old is finger painting in the kitchen, and you've asked her to wash her hands. She runs to the door when the mailman rings, puts her dirty hands on the doorknob, and stains it as well as the wall she is leaning on. Your first instinct? Never mind that. Just take a deep breath, and approach the situation as calmly as you can. She knew to wash her hands, and even if she didn't process that well, she should be more aware of her surroundings, your requests, and how she treats her belongings and others' belongings (your home included). She's old enough now to know not to act so impulsively and to take care of your home. First thing, talk with her about what she did and why it bothers you. Have her own up to it. She may say she was helping by answering the door, or she may just lose interest. It's important she understands that her body is her responsibility and what she did was disrespectful. Continue to remind her of this, and use it as an example as you see other simple opportunities to accept responsibility (hopefully in a positive light). She can start by helping you clean the paint. If it doesn't clean off, you can remind her as you point out the stain. Only once is necessary. She'll see it and remember on her own. Let her talk about it, and you can even model or talk about ways you've learned responsibility like this.

### Thirteen through Eighteen Years Old: Drunken Disorder

Your seventeen-year-old son comes home drunk. He's been out past his curfew and is not what you would consider apologetic or appropriately embarrassed. The best thing to do in the immediate situation is to help him to bed comfortably. Save the lecturing and finger pointing for the next day. You want your son to feel comfortable with you, and while you hope he feels some shame from his digression, you also want him to know that you recognize he's human.

# To Summarize...

- Truly connect with your child when you are together.

- Don't be afraid to be the parent and set limits.

- Listen to your child!

- Step back when you are not able to keep your cool.

# Chapter 24

## Socializing: The Good, the Bad, and the Ugly

**In This Chapter...**

- Fostering healthy relationships
- The art of dealing with others
- Preparing for intimacy
- Why can't we all just get along? And what do we do about it when we can't?

Learning how to support your child in social development (including learning when to back off!) can help you feel more at ease as you watch your child go through the normal ups and downs of growing up. The way children experience friendships, solve conflicts, expand their social circles, and explore new horizons changes as they get older. This chapter will help parents understand what is typical or developmentally appropriate for children when it comes to their social lives and suggest strategies to cultivate socialization for your child in different arenas.

The social lives of our children are perhaps the scariest and best part of our parenting. Parents often worry about what their children are doing or not doing and the influence of someone else's kids on those decisions. How can we expect our kids to resist peer pressure when adults have trouble doing so? Be aware of your child's social life and be a part of it, but don't let it rule your parenting.

Parents consistently tell me what they want most for their children is to experience good relationships. Interpersonal skills are crucial to developing those bonds. Kids learn from a very young age to read the cues that others are giving off. If someone is making eye contact or nodding, they are likely interested. If someone is avoiding eye contact or physically moving away, perhaps the conversation is not so interesting. These cues can be obvious (he hit me; he doesn't like what I'm doing) or nuanced (he's avoiding answering my questions; perhaps he's uncomfortable). The dramatic increase in digital socializing means that kids are less knowledgeable about relationships. You want your child to be able to relate to others, including you. (Read **Chapter 23** for more on relating.)

# Relationships 101

The first relationship your child will have is with you. This relationship will be a model through your child's lifetime. It will be the foundation for all other social interactions. Your child will develop connections (friendly, professional, and intimate) based on the experience of your relationship—so no pressure!

Toddlers are learning to interact with other kids and adults in the world. They want to please you, generally speaking, but they also are learning to live in the world with other people. They will literally test the limits, via pushing kids, biting, grabbing, and they will learn what is appropriate from your feedback and that of other kids and adults. Positive reinforcement (your praise, a special treat, etc.) will help your toddler understand what is appropriate in social settings.

Playdates are a fantastic opportunity for kids to figure out how to be with other kids and adults. Meet up at the park with other kids. If time is tight for you, try swapping out with another parent so you're with the kids only every other time. If you have a babysitter or your child is in a share-care situation, try working out playdates that work with that schedule. However you do it, be sure your child is getting out and about. This doesn't mean you have to go crazy scheduling a playdate every day or at every different park. Make sure that if your child is not already engaged in a regular social setting (classes, school, play groups), you are intentional about setting up playdates.

School offers kids a chance to socialize in a variety of ways. In the younger grades, socializing is a major component of the curriculum. Children in these grades are learning to share, cooperate, and be contributing members of their communities. As they get into the older grades, students learn collaboration and competition. These are social skills they will carry with them throughout their lives. Be sure to continue to set up playdates (or offer opportunities to "hang out," as the term "playdate" definitely ages out).

Tweens and adolescents will want to please you—but less than they want to please their friends. Keep in mind that you may have to take the lead in your relationship with your tween or adolescent. It's worth the investment! Show that you are available when your tween needs you. And your tween may not always reach out, so you will have to do a good amount of reaching. Whenever you have a chance, take a moment to check in. Don't be nosy; be interested. Use open-ended questions, and share from your own life to get the conversation rolling. And when your tween talks, listen.

## Making Friends for Your Child and Yourself

I met another mother in our neighborhood who had a similar schedule to mine, so we met weekly to get our two boys together. It provided us an opportunity to talk about what was going on with ourselves and to share notes about our own parenting experiences. The boys had a chance to be together and learn about sharing when we were at each other's houses, and they were able to have a friend to run around with when we were at the park.

**Pure Genius!**

**Good Conversation Starters with Tweens and Teens**

- 💡 How are things going?
- 💡 What's new?
- 💡 Is there anything going on?
- 💡 Can I share my day with you?
- 💡 I could really use some company right now.

**Perspiration**

Find moments to talk with your adolescent. It's not so easy, and the judgments might come hard. Remember, teens are often more interested in impressing their peers and fitting in than pleasing you (though that is still important to them). Driving is a nice time to connect because you don't have to make eye contact and your child can play with the radio, a favorite pastime for tweens. Try watching a television show or listening to music together. If you show interest in your adolescent's interests, you are more likely to find time together.

Socializing doesn't come easy for all kids. Of course, all kids have their ups and downs, but there are some who do not read social cues easily or at all. If your child is not displaying what you would consider normal empathy or reactions, consider asking your pediatrician or a trusted teacher for recommendations to help practice with social skills. Sometimes it's as easy as some at-home role playing, and sometimes it takes a little more effort. There are a variety of social therapies, including play groups and improv activities. It's better to identify socialization issues early on and deal with them so that you offer your child a better appreciation and enjoyment of relationships.

## Cooperation

My six-year-old son was teaching my nephew to play Parcheesi one day. Parcheesi is a simple game, but it has many rules and takes a great deal of perseverance and patience to get through a full game. My son was not yet expert at teaching, but he sure enjoyed the authority of it. I stumbled upon them midgame, debating whether or not it was part of the rules to advance ten bonus spaces after getting a pawn home. I almost stepped in to protect my nephew, assuming he would be upset being at a disadvantage by not knowing the rules and because my son was advancing ten extra spaces. Before I did, I found myself fascinated by their ability to talk through the disagreement and refer to what Vygotsky (one of the founding fathers of current-day child development and psychology) would call the more knowledgeable other. The idea behind a more knowledgeable other is that one child can learn from another who has the required knowledge base. In this case, my son knew Parcheesi particularly well. This is a natural way to learn. Believe it or not, these two six-year-olds finished that game completely on their own.

There is a sweet spot in childhood between the ages of five and ten where kids can literally be kids. They are old enough to know how to act in most situations. They can be friends, and they are usually nondiscriminating. It's not impossible to see cliques forming at this age, but generally speaking, kids in this age group are inclusive and all about the play.

During this time period, kids will, for the most part, play with other kids without major judgment. They will enjoy each other's creativity during imaginary play, their ability to leap far and gracefully, and their bravery to jump off a high structure. Kids might exclude others but are generally amenable to inclusion with a quick reminder. It's important to talk through inclusion and exclusion with your child during this stage. The more exposure and conversation you offer, the better your child will fare on this front. I once was watching a few kids at the park and saw one hanging out watching my kids play tag with their cousins. I motioned one of my kids over and suggested they include this observer. They were quick to ask the other child to play, likely because they had internalized inclusion as a core value.

Of course, it is inevitable that your child will eventually be excluded or hurt. You can either spend your life trying to avoid

## Make a Date

There are things you can do to encourage social interactions for your child. See which friend your child wants to invite over. You can also talk to your child's teacher, caregiver, or day care provider to find out if there is another potential friend who might be a good match. Set up neighborhood playdates. Reach out to some of your friends with kids and have their families over so you can all enjoy yourselves.

**Inspiration**

it or embrace each challenge as a learning moment to help your child move forward in the midst of pain. Our first instinct is to shelter and protect our kids from hurt and discomfort, but we need to let them experience the pain of life so they can develop resilience and coping mechanisms. It's the bad days that make the great days great! And with pain, your child will learn empathy and begin to understand how words and actions can hurt others. A teenage girl can easily fall into the trap of excluding others with the lure of popularity and feeling like part of the "in" crowd. But upon experiencing exclusion, she will likely learn how hurtful it can be and hopefully, with the right parenting, use that experience to be more cognizant of others' feelings in the future.

In the event your child is struggling with social interactions (and don't just jump to this conclusion), there are social skills groups that help young people with socializing, such as practice with eye contact, social cues, conversation, and friendly competition. Remember that conflict and exclusion are normal aspects of social development. Don't rush your child off to one of these groups just because your child is not exactly like you in the social arena. These groups are for kids who have been recognized as having specific issues in social settings, possibly identified by doctors or teachers. Don't go looking for issues, but know that if your child needs help, help is out there.

## Supporting Your Child's Emerging Identity

Middle school is where many kids begin to develop feelings of self-consciousness and a need to belong. Until now, socializing has mostly consisted of some sort of play or structured time with others. But now the stakes are higher. Now there are issues of fitting in (or, worse, not fitting in), looking okay, dressing right, saying the right phrases, not drawing too much attention to oneself, sitting at the right table, hanging with the right crowd—and the list goes on. You can imagine it's a challenge to keep all that in mind while also doing schoolwork, going to after-school activities, and dealing with your parents and siblings. Think about what it takes for you to take off your "work" hat and put on your "parent" hat during the afternoon or evening transition. Your child has to do the same but has fewer choices in the matter and feels a pressure to conform socially among peers—and also within your household with parents and/or siblings. Focus on transitions, especially after school, and think about how you can make this a more comfortable time for your middle schooler.

Middle-school kids need space to develop. Space does not mean neglect. They are desperate for attention and need it. They will appear not to hear much of what you say, but actually they do (and sometimes in a more amplified voice than you'd like). That's why it's really important to be accepting and nonjudgmental. It's also important to be aware of what you are messaging. Our son used to roll out of bed and into his clothes. When he entered middle school, I mentioned that running a brush through his hair might be a good idea. I didn't require it, but I did say that it's important to realize that peers and teachers can't help but notice appearance. He seemingly ignored me, but sure enough, I noticed that brushing his hair became part of his morning routine. While I don't suggest making your tween super anxious about appearance, it's fine to note it's part of self-care, and in my son's case, he wasn't aware enough. For others, you might want that messaging to include toning down the focus on appearance.

Be aware that in early and full-on adolescence, peer pressure is strong. Kids are taking their cues from other kids and pop culture. Pick your fights. It's not necessarily worth it to fight over clothes. Is the belly button covered? Is there any cleavage or underwear showing? If not, and you just don't like the style, let it go. Is the music not your taste? Is your son hanging out with friends more than doing his homework? Is your daughter on the computer instant messaging more than reading independently like she used to? Have standards, but don't be a dictator. Understand that your child is trying to fit in *and* form an identity. Not all peer pressure is bad. For the most part, you can trust

## Transition Time

Transition from school to home can be a volatile time for a tween. Think of ways to ease the pressure. Consider the following:

- Let your child choose what time is a good time to get started on homework.

- Include your child in as many choices as you can about the schedule (including which, if any, extracurriculars to participate in and chores around the house).

- Ask open-ended questions about the day in general to allow for a conversation your child can steer.

- Allow your child to walk or bike home (if safe) or to have some time at home alone or with friends.

Inspiration

your child to make good choices in friends. We all want to feel accepted and hang out with people who make us feel good. Friends often help kids focus on schoolwork, talk through social problems, and try new challenges, like student council. The best thing you can do is know your child's friends as well as you can and continue to message your standards.

# Intimacy

The first intimate relationship your child will have is with you, other family members, and family friends. Intimacy implies a constant trust and true caring of one another. By elementary school, most kids are capable of enjoying intimate relationships with other friends. They trust one another, share secrets and adventures, and enjoy one another's company. You might see children as young as six forming intimate relationships. Often young children, through adolescence (and even sometimes adulthood), refer to these intimate friends as best friends.

There is a pressure to have a best friend. You might hear adults initiate conversations with kids with a question like "Who's your best friend?" Kids on the playground declaring their best friendship might insinuate that this is a requirement of childhood. It's not. But intimate relationships are important. While your child may not have one best friend, the hope is your child will experience close friendships.

By late elementary and middle school, kids tend to become part of groups, or cliques. Again, this is not a requirement for a healthy childhood, but it is likely that your child will identify with a group of kids. Keep in mind that the groupings can change and your child may feel a part of multiple groups. This is actually a very good sign. You'll want your child to try on different identifiers. Your child might relate better to one group during recess and another for academics. Athletes tend to congregate together. If your child doesn't necessarily have a best friend, sports might create a likely grouping. But make sure your child identifies with other kids in some way. If you're not sure, talk with your child, and don't be afraid to ask your child's teacher or counselor for some perspective.

Many children are not experiencing the intimacy of past generations because they are overscheduled and living in a digital world. That carries over into the dating years. Instead, they are swapping out true relationships for hooking up quickly. Again, your messaging and modeling are key here. It's good to encourage intimate relationships. Are you in a healthy relationship? Your child will likely mimic what is going on in your own home. Have high expectations for yourself and your child.

If your adolescent seems very much attached to a girlfriend or boyfriend, it's okay. Adolescence is the time to experiment with many things, including sexuality and intimacy. They are not the same thing. Don't assume your child is having sex, but certainly be prepared for the possibility. You should share your beliefs and values with your child. Some parents choose abstinence as the approach to sexuality in adolescence. If this is your belief, you can refer to your family doctor for resources and seek support for yourself and your child at a community clinic or center or at your place of worship if you have one.

That said, if your child decides to become sexually active (or feels pressured to), it's better that you have set some ground rules, provided information, and—most importantly—are there for questions and support. You may not approve of adolescents having sex, but it does happen. The best way to be prepared is to talk through your concerns, your beliefs, and your hopes. Keep an open mind and make sure your child knows that you will do your best not to judge and that you are there for support. If you are nervous about this, make sure you lean on your village. Let your child know a few adults to go to. Talk, talk, talk. Your child will hear it. And listen! Read **Chapter 18** for more on health and sexuality.

If you sense your child is not in a healthy romantic relationship, definitely step in. Check in with your child often. If the

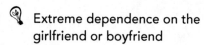

## Signs of an Unhealthy Romantic Relationship

- Extreme dependence on the girlfriend or boyfriend

- A stronger clinging to the nuclear family than usual

- Consistently secretive behaviors (hiding physical parts of the body, not disclosing activities, or lack of communication generally)

- A significant change in behavior (more or less talkative, different style of dress, or staying out more or less)

**WATCH OUT!**

problems seem out of your league, don't be afraid to ask for help. Reach out to your village, your pediatrician, and your own physician. Ask for referrals. It might be difficult to detect trouble in this area, but trust your gut. Better safe than sorry! It's crucial to set high standards for intimate relationships because this is the foundation your child will have for all future romance.

## When Kids Don't Get Along

Your child may be the last one to be picked for a team in PE, may find there are no seats left at the lunch table near friends, may be teased for a poor grade, may be teased for a good grade, or may find all of these to be true. We've all been in this position in some way or another. Even the "popular kids" feel excluded or put upon. In fact, popular kids have a struggle all their own—to stay on top. Your child will likely find a group of friends—and hopefully more than one group. And your child will inevitably find conflict. If not, conflict will find your child. There is no getting along with everyone all the time. So prepare your child and yourself for those tough moments.

Young people are teased, ignored, included, revered, and humiliated. The most important thing you can do for your child's social esteem is to make it clear that your love is unconditional and that you are there no matter what. It's not easy to see your child experience any social discomfort, but remember that from most discomfort will come a lesson and often a deeper understanding of relationships.

When your child is being excluded or teased, resist the urge to dive in. It's almost an instant reaction to internalize the situation and get defensive. You might even say something along the lines of "Well sweetheart, what I would do is..." or "Did you tell a teacher?" The best kinds of responses to a socially hurting child are open-ended questions.

Steer the focus away from rejection, and don't make it a blame game (not to begin with anyhow). Focus on dealing with the current feelings, then talk about what happened—if your child is willing to open up. It's also okay to wait before delving into the issue. And if, after time, your child appears to simply move on, that's okay. Everyone's entitled to a bad day.

If, however, your child appears to be experiencing exclusion or teasing on a regular basis, don't ignore it. Encourage your child to talk to you. If that's not happening, seek out the school counselor or a trusted teacher. Make sure the situation is typical and that your child is not being targeted.

In most instances of exclusion and teasing, the behavior is normal and expected. The word "bully" is overused and misused. For example, I worked with a boy who had a difficult personality. He was in middle school and still displaying many typical social behaviors of an elementary-aged kid. He was playful and fun, and I enjoyed him as a student. He was creative academically but simply not mature enough to handle himself on the playground. Kids picked on him and, for the most part, ignored him because he was, simply put, annoying to them. His parents were concerned he was being bullied, and it was hard for them to see that he needed to work on his own behaviors, as he really was the biggest obstacle between himself and acceptance by the crowd.

This circumstance definitely needed attention and some intervention, but it wasn't bullying. No one was hunting him down. Other kids simply didn't want to be with him, and he needed to do his part in learning the middle school social scene. Luckily, there are a lot of supports out there to help kids in the social arena. This boy worked with an expert outside of school who collaborated with his teachers and counselor.

Sometimes your child is the one causing the pain in someone else. We never want to hear this, but it happens, and it is often more difficult to deal with than when our own child is hurt. In the more extreme situations, and when the other child's parent is involved, it's crucial to make sure you get as much information as you can. Talk with the school representatives involved, including teachers and anyone who might have witnessed the behavior or was involved in the disciplinary actions.

## Talking about Exclusion

Consider using the following to prompt your conversation along:

- 💡 Do you want to talk about it?

- 💡 Do you want some time alone?

- 💡 Is there something I can do to make you feel better?

- 💡 What do you want to do about it?

- 💡 If you could change the way you reacted, what would you do differently next time?

Perspiration

# Socializing Looks Different at Different Stages of Life

## Zero through Five Years Old

Socialization in the early years is about exposing your child to the larger world and defining family and friends. Social interactions are generally supervised and arranged by an adult and include adult intervention. You can nurture socialization with play groups, by speaking directly to your child (no baby talk), and by including young children in the day-to-day experiences of the family. Socializing for very young children can include parallel play with little to no interaction, learning to share, or taking turns.

## Six through Twelve Years Old

Socialization at this stage is as much about self-defining as it is about relating to other people and groups. Parents can support social experiences by encouraging playdates, asking and listening without judgment, and checking in with teachers for any red flags. Socializing in the elementary years can include participating in organized sports, going to the playground with friends, or engaging in a religious or community activity (for example, Boy or Girl Scouts, religious study, or a social justice group).

## Thirteen through Eighteen Years Old

Socialization in the teen years is much more independent of family intervention and inclusion. Parents can support socializing at this stage by allowing independence, offering an open mind, and providing a safe place for friends and peers to hang out. Socializing for adolescents can include dating or going to a dance with a group of friends, hanging out at the mall, going to a party, watching movies, or listening to music with friends.

Talk with the other child(ren)'s parents as well if you are comfortable. Accept that your child has faults and may be at fault here. But *never ever* lose faith in your child. Avoid labeling your child. And *always* stand by your child through necessary discipline from you and from the school.

# Character in Action

### Zero through Five Years Old: The Best Defense Is a Good Offense

You hear a lot of the parents at the preschool making playdates and see a lot of kids going home with other kids. No one seems to be inviting your child over, and you feel left out and hurt. Remember, this is not about you. There are many possible reasons your child has not been invited. The most probable one is convenience. People are likely setting up playdates with families that are conveniently located or have similar schedules. Oftentimes, parents set up playdates with kids of parents they enjoy and it isn't about the kids' relationships, so get over yourself. Of course, there is a chance your child is struggling socially. Talking with the teacher or your pediatrician can help you realize whether your child is simply happier playing independently or needs a little instruction on how to be social. Don't just wait around for an invitation; go ahead and initiate some playdates.

### Six through Twelve Years Old: The BFF Breakup

Your eleven-year-old daughter comes home from sixth grade and is visibly upset. She doesn't say much during the afternoon or dinner. As you head to bed, you notice she's still up and seems quite beside herself. She divulges that her best friend of the past four years has dumped her. Of course, you'd like ten minutes in the room with the other girl and to give the mom of the ex a good talking to. But we must, especially during these times, be brave and stable. It's important for your daughter to see that all is not lost and that the sun will, in fact, rise tomorrow. Do more listening than talking. Ask her how she feels, what she thinks happened, and what she wants to do about it. Honor her feelings. It's okay to feel down in the dumps. Then, most importantly, support her through her decision. It's fine to ask how she's doing the next day, but let it go and don't harp on it. She will have an easier time moving forward if she sees you doing the same.

### Thirteen through Eighteen Years Old: Hot Date

You're running out the door for a business dinner when your fifteen-year-old daughter casually lets you know she's meeting up with a guy she met last week. You have no idea how she met him and don't know him or his family. What do you do? Take a moment to talk if you can to tease out what's going on. Is this a date or a group hangout? How did they meet, and do they have many friends in common?

Don't jump to conclusions, but make sure she will be in a safe spot emotionally and physically. If things are going well and you feel you can trust her, set up some comfortable parameters: Meet in either a group setting or a public setting, make sure there is an early curfew for this first date, and go over personal safety. Make sure she feels comfortable getting out of a sticky situation and standing up for herself. Don't be afraid to role-play some possible scenes. Make sure she know that she can call you if she needs you for anything and that you won't lose your cool but will help her out.

*If you don't have time for all this?* Let her know you need to go quickly and don't want her to go out without a discussion first. It's not a no; it's a no for tonight. She will undoubtedly be disappointed—and likely angry too. Let her know that she can put all the blame on you when supplying her answer to this boy and that you promise to explore this just as soon as you can. You can even make time after your meeting that night.

## To Summarize...

- ✐ Healthy relationships start with you!

- ✐ It takes all kinds to forge strong relationships.

- ✐ Honor and enjoy your child's identity.

- ✐ Be aware of red flags with particularly difficult relationships.

# Chapter 25

## Raising a Family

Parenting is about raising a family as much as it is about raising an individual child. As you parent your child, you will grow as an individual, as a parent, as a child of your parents, and as a partner to whomever is working beside you in this great adventure. Make this process about the family, not about only you—but you, your successes, your shortcomings, and how they work within the family. Make it about what you are together.

Your family unit is not static. It will change dramatically over the course of raising your child or children. You must remember that you are constantly adapting to the changing needs of your child, your spouse, yourself, and your

### Words to Parent By

*It's not what you leave to your children; it's what you leave in your children.*

Unknown

**Quote**

family as a unit. I've talked about values, and these are for you, your child, and your family. You can base any decision you make around the values in this book. No matter whether you are deciding on feeding routines with your infant, whether you or your wife should take some time to be home with your child, or whether or not your seventeen-year-old is ready for sex, you can count on your own resilience, responsibility, and education. You can also count on the fact that you are raising your child with values. So while your family members' opinions may differ and arguments may ensue, you can always go back to your foundation in these values.

## Raising Your Child

Your experience as a child will undoubtedly play a role in your decision making as a parent. You will likely attempt to re-create some special moments for your child that you still hold dear, like the first time you went on a roller coaster with your dad. And, you'll likely change some things based on bad experiences you had, like maybe you don't need to comment on every calorie your child takes in the way your mom did. These are conscious decisions you will make based on your experience.

There are many subconscious decisions you will make based on your experience as well. It's important to keep in mind that you are raising your child, not reliving your own childhood. Enjoy what you can, but parenting is not a vicarious experience. Honor your child, and make decisions that will help nurture that unique individual.

## Raising You

As you parent, you will inevitably learn many things along the way. You will experience emotions you've never known. You will be forced out of your comfort zone on a very regular basis. And if you're smart, you'll take advantage of this opportunity to grow.

Think of parenting as an ongoing science experiment and therapy exercise all in one. You get to hypothesize what will work, try new things (pretty much daily), conclude what worked and didn't, make adjustments, and then continue. All the while, you will work through feelings of excitement, love, anger, frustration, joy, and despair. Now add your child, your partner or spouse, your parents, your village, your child's teachers and coaches, your local librarian, and a few others into the mix, and you've got your new life.

# Raising Your Partnership and Village

You will make connections with others that will run deep. A bond with your child is a bond worth having. Naturally, if you are coparenting, your relationship with the other parent will be crucial to this experience. Try to keep it strong and enjoy it. Depend on one another, and let someone help you in this daunting task of child rearing.

"A friend in need is a friend indeed!" Look back to **Chapter 21** for more on creating your village. There is no way to describe a friend who has been there for you when you needed help most—be it a colleague who takes you to the hospital for your child's broken limb, a neighbor who can help with a last-minute carpool when you're stuck twenty miles from the school, or a fellow congregant your child can go to talk to about sex and drugs. Your relationships within your village will serve you well, so invest time and energy into them.

What is your relationship like with your parents? Are you in touch? Are you close? Parenting can often bring us closer to our own parents. If you're fortunate enough to still have your parents in your life, lean on them and allow them to be a part of this wonderful time. Model what a devoted child does, and take care of your parents. I met four of my grandparents but knew only one well. One passed when I was three, and two more shortly after. I recall their presence—but not their personality.

## The Long View

Remain humble with confidence. Know that you're in it for all the right reasons and that you are making the best decisions you can in the moments you have to make them. Know that you're reflecting on these decisions to be sure you do it even better next time.

**Inspiration**

I do remember my one grandmother, and she was a kick in the pants! My mother was devoted to her. We would visit regularly. And when we were not with her, my mother called her daily. She taught me the importance of the parent-child relationship from both directions.

## Raising the Bar

Whenever it was time for a big test, report card, or athletic competition, my mother would always say, "Do your best; it's all anyone can ever ask of you." Knowing that's what she expected sure made it easier to come home with a C. If I had truly tried my best, then that was a well-earned grade. And if I hadn't tried my best—well, there was definitely room for improvement, and I knew it.

Have high expectations of yourself and your child. No, don't be the tiger mother who intimidates her children (and other parents for that matter). Be a loving and honest parent who expects the best whenever possible. Don't settle for second best, but be okay with it when it happens. And then be the parent who understands when things don't go as planned or expected. "When your child lies, throws a fit, or gets cut from the team, or when your child is dumped or faces true danger, remember that this is your child. You don't have to be happy with the situation, but you must always be your child's number-one advocate, even when your child is self-advocating.

Increasing your expectations for yourself will help you be a better parent. Expect yourself to be supportive of your child. Expect yourself to embrace the challenges you face. You won't always say the right thing in the moment, but when that happens, expect more of yourself in your reflections. Hold yourself to a higher standard, especially when you disappoint yourself. Picture your toddler throwing a fit. He's frustrated you've taken him out of the sandbox and are going home. You raise your voice, say things in the park you wish you hadn't, and physically remove him and take him home. You haven't met your high standard, but you did the best you could. So hold yourself to a higher standard in the moments after—once he's napping and you have some room to breathe. Understand he was tired and hungry, and make a plan for the next time he throws a fit so you will be better prepared and feel better about the outcome. It's no use beating yourself up over your reaction, but at the same time, it's a waste of angry feelings if you don't learn from it and improve next time.

### Disappointment Do-Over

Remind yourself that when you're disappointed in your actions, you can do better just by learning from your own mistakes. The lesson will be worth it the next time when you do it differently.

**Perspiration**

Fast forward to your tween. She's cleared the history on her iPad when you've asked her not to. This time, you remained calm and talked to her about it. Good for you. Here's where you raise the bar for your child. Okay, she screwed up and you're angry and disappointed. You could take away privileges (and you might), but the way she'll really understand the seriousness of the situation is if you remind her that you expect more of her. She must do better because it's her own security at risk when she engages in risky Internet behavior. And she's only hurting herself more by hiding it. Tell her it's normal to be curious about whatever she is hiding and it's normal for her to hide it. But now that she's been caught, you need to also let her know that she's in a position to help or hurt herself. Setting this high bar will help her know that you are setting her up for success and not simply punishing her.

## Raising the Roof

Have fun as a parent. Enjoy these moments with your child, with your family, and with your friends. Life is not a guarantee. Take the value lessons from this book and bring them together to help you and your family grow. Take the job seriously and don't back down. But find the fun between the serious conversations. The best insurance for a lasting family relationship is to cultivate a strong relationship with your child in the early years. The child who enjoys the companionship of parents will have a long-lasting relationship with parents.

When you're in the moment, let it last. If you're enjoying a family game night and it's time for bed and the kids are asking for more, consider letting them stay up a little later to enjoy the moment. Allow more late movie nights during the summer when the kids can sleep in the next day. Go out on a school night for an ice cream. Being spontaneous is often a great idea given

## Take a Moment

Carve out regular moments in your busy schedule to be with one another. All of these options—scheduled family time, impromptu outings—routine activities or not, will encourage a relationship that, if fostered, will continue through your child's adulthood.

**Inspiration**

the hectic nature of family lives these days. You don't always have to break the rules to have fun. Plan a fun outing with just one child or with the family.

I teach on Tuesday nights, and I often return home to my little one snuggled sound asleep in bed, a smell of fish in the house, and my two older kids (often roughhousing but also sometimes cuddling cutely) with their father watching a cooking show. Sure, we try to limit media time, but what my husband has realized is that Mom's night out teaching is an opportunity for him to be with his kids and do something special. He and our youngest prepare "exotic fish night" menu items while the older two are at their after-school activities and finishing homework. (Of note, I don't care for fish, and apparently the rest of my family does, so this has provided them with an outlet for their fish fantasies.) Then when the youngest goes to bed, the older two enjoy exploring my husband's interest in cuisine with him. What started as a fun and impromptu activity one night while I was out has become a regular part of their routine when I am in the midst of a teaching semester.

My husband travels frequently for work. When he is away, we have special things we do. I am not sure how this happened, but we began drinking tea out of my pewter tea set that used to sit unused for years on a tray in our dining room. We often light candles and snuggle up for books in my bed instead of my children's beds for story time. What my husband and I are doing in these situations is creating a special place for our family where we can support each other in our professional lives while also enjoying the family we have built together. My nights teaching and his travel schedule could be seen as inconvenient and difficult challenges for two working parents. But instead of dwelling on the challenges, we work out carpools and schedules that allow us to find joy in what would otherwise just be considered difficult.

The whole point of parenting is to raise a family. Make your family one that you enjoy. Find what works, and don't be afraid to let go of what doesn't. Make your best decisions and reflect on them to see what works and what doesn't. Be proud of yourself and be proud of the family you are building together. This will be your support and your joy for the rest of your life.

# To Summarize...

- The values in this book are ones you and your family can live by.

- We continue to grow as parents as we nurture our children.

- Expect a lot of yourself and your child.

- As we raise children, we raise a new family unit—one we want to have for life.

# Resources

## Family Organizations and Websites

- American Academy of Pediatrics (aap.org)

  This is a natural first stop for questions and resources about physical and mental health for children.

- Challenge Success (challengesuccess.org)

  Challenge Success focuses on research-based practices to help schools and families address issues of stress and increase academic engagement.

- Child-Welfare Information Gateway (childwelfare.gov)

  The Child-Welfare Information Gateway is a national organization that can connect you to professionals and other resources for questions and needs about family, including abuse, neglect, care, and health.

- Common Sense Media (commonsensemedia.org)

  Here is a great resource to help you better understand the media your child is interacting with. You can find detailed reviews of movies and more. Additionally, Common Sense Media provides resources on how to talk with your child about media and offers some places to start with user agreements.

- Great Schools (greatschools.org)

  You can find some good, basic information about schools on this website. Don't rely too heavily on the opinions, but you can get some good facts.

It's My Life (pbskids.org/itsmylife)

This is PBS's insider website, where kids can look up information about a variety of topics, ranging from family to academics.

Mayo Clinic: Children's Health (mayoclinic.org/healthy-living/childrens-health/basics/childrens-health/hlv-20049425)

Here is a website with some valuable resources dedicated to children's health.

Motherlode: Living the Family Dynamic (parenting.blogs.nytimes.com)

This blog provides a variety of perspectives on a range of parenting topics, including some controversial issues and opinions.

National Alliance for Youth Sports (nays.org)

You can go here for some information about what's going on and what to look for in youth sports.

National Sleep Foundation (sleepfoundation.org)

This website is a great resource dedicated to promoting and supporting healthy sleep habits. Find facts about sleep as well as strategies to get more.

PBS Parents (pbs.org/parents)

Parents can look here for information about kids. Includes topics such as friendship and involvement.

Red Tricycle (redtri.com)

This is a website that promotes family activities local to your area. You can subscribe to receive local postings about seasonal activities. Keep in mind this website has a lot of advertisements and sponsorship.

## Books to Love and Live By

🔦 *Alone Together: Why We Expect More from Technology and Less from Each Other*, by Sherry Turkle

Turkle takes a deep look at the impact technology has on developing interpersonal skills.

🔦 *The Blessing of a B Minus: Using Jewish Teachings to Raise Resilient Teenagers*, by Wendy Mogel

Mogel has written a great read for parents of adolescents or tweens that paints the importance of owning responsibility and developing independence.

🔦 *The Blessing of a Skinned Knee: Using Jewish Teachings to Raise Self-Reliant Children*, by Wendy Mogel

Here is another book by Mogel with a down-to-earth perspective that helps you keep the big picture in mind.

🔦 *Building Resilience in Children and Teens: Giving Kids Roots and Wings*, by Kenneth R. Ginsburg

Here is an insightful book that will help you with practical strategies as you navigate the day-to-day. This book also offers online films to drive its points home and to make it easier for readers to share its ideas with others.

🔦 *Bully Nation: Why America's Approach to Childhood Aggression Is Bad for Everyone*, by Susan Eva Porter

Porter provides a fresh look at a national problem with some great insight.

🔦 *Crazy Busy*, by Edward M. Hallowell

Hallowell does a terrific job of outlining tried-and-true strategies for ADD patients in an effort to help busy people apply them to our ADD lifestyles.

*Drive: The Surprising Truth about What Motivates Us*, by Daniel H. Pink

Pink takes a deep look at motivation and explores the connection between performance and self-satisfaction. This book will help you understand the importance of owning your decisions and actions.

*How to Talk So Kids Will Listen & Listen So Kids Will Talk*, by Adele Faber and Elaine Mazlish

This is a fantastic book to help you walk through, rethink, and rework your communication style with your child.

*Mindset: The New Psychology of Success*, by Carol Dweck

This is a wonderful piece that describes the concept of growth mindset and how to foster it as we frame our own thinking.

*Nurture Shock: New Thinking About Children*, by Po Bronson and Ashley Merryman

This book offers a modern-day take on the research and themes in parenting.

*The Power of Play: Learning What Comes Naturally*, by David Elkind

Elkind describes the importance of play in the development of children.

*The Price of Privilege: How Parental Pressure and Material Advantage Are Creating a Generation of Disconnected and Unhappy Kids*, by Madeline Levine

Levine describes a phenomenon that is happening across the nation. She explores the roots of teenage stress in privileged families and offers a pragmatic view.

*Teach Your Children Well: Parenting for Authentic Success*, by Madeline Levine

This is a must-read—for parents of all ages. This book will provide you with a great understanding of emotional development throughout the ages with a wonderful set of anecdotes to help illustrate key points.

*Teaching Kids to Be Good People*, by Annie Fox

Fox offers practical suggestions for helping kids understand what it is to be good and how to foster that internally.

*Uncommon Sense for Parents with Teenagers*, by Mike Riera

Riera uses humor and reality to help you understand and connect with your teen through better communication.

*What to Expect When You're Expecting* (and subsequent books in that series), by Heidi Murkoff and Sharon Mazel

This is a fantastic primer for expecting and new parents. There are follow-up books that help identify important benchmarks in a child's development and suggestions for common concerns and questions.

# T

# V

# Just Released from For the GENIUS Press:

Caregiving is a universal concern today. Sooner or later, you will be called to care for a loved one. An aging parent. An ill spouse, partner, friend, or child. And ultimately, you, too, will need additional care. Are you prepared to provide care? To receive care? These are important questions to consider before the caregiving crisis lands on your front porch. *Caregiving for the GENIUS* offers you the motivation, inspiration, and education necessary to be proactive instead of reactive when it comes to caregiving. Prepare to care—pure genius!

Thomas Edison famously said that "genius is 1 percent inspiration, 99 percent perspiration." Reading *Fundraising for the GENIUS* shows that you have the inspiration to master the art and science of fundraising for your nonprofit organization or institution, while the author helps you with the perspiration part by showing you how to dramatically increase your fundraising results. She employs tried-and-true methods used by the most successful nonprofits and institutions, and shows you to develop an integrated fundraising program that allows you to leverage your human and financial resources to create a strong organization.

## http://ForTheGENIUS.com

Wondering how Obamacare—the Patient Protection and Affordable Care Act—fits in with your retirement plans? In a nonpartisan approach, the author explores the topic in the full context that gave rise to the Affordable Care Act and how it's transforming the health care landscape. ***Obamacare for the GENIUS*** will provide a fuller appreciation for how *you* will be impacted, and you will learn key strategies to make the right decisions that impact the health care you and your loved ones receive.

In ***Retiring for the GENIUS,*** we explore YOUR retirement, on YOUR terms. You'll gain a better understanding about what you've accumulated so that you can decide how to use those resources effectively throughout your retirement years. After all, if you don't know how every piece in your financial puzzle fits into your life, how can you build confidence about your financial future?

http://ForTheGENIUS.com

CPSIA information can be obtained at www.ICGtesting.com
Printed in the USA
BVOW01s1208161014

371030BV00004B/10/P